VOTES
WITHOUT POWER

The Hong Kong
Legislative Council Elections
1991

Vote: it's power in your hands!

Hong Kong Government

The perverse and unorthodox argument of this little book is that voters are not fools.

V.O. Key, Jr.

VOTES WITHOUT POWER

The Hong Kong Legislative Council Elections
1991

Editors

Rowena Y.F. Kwok   Joan Y.H. Leung   Ian Scott

Contributors

Elaine Chan   Rowena Y.F. Kwok   Beatrice Leung
Joan Y.H. Leung   Ian Scott   Fred Yeung

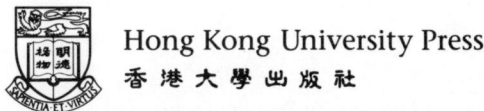

Hong Kong University Press
香港大學出版社

Hong Kong University Press
The University of Hong Kong,
139 Pokfulam Road, Hong Kong

© Department of Political Science, The University of Hong Kong, 1992

ISBN 962 209 317 5

Cover photograph courtesy of the Hong Kong Government

Printed in Hong Kong by Liang Yu Printing Factory Ltd.

Contents

Tables   vii

Figure   ix

Maps   ix

Plates   ix

Contributors   xi

Abbreviations   xii

Preface and Acknowledgements   xiii

1   An Overview of the Hong Kong Legislative Council   1
    Elections of 1991
    Ian Scott

Part I
Voting Behaviour in Kowloon Central

2   Kowloon Central: The Constituency, the People   31
    and the Candidates
    Rowena Y.F. Kwok

3   Political Orientations: Turnout and Vote Choice   49
    Joan Y.H. Leung

4   Issue Voting: Policy Positions and Voting Inclinations   79
    Rowena Y.F. Kwok and Elaine Chan

5   Voting Criteria: Ideal and Actual Choices in Candidate   99
    Selection
    Fred Yeung

6   Voter Consistency: Turnout, Choice and Criteria   125
    Elaine Chan and Fred Yeung

7   Summary Findings and Implications   143
    Joan Y.H. Leung

Part II
Catholic Voting Behaviour

8   The Catholic Voter   151
    Beatrice Leung

Part III
The Electoral Process

9   Government and the Electoral Process: 187
    The Need for Review
    Rowena Y.F. Kwok

Appendices

A   Election Results   212

B   Research Design   220

C   Survey Questionnaires   225

D   Profile of Survey Respondents   259

Bibliography of Hong Kong Electoral Materials   263

Index   275

Tables

1.1	The Hong Kong Legislative Council, 1991: composition and electorate	4
1.2	Direct election results: summary	5
1.3	Functional constituency results: summary	11
2.1	Kowloon Central: distribution of population by housing type	36
2.2	Population and registration by constituency	38
2.3	Kowloon Central: voting records (1982-1991)	39
2.4	A profile of the candidates in Kowloon Central	44
2.5	The election results in Kowloon Central	45
3.1	Respondents' identification of candidates' political stance	51
3.2	Respondents' identification of candidates' political affiliation	52
3.3	Comparison between voters and non-voters: socio-economic status	58
3.4	Voters' reasons for not going to vote	61
3.5	Voters' most important reason for going to vote	62
3.6	Comparison between voters and non-voters: political orientations	64
3.7	Comparison between voters and non-voters: attitudes towards social policies	66
3.8	Preference to leave government to capable leaders rather than requiring constant citizen scrutiny	66
3.9	Intention to vote on the basis of candidates' political stance	67
3.10	Intention to vote on the basis of candidates' political group affiliation	68
3.11	Understanding of candidates' platforms	68
3.12	The most important reasons for the choice of candidates	69
3.13	Single votes	71
3.14	Paired votes	71
3.15	Voters' socio-economic status and vote choice	72
3.16	Voters' political orientations and their choice of candidates	73
4.1	The most salient problem confronting Hong Kong	86
4.2	Candidates' political stance as perceived by respondents	87

4.3   Voting on the basis of candidate's political stance   88
4.4   Acceptance of China playing a decision-making role in   89
      the internal affairs of Hong Kong
4.5   The importance of accepting China's views in Sino-   90
      Hong Kong disputes
4.6   Confidence in a stable and prosperous Hong Kong   91
      after 1997
4.7   Intention to emigrate if the opportunity arises   92
4.8   Preference to leave government to capable leaders   92
      rather than requiring constant citizen scrutiny
5.1   Pattern of match of the three most important voting   107
      criteria employed in choosing two candidates
5.2   Percentage mentions of the three most important voting 108
      criteria
5.3   Percentage mentions of the single most important   109
      voting criterion
5.4   Rank order of the four major criteria identified   110
5.5   Percentage mentions of the three most important voting 115
      criteria under reclassified categories
6.1   Consistency of voting intentions and turnout   128
6.2   Voting intentions and actual turnout rates   128
6.3   Consistency of pre-election and post-election vote   131
      choices by respondents
6.4   Consistency of pre-election and post-election vote   131
      choices by vote
6.5   Consistency in the three most important candidate   133
      selection criteria in the pre-election and post-election
      surveys
8.1   Distribution of respondents by parish   157
8.2   Catholic voting rates in the 1991 elections   159
8.3   Voting rates in four Catholic parishes in the Legislative 159
      Council elections, 1991
8.4   Voting rates in two Catholic parishes in the Urban   160
      Council elections, 1989
8.5   Reported Catholic voting rates in Urban Council   160
      Elections, 1989 and 1991

8.6   Comparison of Catholic registered voters with   161
      general registration rates
8.7   Rank order of influence on Catholic voters' choice   163
      of candidate
8.8   Age and sources of influence   168
8.9   Income and sources of influence   169
8.10 Catholic orientations towards the election and future   171
      political development by parish
8.11 Orientations towards the election and political   172
      development by participation in Catholic groups' activities

Figure

9.1   The Registration and Electoral Office: 191
      Organizational Chart

Maps

2.1   Legislative Council electoral boundaries   32
2.2   Kowloon City District   33
2.3   Wong Tai Sin District   35

Plates

1.   Newly elected United Democrats after meeting the   6
      Governor
2.   Chan Yuen-han campaigning   42
3.   Registration of voters in a Catholic church   154
4.   A returning officer emptying one of the ballot boxes   194

Contributors

Elaine Chan
> Demonstrator, Department of Political Science,
> The University of Hong Kong

Rowena Y.F. Kwok
> Lecturer, Department of Political Science,
> The University of Hong Kong

Beatrice Leung
> Demonstrator, Department of Political Science,
> The University of Hong Kong

Joan Y.H. Leung
> Senior lecturer, Department of Public and Social Administration,
> City Polytechnic of Hong Kong

Ian Scott
> Professor and head, Department of Political Science,
> The University of Hong Kong

Fred Yeung
> Post-graduate student, Department of Political Science,
> The University of Hong Kong

Abbreviations

ADPL	Association for Democracy and People's Livelihood
CIC	Christian Industrial Committee
FTU	Federation of Trade Unions
Hong Kong Alliance	Hong Kong Alliance in Support of Patriotic and Democratic Movements in China
HKCA	Hong Kong Civic Association
HKCF	Hong Kong Citizen Forum
HKDF	Hong Kong Democratic Foundation
HKRC	Hong Kong Reform Club
I	Independent
LDF	Liberal Democratic Federation of Hong Kong
MP	Meeting Point
NHKA	New Hong Kong Alliance
REO	Registration and Electoral Office of the Hong Kong government
SCMP	*South China Morning Post*
TUC	Trades Union Council
UDHK	United Democrats of Hong Kong

Preface and Acknowledgements

Hong Kong's first direct elections to the legislature in 150 years of colonial rule might conceivably have been an important stage in the development of representative government, the emergence of political parties and the growth of political awareness. The elections may yet prove to be a watershed in progress towards an accountable and democratic government, but present indications suggest otherwise. The Chinese government, in particular, has no intention of permitting a popularly elected government to rule Hong Kong after 1997. Britain and China have already agreed that future constitutional developments must accord with the Basic Law, the document which provides for the governance of Hong Kong after the resumption of Chinese sovereignty. In real political terms, this simply means that the formidable executive powers of the Hong Kong government will be transferred to the government of the People's Republic of China. In this scheme of things, direct elections and the legislature itself are relatively unimportant. The executive will be accountable, in practice, to the Chinese government rather than to the legislature. And, in any event, directly elected seats will constitute not more than half the seats in any future legislative body. In this context, the 1991 elections were seen by the governments concerned as valuable, principally because they might relieve insistent local pressure for greater representation and provide some legitimacy for decisions which would be taken elsewhere.

There are, of course, dangers for governments which seek to preserve power by such means. Elections arouse expectations. The level of political awareness is invariably raised, even if only temporarily, because citizens are assailed with promises of better futures, solutions to intractable problems and the end of perceived evils. In addition, as the Hong Kong government has already found out, elected members with a popular mandate can prove recalcitrant when faced with demands from a political executive with no such mandate. The 1991 elections also focused concern on a related problem of critical dimensions, that of popular support for the transition to Chinese rule. The single, most important finding of our survey research is that the electorate favoured those candidates who were seen to stand for Hong Kong's autonomy from China and were opposed to those candidates who were even remotely perceived to be sympathetic to the Chinese government. Even those voters who did choose pro-China candidates were adamant that China should not interfere in Hong Kong affairs. The political sentiments of the majority of the people are thus running on a collision course with the Chinese government's increasingly explicit attempts to exert direct political control over the territory.

The Chinese and Hong Kong governments had vested interests in explaining the 1991 election results in ways which sought to show that they retained support (see Chapter 1). Both chose to set the landslide liberal victory against an allegedly low turnout rate. Our survey shows that there is no reason for either government to be sanguine about its support among those who did not vote; the electorate, as a whole, has little faith in the Hong Kong government and even less in the Chinese government. Turnout, we shall show, is far less significant, because of a faulty electoral register and of similarities in the views of voters and non-voters, than the expressed preferences of those who did vote. And there is no evidence to support the view that the voters were ill-informed. On the contrary, the majority had substantial knowledge of the candidates and their political stance and cast their ballots accordingly.

The single act of voting carries with it the possibility of multiple interpretations of what that vote actually means. In order to find out what is in the electorate's collective mind, some form of survey research is essential. Since these were the first direct elections in Hong Kong's history, we felt that we should seek to ascertain the views of the electorate in face-to-face interviews on the salience of policy issues to vote choice, their political orientations towards candidates and the criteria which they used to guide their choice (see Chapters 3-6). Funded by an earmarked University and Polytechnic Grants Committee research grant awarded by the Committee on Research and Conference Grants of The University of Hong Kong, we conducted structured interviews with 1,046 registered voters before the election and followed this with a further 570 interviews from the same sample after the election. We were also able to hold interviews with an additional 141 respondents who had not been contacted in the pre-election survey.

The design of the questionnaire was a difficult, and sometimes frustrating, task and we are most grateful for the help of Dr John Bacon-Shone, Director of the Social Sciences Research Centre, The University of Hong Kong, and Robert Chung, a research officer in the centre. They not only saved us from making invalid inferences from the statistics, but were also generous in sharing the data from their own surveys with us and suggested improvements to earlier drafts of these chapters. The first version of the questionnaire was produced in February 1991 in time for the District Board elections. We conducted a pilot survey of voter attitudes in those elections and further refined the questionnaire as a result. At that point, we were fortunate to have a visit, funded by the British Council, from Professor Ivor Crewe of the Department of Government at the University of Essex, who is one of the world's leading authorities on electoral survey research. Professor Crewe cast a critical eye over our questionnaire and we made further improvements in line with his suggestions. Subsequently, a member of the research group, Fred Yeung Yiu-mo, attended the Essex summer school on data analysis and was able to make additional amendments to the questionnaire on the basis of his work in England. We would also like to thank Anthony B.L. Cheung, Ernest Chui Wing-tak and Law Chi-kwong for giving advice on the research design and Linda Cho of the Social Sciences Research Centre for assistance in the sampling process.

The final questionnaire was produced in early September and an English version was prepared by Terry Lui. At this stage, we spent a week training the 86 student interviewers who were to administer the questionnaire in the field. We are grateful to members of the Language Centre, The University of Hong Kong, Nigel Bruce, Shelagh Byron and Lily Leung, and to post-graduate students in the Department of Political Science, Winnie Lam, Trini Leung, Kevin May, Pak Fung, Sebastian Tse and Eric Wan, who assisted with this essential work. We owe a particular debt to Richard Lui, who supervised the interviewers and administered the entire survey very efficiently, and to Stephanie Lai, who prepared the data set and supervised data entry. Without the students who conducted the interviews, often under difficult conditions, we would not have had the raw data on which some of the chapters are based. Their participation and enthusiasm were clearly indispensable for the success of the entire project. We are grateful also to Elaine Chan, who tabulated the results from the returned questionnaires and, in addition to her own contributions to this volume, provided many of the statistical tables which are used in other chapters. Adeline Lee Fung-ping and Eddy Fong assisted in the compilation of the background research material on the constituency and in preparing the bibliography.

Our survey was a representative sample of electors, derived from the electoral register. Officials of the Registration and Electoral Office of the Hong Kong government were helpful in enabling us to identify our sample and also provided us with much useful information on voter registration and turnout. We would also like to thank those candidates in Kowloon Central who agreed to be interviewed by members of the research team. Although the central focus of this study was the survey research in Kowloon Central constituency, we also looked at the elections in their wider context and in relation to the voting behaviour of a particular group of Catholics. In this respect, we owe a debt of gratitude to Peter Cheung of the Catholic Institute of Religion and Society and to Wilfred Lai Ming-fai for tabulating the data derived from a survey of four Catholic parishes.

In preparing this book for publication, we have also incurred some debts of gratitude. We would like to thank the Cartographic Unit of the Department of Geography and Geology, The University of Hong Kong and Richard Irving of the same department, for their work on the maps, and Grania Skeldon for her help with the copy-editing. Acknowledgement is also due to *South China Morning Post* for providing the photographs on pages 6, 42 and 194, and to *Kung Kao Po (Chinese Catholic Weekly)* for the photograph on page 154. Lastly, we are especially grateful to Ann Wan, who typed the manuscript and for the logistical support provided by Rosita Wan and Linda Chow. The mistakes, of course, are our own responsibility.

Rowena Y.F. Kwok
Joan Y.H. Leung
Ian Scott

December 1991

1

An Overview of the Hong Kong Legislative Council Elections of 1991

Ian Scott

In a celebrated article published in 1955, V.O. Key sought to identify the characteristics of what he called 'critical' elections. There were, he felt, three essential features which served to distinguish these kinds of elections from more commonplace varieties. First, critical elections were those 'in which more or less profound readjustments occur in the relation of power within the community';[1] secondly, in such elections, the depth and intensity of electoral involvement would be high; and, thirdly, the election would provide the means by which 'new and durable' political groupings were formed. These criteria have been used to pass judgement on the significance of many elections. Most British commentators, for example, seem to agree that the elections of 1906 and 1945 were critical elections.[2] Key himself felt that the American presidential elections of 1896 and 1928 met the conditions of his categorization.[3] Palmer argues that the Ceylonese election of 1956 might also be included.[4] And so, too, could all the pre-independence elections in British colonies in Africa, which were usually marked by high turnouts, a commitment on the part of the colonial government to hand over power to nationalist leaders and the emergence of a mass party.[5]

Hong Kong's 1991 Legislative Council elections were officially declared to be critical elections. The Hong Kong government informed the public — in advance of the event — that the elections were 'historic'. The spokesmen noted that it was the first time that Hong Kong voters had been permitted to elect some members of the legislature under full adult suffrage. Senior government officials called for a high turnout and suggested that, if the elections were a 'success', they might serve to speed up the pace of democratic reform.[6] There were even vague promises, subsequently retracted, that British ministers might be prepared to talk to their Chinese counterparts to persuade them to consider a legislature which would contain a higher proportion of directly elected members. But, in all this, there was a degree of ambivalence and of ground-shifting. The government's television advertisements might proclaim that the elections meant 'power in your hands', but the constitutional framework, as many voters were aware, was not designed to achieve that end. The government might appeal for a high turnout but the electoral register was out of date. And that patronizing and insidious word 'success' could be interpreted to mean precisely what the government chose it to mean.

To evaluate whether these elections were indeed critical, and in what ways, we must return to Key's criteria. Did the elections result in a profound shift of power? Did the elections engender a high level of public interest and voter turnout? Did the elections see the emergence of 'new and durable' political groupings? We consider these questions in turn.

POWER AND THE POLITICAL SYSTEM

The parameters of the 1991 Legislative Council elections were deliberately set to prevent a dramatic shift in power alignments in Hong Kong. These arrangements centred on the expectation that power would remain firmly lodged with Hong Kong's colonial and bureaucratic executive until 1997 when it would then be transferred in effect to the government of the People's Republic of China. Lip-service is still paid to the Sino-British agreement of 1984, which formally provides for 'a high degree of autonomy' for the territory after 1997 under the 'one country, two systems' concept.[7] But there is little public confidence that the Chinese government, if it retains its present inclinations, will respect the autonomy of its future special administrative region. The constitutional arrangements spelled out in the Basic Law, a Chinese document which is intended to apply to Hong Kong after 1997, and the political developments agreed to by the British and Chinese governments in the transitional period are clearly not aimed at the establishment of anything which could remotely be considered a popularly elected or supported government.[8]

Seen in this light, the 1991 Legislative Council elections were simply a sop to democratic sentiment, a concession designed to ensure that conservative business and professional élites in collaboration with senior civil servants would remain the key decision makers. The composition of the 60-member legislature was intended to bring about that result. Only 18 members of the Council were to be directly elected. A further 21 were to be elected from functional constituencies, mostly on very restricted franchises. The Governor personally was to appoint an additional 18 members, including the Deputy President of the Council. And there were three remaining official members, the Chief Secretary, the Financial Secretary and the Attorney General (Table 1.1). This arrangement was designed to ensure 'convergence' with the Basic Law and anticipated the future legislature of the special administrative region which was to have 20 directly elected seats, 30 functional constituency seats and ten members appointed by a selection committee.

When the composition of the legislature was decided in 1988 and 1989, the Hong Kong government probably thought that the directly elected seats would produce a mixture of liberal, rural conservative and business representatives and perhaps some members of 'united front' organizations which had the support of the People's Republic of China. The constituencies were established as two-member seats which, it was assumed, would produce an appropriate mix if Hong Kong voters cast their ballots for prominent individuals rather than a 'party' label. This was an entirely reasonable assumption since, at that time, there were no formal political parties in Hong Kong. If matters had worked out as the government expected, then the 1991 Legislative Council elections would have resulted in comparatively little change because the government would have been able to claim that those who had been elected represented a broad and disparate spectrum of opinion. It would then have been able, as it had done so often in the past, to interpret the 'consensus' to its own advantage.[9]

Table 1.1 The Hong Kong Legislative Council, 1991: composition and electorate

Mode	Number	Registered electorate	Turnout	Votes cast	Percentage turnout
Directly elected	18	1,916,925	750,467	1,369,313[a]	39.15
Functional constituencies[b]	21	48,756[c]	22,919	—	47.0
Appointed by the Governor	18[d]	—	—	—	
Officials	3	—	—	—	
	60				

Source: Compiled from information supplied by the Registration and Electoral Office of the Hong Kong government.

[a] Each voter was entitled to cast two votes. There were 1,609 invalid ballots.
[b] Elections in functional constituencies are by 'preferential elimination'.
[c] This was the registered electorate for the contested constituencies only. The total registered electorate for functional constituencies was 69,825. Twelve seats were uncontested.
[d] Including the Deputy President of the Legislative Council.

But the direct elections did not produce the results which the government had originally expected. One party, the liberal United Democrats, won 12 of the 18 seats. Two other seats went to an allied group, Meeting Point, whose candidates were not opposed by the United Democrats. Yet another liberal group, the Association for Democracy and People's Livelihood, won a seat in Kowloon West. Of the remaining seats, one went to a liberal independent, one to an independent incumbent and the other to an incumbent rural conservative (Table 1.2). In short, the results of the direct elections were a liberal landslide. The United Democrats alone received 45% of the vote. If votes for allied groups and sympathetic independents are included, approximately 67.5% of the voters cast their ballots for liberals.

The other parties and political groupings fared very badly. The conservative Liberal Democratic Federation, composed mainly of business and professional groups favouring collaboration with China,

Table 1.2 Direct election results: summary

Affiliation	Candidates	Seats	Percentage of vote
Liberals[a]:			
United Democrats	14	12	45.14 ⎤
Meeting Point	3	2	7.20
Association for Democracy and People's Livelihood	3	1	4.44 ⎬ 58.22
Hong Kong Democratic Foundation	1	0	1.44 ⎦
Liberal Independents	5	1	9.35
Conservative[b]:			
Liberal Democratic Federation	5	0	5.09
Pro-China[c]:			
Federation of Trade Unions	1	0	3.28 ⎤
New Hong Kong Alliance	2	0	0.87
Hong Kong Citizen Forum	1	0	2.18 ⎬ 7.88
Kwun Tong Man Chung Friendship Promotion Association	1	0	1.55 ⎦
Other Groups:			
Reform Club	1	0	0.60
Civic Association	1	0	1.03
Trades Union Council	1	0	0.25
Other Independents[d]	15	2	17.55
	54	18	99.97

Source: Calculated from *The Hong Kong Government Gazette Extraordinary* 133(41), 20 September 1991. For detailed results, see Appendix A.

[a] Most liberals stood for constitutional reform, including a directly elected legislature. Many supported the pro-democracy movement in China.
[b] Composed largely of business and professional groups opposed to rapid progress towards representative government. Many favoured collaboration with China and acquiescence to the views of the Chinese government on political development.
[c] 'United front' organizations which took the Chinese government's line and received financial and other support from that source.
[d] Includes rural conservatives, one of whom was re-elected, some candidates who were probably pro-Beijing or who supported the Liberal Democratic Federation but did not directly identify themselves as such, past political notables without specific affiliations and an incumbent member who was re-elected but who did not belong to any political grouping. The elected independent rural conservative, Tai Chin-wah, whose qualifications to practise as a solicitor were being investigated by the police, did not take his seat. The subsequent by-election was won by a Meeting Point candidate.

Percentages do not add up to 100% because of rounding.

polled only 5.1% of the vote. None of its candidates were elected. Candidates running for pro-China 'united front' organizations received only 7.9% of the vote and were also easily defeated. Chan Yuen-han, the Federation of Trade Unions' candidate in Kowloon Central, polled approximately 11,000 votes less than the second place United Democrat, Dr Conrad Lam Kui-shing, and was 23,000 votes behind the winner, United Democrat Lau Chin-shek. In Island East, Cheng Kai-nam, who had the support of a pro-China group, Hong Kong Citizen Forum, polled 29,902 votes against the United Democrats' leader, Martin Lee Chu-ming, who received 76,831 votes. Lee and his fellow United Democrat, Szeto Wah, who had been labelled 'subversives' by the Chinese government and expelled from the Basic Law Drafting Committee following their support for pro-democracy groups in China, received the highest number of votes cast for individual candidates.

What explains this liberal sweep? We should first consider arguments variously put forward by members of the Hong Kong and

Plate 1 Newly elected United Democrats after meeting the Governor (Lau Chin-shek in the white shirt and Conrad Lam Kui-shing to the right)

Chinese governments which essentially sought to discredit the view that the results were representative of Hong Kong public opinion. On the eve of the elections, when it was already clear that there would be a substantial liberal victory, Hong Kong's highest ranking civil servant, the Chief Secretary, Sir David Ford, said on television that the elections should be seen in the context of a 50% registration rate, of whom perhaps only 50% might turn out at the polls. The implication was that those elected represented one quarter of the eligible electorate and that there remained, in consequence, a majority who were not represented. The government, Ford appeared to be saying, reserved the right 'to balance' the legislature by appointing members who might be thought to represent those who had not registered or had not voted.

The problem with this argument, of course, is that, other than by surveys, there is no way of knowing how those who were not registered or did not cast their ballots would have voted. They might, quite conceivably, have voted in the same way as those who did vote. In fact, our surveys suggest that the views of voters and non-voters were not strikingly dissimilar. Both groups, for example, were adamantly opposed to Chinese government intervention in Hong Kong affairs and both strongly preferred liberal candidates.[10] In addition, 20% of the eligible population did actually vote and, in other contexts, this would be taken as a more than adequate indication of the people's preferences. Most governments in Western democracies are not elected by a majority of the eligible voters or even by a majority of the voters. The Conservative Party in Britain in the 1987 election, for example, obtained 42.3% of the votes on a 75% turnout. This translated into 374 seats out of 650 and was regarded as a substantial victory.[11] No winning British party this century has ever received the votes of a majority of the eligible voters and only twice has a winning party been able to secure an absolute majority of those who did cast their ballots.[12]

There may, of course, be many reasons why people do not vote. Hong Kong census statistics show that, at any one time, over 150,000 residents may not be in the territory.[13] Some voters may have refrained from casting their ballots as a protest against government policies. Others, whose names were still on the register, were dead or had emigrated. Still others, a significant majority of non-voters in our sample, did not vote because they felt that their vote would have no effect, that the individual was powerless to change the course of political history (see Chapter 3). In none of these cases, however, was it appropriate for the government to claim the right to appoint individuals to the legislature to represent views other than those of the liberal majority. Yet this is precisely what the Governor chose to do when, following the election, he appointed 17 members to the legislature, none of whom were specifically identified with liberal groups.[14]

The government's arguments fail for another reason. The actual turnout in the direct elections was 39.15%, a figure which was sufficiently low for various commentators, including the Chinese government and the English-language newspaper, the *South China Morning Post (SCMP)*, to imply that the results were not representative.[15] It is clear, however, from the electoral survey results that a major reason for the low turnout was that the electoral register was badly out of date. It had not been revised since 1982. New voters had only been added to the register on their own initiative and the names of voters who had left Hong Kong had not been removed from the register.

The government made no attempt to play a more positive role in the registration process. The issuing of new identity cards to all adult citizens in the years preceding the elections offered an excellent chance to register voters at no extra cost. Alternatively, the decennial census held in March 1991 might have been adapted to compile a more accurate register. Neither opportunity was taken. The result was that many voters had moved elsewhere in Hong Kong and so did not receive polling cards or campaign literature. Others, some 300,000 of a population of 5.5 million, had emigrated since the signing of the Sino-British agreement in 1984.[16] Thirty-five thousand people were added to the register shortly before the elections because they had moved to other constituencies, but it is very doubtful whether this came remotely close to solving the problem. Our surveys in Kowloon Central showed that some 14% of the voters could not be contacted at their homes, even after repeat visits. In other constituencies, with greater mobility rates, the percentage of those who should not have been on the register might have been even higher. The effective voting rate, Robert Chung has suggested, was probably about 48%.[17] Under the circumstances, the turnout rate does not lend itself to the interpretation that the results were unrepresentative. They were representative of those who were able to vote and they constituted a higher percentage of the eligible electorate than both the Hong Kong and Chinese governments were willing to recognize.

The argument that the direct election results were not representative was quickly picked up by the New China News Agency, China's diplomatic arm in Hong Kong, and by Mr Lu Ping, the director of the Hong Kong and Macau Affairs office of the Chinese government. Lu Ping, who had earlier warned the Governor not to appoint Martin Lee and Szeto Wah to the Executive Council, was quoted as saying that more than 80% of eligible voters had not voted in the elections and that 'people in Hong Kong will sooner or later be able to see clearly what is real democracy'.[18] He also warned that 'Beijing would not tolerate Hong Kong legislators challenging its rule after the transfer of sovereignty'[19] or pressing for more directly elected seats in the legislature. He exhorted members of the Legislative Council to be loyal to the Basic Law and to work for the long-term prosperity and stability of Hong Kong. The Chinese government also declined to recognize the legislature before 1997, claiming that it was only an advisory body and, in the words of Zhang Junsheng, a vice-director of the New China News Agency, 'certainly not a representative one'.[20]

It is not clear what the Chinese officials meant by representative or democratic. It is possible either that they meant to imply that the present political arrangements in Hong Kong did not reflect the wishes of the population which would be better served under Chinese sovereignty or that the elections themselves were not representative because only 20% of the eligible electorate voted. In the former case, the evidence from the elections itself and from opinion polls conducted before the elections does not suggest that most Hong Kong people were positively looking forward to the assertion of Chinese sovereignty over the territory in 1997. A poll conducted in June 1991, for example, found that only 21% favoured a return to China while 73% preferred options such as becoming independent (29%), becoming part of Britain (26%) or part of the Commonwealth (19%).[21] The Chinese government is not generally regarded in Hong Kong as a model for 'real democracy'; words such as representative and democratic are not, in their normal usage, usually associated with the regime in Beijing.

If the argument, on the other hand, is that the elections were not representative, then the critical question is whether the direct election results or the allocation of seats is being considered. I have argued, to this point, that the results of the direct elections do provide an adequate and representative indication of the political preferences of the Hong Kong people. However, if one takes the allocation of seats as the principal criterion of representativeness, then there seems no doubt that the composition of the legislature, which includes 21 functional constituency members and 18 appointed members, does not properly reflect the views of the whole population. Table 1.3 shows the results and the size of the electorates in the functional constituencies. It is immediately evident that the government's decision to grant functional constituency status to particular occupational groups was heavily biased towards the business and professional sectors.[22] It is also clear that, in most cases, the electorate for these constituencies is very small. So-called 'representative' organizations determine who will constitute the electorate with the consequence that the results are open to manipulation and can often be determined in advance.[23] In the 1991 elections, 12 of the 21 functional constituencies were uncontested. The two constituencies with the largest electorates, Health Care and Teaching, were both won by United Democrats. Of the remainder, members of the liberal Hong Kong Democratic Foundation won two seats (Commercial (1) and Medical and Health (1)) while the others mostly went to businessmen and professionals associated to varying degrees with conservative and pro-Chinese government positions. Taking into account the Governor's 17 appointees (excluding the Deputy President of the Council), the legislature as a whole still has a predominantly conservative bias even though the vast majority of the electors preferred liberals.

Both the Chinese and the Hong Kong governments are fully committed to retaining the functional constituency system. In 1995, under an annex to the Basic Law, the number of functional constituency seats will increase to 30, the number of directly elected seats to 20 and ten members will be selected by an election committee composed mainly of members appointed from functional sectors and from Hong Kong delegates to the Chinese National People's Congress.[24] Despite abundant evidence that the functional constituency system does not permit

Table 1.3 Functional constituency results: summary

Functional constituency	Electorate	Turnout	Percentage turnout
Commercial(1)	1,609	911	56.6
Commercial(2)	2,348	Uncontested	
Industrial(1)	460	Uncontested	
Industrial(2)	1,366	390	28.6
Finance and Financial Services(1)	234	Uncontested	
Finance and Financial Services(2)	694	556	80.1
Labour[a]	378	Uncontested	
Social Services	181	Uncontested	
Medical and Health Care(1)	4,031	Uncontested	
Medical and Health Care(2)	10,636	Uncontested	
Teaching	38,678	17,034	44.0
Legal	1,240	714	57.6
Engineering, Architectural Surveying and Planning(1)	2,805	1,511	53.9
Engineering, Architectural, Surveying and Planning(2)	1,481	1,039	70.2
Accountancy	2,276	Uncontested	
Real Estate and Construction	373	Uncontested	
Tourism	847	728	86.0
Urban Council	40	Uncontested	
Regional Council	36	36	100.0
Rural	112	Uncontested	
Total	48,756[b]	22,819	47.0

Source: Registration and Electoral Office of the Hong Kong government.

[a] There are two seats for the labour functional constituency.
[b] In contested constituencies only. The total registered electorate for functional constituencies was 69,825.

adequate choice and that it discriminates between voters by allowing some to cast more ballots than others, it is attractive to the Chinese government because it enables political control to be exercised more easily. The Chinese strategy for Hong Kong appears to be to rule through surrogates and collaborators; the functional constituencies, with their small electorates, allow for greater manipulation in the selection of candidates than the large electorates in the directly contested seats. As a corollary, the Chinese leadership's opposition to democratic constitutional reform probably stems principally from the fear that, if free elections were held to a wholly directly elected legislature, the result would be an assembly largely antagonistic to future Chinese plans for the territory. The paradox is that it is precisely the Chinese government's intransigent position on constitutional reforms and civil liberties which is fuelling support for the liberals. The evidence from the 1991 elections showed that the single most important variable determining voter support for candidates was their stance towards the Chinese government.

There are a number of separate factors which can be adduced to support this conclusion. The most obvious is that all candidates who supported, or were thought to support, the Chinese government lost. Beyond this, however, it is clear that even candidates who ran under a liberal banner but who were thought to have pro-China sympathies were defeated. In Kowloon West, for example, the Association for Democracy and People's Livelihood put up two candidates. The leader of the Association, Frederick Fung Kin-kee, had long-established roots in the constituency and was duly elected with 28.9% of the vote. His running mate, Law Cheung-kwok, was widely suspected of having strong links with the Chinese government. He received only 13.6% of the vote and finished fourth.

Suspected pro-China sympathies probably also lost the election for other candidates. In some cases, the voters may even have preferred the Beijing-supported candidates for their personal qualities to the liberals who were elected. Both the data from the Kowloon Central constituency survey and exit polls conducted by the Social Science Research Centre at The University of Hong Kong suggest a 'coat-tails' effect where the winning United Democrat pulled his less popular colleague into office with him.[25] This can be ascertained by examining the voters' preferred pairings for candidates and by contrasting this with the number of single votes cast. In many cases, the leading United Democrat candidate had a substantially greater number of votes than his fellow party member (see Appendix A) who, in turn, received few votes that were not paired with those of the leading candidate. Thus, we might conclude that some liberals won because of what they were perceived to stand for rather than for their own personal attributes.

The perception of what the liberals did stand for, other than on the China question, is rather more difficult to assess. It is clear that the 1991 election was not an election which was fought on traditional policy issues. One study of party platforms suggests that there was little difference between the contending groups; most platforms were bland statements of support for generally liberal policies.[26] The critical issues in personal debates between candidates were their positions on Chinese intervention in Hong Kong affairs and their past record of support for constitutional reform in the territory. Judging from the Kowloon Central survey, however, voters did have strong views on a number of policy issues, such as the repatriation of the Vietnamese boat people. Yet this does not seem to have been the critical factor influencing their choice of candidate. Many liberals were equivocal on the boat people issue but were none the less elected. Emily Lau Wai-hing, for example, was elected in New Territories East on an election manifesto which was strong on human rights and freedoms, on maintaining Hong Kong's autonomy and in advocating a directly elected Legislative Council.[27] She said nothing in her manifesto about the Vietnamese boat people housed in camps in her constituency. Yet she was elected with support which appeared to increase over the course of the campaign. It is difficult not to conclude that her long past record of standing up for the political rights and liberties of Hong Kong people and against Chinese interference in the territory was the principal reason why she won comfortably over the incumbent independent, Andrew Wong Wang-fat.

Conventional policy issues probably did not play much part in determining voter allegiance for two reasons. First, there seems to have been widespread awareness that the Legislative Council did not make policy and was relatively powerless *vis-à-vis* the executive. In a poll conducted shortly before the elections, only 28% of the respondents thought that the Legislative Council would have the power to govern Hong Kong after the election whereas 52% thought that power would rest with the Governor, the Executive Council or the British or Chinese governments.[28] Secondly, the parties and the candidates did not act as though policy questions, other than the China question, were important. Although the parties did have platforms, they were often vaguely expressed, mainly 'motherhood' promises about pressing government to control inflation, to improve law and order, to spend more on social policies and services and to clean up the environment. Where intense debate between candidates over policy issues did take place, it was normally conducted in the knowledge that they would not be called upon to put their recommendations into effect. Much of the campaign literature consisted of self-promotion, short on policy substance and usually restricted to recounting educational background and public service record. Most candidates also sought endorsements from local notables or party leaders who might be expected to help their cause. This was characteristic of previous election campaigns in Hong Kong and was probably based on the assumption that voters would cast their ballots on the basis of the personal qualities of the candidate. If parties and groups are not contesting an election and if the platforms of the candidates are vague or indistinguishable, then this is a reasonable premise since the voter would have no other basis on which to make a choice. However, when parties enter the contest, as they did for the first time in 1991, there is always the possibility that they may be able to structure voters' preferences on a particular issue to their own advantage. The liberals seem to have been able to do this with the China issue although it seems likely that they were able to capitalize not only on immediate grievances sparked by the campaign but also on rather more long-standing resentment which went back to the Sino-British agreement of 1984 and its aftermath.

When we say that a party or a group has the ability to structure voter preferences, we mean that they can make a particular issue seem salient to voters and to persuade them, in consequence, to cast their ballots for those who seem most concerned about that issue. This was not an entirely new development in Hong Kong. There had been elections earlier in 1991 for both the District Boards and the Urban and Regional Councils. In the Kowloon Central constituency survey, nearly 65% of the sample had voted in previous elections and, of these, a surprising 52.6% had voted more than three times.[29] The District Board elections, in particular, had resulted in liberal victories after campaigns which had focused, albeit rather less intensely, on democratic concerns similar to those expressed in the 1991 Legislative Council elections.[30] There was also evidence in New Territories District Board and Regional Council elections that rural conservatives had firm support among the electorate, presumably on the grounds that they best represented the interests of villagers. This support appears to have been maintained in the Legislative Council elections. In New Territories West, for example, Ng Ming-yum, running for the United Democrats, drew strong support from voters in the urban areas of Tuen Mun who had previously elected him as a District Board member. However, one of his opponents, Tai Chin-wah, a conservative incumbent, was still able to take second place by retaining his rural support.[31] The by-election in December 1991, which resulted from Tai's inability to take his seat following police investigations of his qualifications to practise as a solicitor, confirmed that there was strong support for rural conservatives in the constituency. Although a member of the liberal group, Meeting Point, won the election, his margin of victory over the rural conservative was only a few thousand votes. Thus, some voter preferences appear to have been structured before the 1991 elections. However, the territory-wide scope of the election, the number of new voters (approximately 250,000 more than those who voted in the District Board elections in the previous March) and the significance of the anti-Chinese government vote all suggest that the liberals were able to win support from among first-time voters and might possibly have created more long-term stability in voting patterns.

It is difficult to attribute the anti-communist vote to a specific cause because it could conceivably be related to any or all of the following: the Hong Kong people's past experiences with the Chinese government; events associated with the Sino-British negotiations on the future of the territory both before and after 1984; the Beijing massacre in 1989; the actions of the Chinese government during the election campaign; and general apprehension about future Chinese government policies towards the territory. These factors are considered in turn.

Past Experiences

Approximately 35.6% of Hong Kong's population were born in China.[32] Many people came to the territory as refugees in large waves of emigration after 1949, in the period from 1958 to 1962, or during the Cultural Revolution. Academic commentators and politicians alike are agreed that there remains great affection for China in a patriotic sense but little respect for its government.[33] The Cultural Revolution, and later the Beijing massacre, significantly influenced the political attitudes not only of those who were born in China but also of their children who were born in Hong Kong. The suffering of relatives in China during the Cultural Revolution made a particularly strong impact on Hong Kong people and helped to create an atmosphere of mistrust of the Chinese government which persisted throughout the Sino-British negotiations and beyond.

The Sino-British Negotiations

The 1984 agreement was negotiated without the participation of Hong Kong representatives and without the consent of the Hong Kong people. An assessment office was set up to ascertain their views but it was essentially an exercise in ratifying an ultimatum from the British government to accept the agreement or take the consequences.[34] The British and Hong Kong governments also sold the agreement to the Hong Kong people on the grounds that it would protect their civil liberties, lead to an elected legislature, maintain 'a high degree of autonomy' after 1997 and promote continued economic growth.

By 1991, with the exception of economic prosperity, the grounds on which the assessment office claimed the agreement had been accepted had either been directly re-negotiated or become largely implausible. The promise in the agreement, for example, of an elected legislature to which the executive would be accountable had been undermined by the Basic Law and by China's refusal to permit more directly elected seats. In January 1986, the British and Chinese governments negotiated an agreement whereby Britain conceded that constitutional developments in Hong Kong in the transitional period would 'converge' with the Basic Law which was then still to be drafted by China.[35] However, an earlier white paper had promised that there would be a review of constitutional developments in 1987 and that the question whether there would be direct elections to the legislature in 1988 would be considered.[36] It seems clear from opinion polls that at least a plurality, and probably a majority, of Hong Kong people were in favour of the introduction of direct elections at that time.[37] Because of the British government's agreement with China, however, the Hong Kong government was forced to resort to the expedient of counting cyclostyled petitions from Chinese 'united front' organizations as part of assessed opinion against introducing direct elections.[38] Such tactics inevitably caused a backlash. The liberals probably gained support from those who saw the government's decision not to introduce direct elections as a violation of promises made in 1984 and as frustrating the democratic aspirations of the population.

The future autonomy of the territory was also a critical issue in post-1984 Hong Kong. The Basic Law, which included provisions for the stationing of People's Liberation Army troops in Hong Kong and for the declaration of a state of emergency at the wish of the Chinese government, soon illustrated the very limited self-government which Hong Kong was likely to enjoy after 1997.[39] The conclusion of another agreement between Britain and China in July 1991 to build a new airport in Hong Kong was further seen as compromising the territory's political and economic autonomy in the transitional period.[40]

Finally, civil liberties were called into question, partly because the Hong Kong government tried to introduce some ill-advised measures which raised questions about press freedom and judicial independence.[41] The Beijing massacre and the subsequent treatment of dissidents in China focused attention on the future sovereign power's view of political and civil liberties and did nothing to assuage local fears. In one sense, the 1991 direct elections results can be interpreted as a referendum on the past seven years. The elections represented the first opportunity that Hong Kong people have had to express themselves on a territory-wide basis on the Sino-British agreement and its aftermath. The election results were a vote against the Chinese government and against communism but also probably indicated a negative judgement on the facile role which the British and Hong Kong governments had played in failing to introduce representative government, to insist on autonomy and to protect civil liberties. The Beijing massacre was evidence, if evidence were needed, that the fears of the Hong Kong people were fully justified.

The Beijing Massacre

It may be too soon to estimate the full impact of the Beijing massacre on the political attitudes of the Hong Kong people. Over one million people (or 20% of the population) were estimated to have taken to the streets in one or more of the rallies organized in support of the pro-democracy movement in May and June 1989. The massacres were seen live on television and were widely condemned in the media, including one communist newspaper. The organization formed to aid the pro-democracy movement, the Hong Kong Alliance, was led by liberals and was denounced by the Chinese government as subversive. None the less, its leaders were still able to mobilize tens of thousands of supporters on the anniversaries of the massacre. It is not clear, however, that all the supporters of the Hong Kong Alliance were necessarily committed to the liberals' vision of a democratic future which, in any event, was rather vaguely stated. What united them — and what may have been reflected in the 1991 direct elections results — was a profound distaste for the Chinese system of government, for its political values and for the implications which this had for Hong Kong.

The Chinese Government's Campaign Tactics

Following the election campaign, the Chief Editor of the communist newspaper, *Ta Kung Pao,* concluded that Chinese official behaviour towards the election could be characterized as minimal involvement:

> There was no organized fielding of candidates. For the 18 seats con-
> tested in the direct elections, there were only three candidates from
> established pro-Beijing circles, and they had all decided to run on
> their own initiatives. There was no Chinese official attempt to con-
> tact more would-be candidates with enticement to run.[42]

He went on to point out in the same paper that no senior ranking local employee of official Chinese establishments in Hong Kong ran; that there was no attempt to remove the clause barring local people sitting on Chinese national or provincial legislatures from running; that there was no Chinese government support for any candidate; that there were no 'united front' tactics; that there was only limited, localized mobilization of support; and that no attempt was made to exclude any particular group.

It would perhaps have been more helpful for China's cause if these points had been made before the elections. There was evidence during the campaign that the New China News Agency was actively involved in supporting candidates and no doubt at all that it would have claimed the patriotic support of the Hong Kong people for the Chinese government had its candidates won. The difficulty for most candidates with Chinese connections was that they were aware that a pro-Beijing stance was a considerable electoral liability and that they took steps, accordingly, to distance themselves from the Chinese government and the New China News Agency. The fact remains that the New China News Agency did encourage particular candidates to run — in Hong Kong Island West, for example — and that it may not have exercised 'united front' tactics in that constituency only because the Agency itself was divided on the issue of whom to support.[43] The Chinese government did provide funds for preferred candidates of at least $100,000 and used such organizations as the Federation of Trade Unions to mobilize voters.[44] Finally, although it was later to claim that too much was made of this, the New China News Agency did warn Hong Kong voters to take candidates' attitudes to relations with mainland China into account when casting their votes.[45]

The Chinese government's role during the campaign does not seem to have influenced the vote significantly except perhaps to confirm the already established suspicions of the voters. There was some hardening of the Chinese position on democracy following the failed Soviet coup in August but there is no evidence that this had an impact on the elections. Given the financial and logistical support enjoyed by candidates backed by the Chinese government, it is surprising that they were able to garner so few votes.

Future Apprehension

Little more need be said about the growing apprehension with which Hong Kong people view the Chinese takeover in 1997. Before the 1991 elections, there were essentially two views on how the population should respond to this situation. One view held that the appropriate way to deal with China was through élite interaction, conceding the political demands of the Chinese leadership but seeking to preserve economic integrity and prosperity and to demonstrate, through this, the usefulness of the territory to China's modernization programmes. The second view, that of the liberals, was that, while there was a need to communicate with the Chinese leadership, this was best done on the solid foundation of a system which guaranteed civil and political liberties and which allowed properly elected representatives to present the views of the Hong Kong people. The latter position appears to have been supported by a solid majority of voters in the 1991 elections, but it was possibly not so much a consequence of the election campaign as an outcome of previous debates on constitutional issues.

If the 1991 election results can be interpreted as a referendum on the past rather than as an immediate response to the campaign, what conclusions can be drawn for the structuring of voter preferences? The liberals attracted two-thirds of the vote but it would seem that this vote was largely an anti-Chinese government vote rather than a vote for a particular political party. The United Democrats have yet to succeed in institutionalizing their political party; voters do not vote for the candidates because they are United Democrats but because they are perceived to be the group which has stood up most strongly for Hong Kong interests and in opposition to the Chinese government. To the extent that voter preferences are stable and rooted in history, it is that historical element rather than party loyalty which predominates. Provided that the United Democrats continue to occupy that part of the political spectrum they will continue to enjoy support but the fact that their candidates lost to other liberals in some constituencies does not suggest that they are necessarily in a monopoly position.

Finally, we may return to Key's criterion of a critical election: the extent to which the election represented a profound readjustment in power relations. In formal terms, there were no changes in power relations after the 1991 elections. Informally, however, the results from the direct elections can scarcely be ignored. They mean, first, that the Chinese government has no mandate from the people of Hong Kong to interfere in the affairs of the territory either before or after 1997. Secondly, the Hong Kong government, which is not elected, has no mandate to claim that it acts with the support of the people of Hong Kong, while the liberal opposition can speak from a basis of popular backing. There have already been some signs that the relationship between the executive and the legislature is changing, with the newly elected members, and some appointed members, seeking greater accountability. Thirdly, as a corollary, that the government's legitimacy and, in consequence, its ability to formulate and implement policy is considerably impaired. The election may not have resulted in a shift in power but it did suggest that the community was fundamentally disenchanted with both the existing and planned future political arrangements.

POLITICAL PARTICIPATION AND INVOLVEMENT

We can deal with the second of Key's criteria — the level of political involvement in the election — rather more briefly. The usual indicator of high involvement in an election campaign is the turnout rate. However, as we have seen, the turnout rate of 39.15% in the direct elections is, in important respects, misleading and represents a considerable underestimate of the percentage of registered voters actually casting their ballots. None the less, the qualitative indicators suggest that voters were not as highly committed to participation as one might expect in a 'critical election'. That is not to say that they were uninformed or that they were apathetic. Rather, voting seemed to constitute a single act in which voters expressed a preference rather than a process in which they might participate. There were no tumultuous or well-attended rallies, no landmark speeches and not much by way of active involvement in the campaign. The media did give the election a high level of coverage which kept the electorate well-informed of the candidates' positions but this did not usually lead to impassioned or didactic debates over policy issues either among candidates or between candidates and the electorate.[46] Voting itself seemed little more than a minor deviation from a normal Hong Kong Sunday. There were small groups of occasionally raucous candidates' supporters outside the polling stations, who sometimes made it difficult to vote, but the process of voting itself was conducted very peacefully, almost without incident.

There may be many reasons why Hong Kong voters were not deeply involved in the electoral process but the following considerations may be germane. First, the Hong Kong public has traditionally distanced itself from politics and from government. Although this view has changed gradually over the years, it is still a fairly widely held value that people should not be involved in politics. Secondly, the elections were not elections about winning political power. Control remained in the hands of the executive. The direct elections results did not change that fact, although they may have reduced further the extent to which the executive could treat the Legislative Council as a rubber stamp for its policies. Thirdly, the relatively recent emergence of political parties and political groups meant that there was only a limited organizational framework through which individuals could participate. The political parties did not have mass memberships or established district-level organizations; nor did they invite active participation from the electorate. These factors may become of less significance over time. The electoral process itself increased political awareness which, in turn, might possibly be expected to lead to greater involvement.

THE DURABILITY OF POLITICAL GROUPS

Key's third criterion has already been partially considered in our treatment of power relationships and political involvement. It is too early to say whether the political groups which emerged for the 1991 elections will prove to be durable. The United Democrats had been in existence for just over a year when the election was held.[47] The party is itself a coalition of various liberal groups and there is tension among them, particularly over party support for candidates in elections. Candidates with strong liberal credentials who did not receive the party nomination ran against United Democrats and some received a significant proportion of the vote. It is possible, however, that the strong showing of the party in the election will tend to discourage other liberal independents in future. The election results suggest that the only real challenge to the United Democrats comes from those who were perceived to have better liberal credentials than party candidates or from those who had established a strong local base of support. The party did not challenge Frederick Fung Kin-kee, the leader of the Association for Democracy and People's Livelihood, in Kowloon West, although this may change in the future.[48] Its candidates lost to a prominent liberal, Emily Lau Wai-hing, in New Territories East. And the labour activist, Lau Chin-shek, could probably have won under any label in Kowloon Central. Party loyalty, in short, has still to be established. In most constituencies, the United Democrats offered the best liberal alternative but, where there were choices, the voters were willing to consider those whose liberal political orientations best matched their own inclinations.

For the other declared party, the conservative Liberal Democratic Federation, the elections were little short of a disaster. Yet the party does have considerable financial and political resources and it is likely to remain an influence in Hong Kong politics although possibly in some reconstituted form. The party never claimed to seek a mass base, as the liberals did, and it has remained a collection of notables with ties to China and the Hong Kong governmental system rather than a distinctive organization. Its best prospects for the future, as one of its leaders, Maria Tam Wai-chu, candidly admitted, is the hope that the Hong Kong voter will see the need for a bridge with China in 1995. If the strong historical sensibilities of the voters remain in place, this may be a forlorn hope. None the less, because the functional constituencies are so strongly biased towards business and professional groups, it seems likely that the party will continue to enjoy political influence disproportionate to its popular support.[49]

Lau Siu-kai has suggested that the objective constraints to party development in Hong Kong are considerable.[50] No doubt in the constitutional context which the Chinese, British and Hong Kong governments have sought to establish there is little room for any party other than the Chinese Communist Party. There are also considerable constraints in terms of the organizational effort which the party — in this case, only the United Democrats are relevant — would need to make to establish a permanent base in the society.

Key's criterion, however, is not simply related to the likelihood of the political group enduring but also to the question whether the election results provide the means for creating durable political groups. Lo Chi-kin has remarked, for example, that the parties in the 1991 election were often less well-organized than the independent candidates.[51] As we have seen, the support for the United Democrats has not yet been structured into party loyalty; voters do not support the United Democrats in the same way, say, as they might support a football team. They support them, rather more rationally, because they represent a very specific viewpoint with which the voter agrees. There is the possibility of structuring that perception into more long-term durable support which might enable the party to retain voter support on wider policy issues, but this would require a more coherent policy message than the party has at present and a much more extensive organization.

CONCLUSIONS

If we examine the assumptions behind Key's criteria, the most obvious omission in the Hong Kong context is the notion that the democratic process will be allowed to proceed unhindered. If Hong Kong were a colony which was moving towards independence, then the 1991 elections would have significantly aided the emergence of a mass party and the further development of representative government. In Key's terms, they would have been critical elections. They may yet prove to be so. The Hong Kong voter delivered the unequivocal message that the territory should have an autonomous, free and democratic future untroubled by interference from the Chinese government. The results gave victories to a solid block of liberals, now composing over one-third of the members of the Legislative Council and 17 of the 18 members who are directly elected. Under most circumstances, this would represent a significant realignment of power away from the conservative and business groups who, together with the bureaucracy, have dominated Hong Kong's political system for so long. But that is not the way in which the political die have been cast. The Chinese government has set itself against future constitutional changes for more directly elected seats. It has declared that it has the right, and will actively exercise that right, to intervene in Hong Kong affairs before and after 1997. The 1991 elections results show that, if the Chinese government chooses to take this course of action, it will do so against the democratically expressed wishes of the Hong Kong people.

NOTES

1. V.O. Key, Jr., 'A Theory of Critical Elections', *Journal of Politics* 17 (February 1955): 3-18. Key also used the closely related concept of the 'realigning election' which was taken up in the classic study by Angus Campbell *et al., The American Voter* (New York: Wiley, 1960), pp.534-

536. See also Walter D. Burnham, *Critical Elections and the Mainsprings of American Politics* (New York: W.W. Norton, 1970); Jerome M. Chubb, William H. Flanigan and Nancy H. Zingale, *Partisan Realignment: Voters, Parties and Government in American History* (Beverly Hills: Sage Publications, 1982); James L. Sundquist, *Dynamics of the Party System: Alignments and Realignment in the United States* (Washington, D.C.: Brookings Institution, 1983); and Byron E. Shafer, 'The Election of 1988 and the Structure of American Politics: Thoughts on Interpreting an Electoral Order', *Electoral Studies*, 8,1 (December 1989): 5-21. A further related concept was the notion of 'dealignment', where traditional electoral loyalties had been undermined but where no new permanent voting patterns had been established. See Burnham, *Critical Elections* and Bo Sarlvik and Ivor Crewe, *Decade of Dealignment* (Cambridge: Cambridge University Press, 1983).

2. For a contrary view of the 1906 election, however, see Kenneth D. Wald, 'Realignment Theory and British Party Development', *Political Studies*, 30, 2(June 1982): 207-220.

3. V.O. Key, Jr., *The Responsible Electorate: Rationality in Presidential Voting* (Cambridge, Mass.: The Belknap Press of Harvard University Press, 1966).

4. Norman D. Palmer, *Elections and Political Development: The South Asian Experience* (Durham, N.C.: Duke University Press, 1975), p.16.

5. See, for example, David C. Mulford, *The Northern Rhodesian General Election 1962* (Nairobi: Oxford University Press, 1964).

6. See, for example, *SCMP,*12 September 1991. The notion that the elections might, or might not, be a 'success' seems to date from a statement made a year earlier by the Earl of Caithness, the British minister responsible for Hong Kong.

7. *An Agreement Between the Government of the United Kingdom of Great Britain and Northern Ireland and the Government of the People's Republic of China on the Future of Hong Kong* (Hong Kong: Government Printer, 1984).

8. *The Basic Law of the Hong Kong Special Administrative Region of the People's Republic of China* (Hong Kong: The Consultative Committee for the Basic Law of the Special Administrative Region of the People's Republic of China, April 1990).

9. See, for example, Ian Scott, *Political Change and the Crisis of Legitimacy in Hong Kong* (London: Hurst, 1989), Chapter 7.

10. See Chapter 4 and Social Sciences Research Centre, The University of Hong Kong, 'Public Opinion Programme', 11-13 September 1991, sponsored by Asia Television Limited (mimeo).

11. F.W.S. Craig, ed., *British Electoral Facts 1832-1987*, 5th ed. (Dartmouth: Parliamentary Research Services, 1989).

12. Ibid.

13. *Hong Kong 1991 Population Census: Tabulations for District Board*

Districts and Constituency Areas: Living Quarters, Households and Population by Type of Living Quarters (Hong Kong: Census and Statistics Department, 1991), p.13.

14. Most were professionals and business people chosen from among those who had loyally and conscientiously served on government committees.

15. *SCMP,* 17 September 1991.

16. See Ronald Skeldon, 'Emigration, Immigration and Fertility Decline: Demographic Integration or Disintegration', in Sung Yun-wing and Lee Ming-kwan, eds., *The Other Hong Kong Report* (Hong Kong: The Chinese University Press, 1991), pp.253-258.

17. Robert Chung, 'What Went Wrong With the Turnout Rate?' (unpublished manuscript).

18. *SCMP,* 9 October 1991. See also 'Lu Ping on the Elections', *Wen Wei Po,* 20 September 1991.

19. *SCMP,* 9 October 1991.

20. *SCMP,* 3 October 1991.

21. *Sunday Morning Post,* 30 June 1991.

22. This has been the government's objective since 1984 when the scheme to introduce functional constituencies was mooted in a green paper. The green paper argued that: 'Full weight should be given to representation of the economic and professional sectors of Hong Kong which are essential to future confidence and prosperity. Direct elections would run the risk of a swift introduction of adversarial politics, and would introduce an element of instability at a critical time.' See *Green Paper: The Further Development of Representative Government in Hong Kong* (Hong Kong: Government Printer, 1984), p.9.

23. The elected Regional Council functional constituency member, for example, was charged after the election with attempting to bribe an elector, *SCMP,* 20 December 1991. The functional constituency system has been widely criticized. See Electoral Reform Society's *Report* (London: 1991, mimeo), s.5; Ian Scott, 'Functional Constituencies and Representation', paper presented at a conference on 'Democracy and Political Development: Hong Kong Characteristics', organized by the Hong Kong Democratic Foundation, 19 May 1991; Ian Scott, 'Digging a Hole for Functional Constituencies', *SCMP,* 21 September 1991. For the government view, see the paper given by the Secretary for Constitutional Affairs, Michael M.Y. Suen, 'The Hong Kong Electoral System and Its Future Development', at a conference on 'Democracy and Political Development : Hong Kong Characteristics', organized by the Hong Kong Democratic Foundation, 19 May 1991. See also Hong Kong Democratic Foundation, 'Electoral Reform Proposals' (mimeo), November 1991.

24. *The Basic Law,* pp. 65-67.

25. This was particularly evident in Island East, where the United Democrat leader, Martin Lee Chu-ming, was running.

26. Lee Ming-kwan, 'Issue Positions Assumed by Candidates Standing for Elections to the Legislative Council, 1991', paper presented at a conference on 'Politics and the 1991 Elections in Hong Kong', City Polytechnic of Hong Kong, 27 October 1991.

27. 'Emily Lau Wai-hing's Election Manifesto', n.d. (mimeo).

28. *Sunday Morning Post,* 15 September 1991.

29. If we exclude non-voters in the Legislative Council elections, the percentage is even higher (see Chapter 3).

30. *Hong Kong Standard,* 5 March 1991. The United Democrats, for example, saw 56 of its 80 candidates returned.

31. Exit polls conducted by the Social Sciences Research Centre, The University of Hong Kong, conclusively show the bifurcated nature of political support in this constituency. Ng Ming-yum had previously won a District Board seat in Tuen Mun in the March elections, polling more votes than any candidate in the territory, *SCMP,* 5 March 1991.

32. *Hong Kong 1991 Population Census: Summary Results* (Hong Kong: Census and Statistics Department, 1991), p.40.

33. A liberal legislator who was elected in the Kowloon Central constituency, Dr Conrad Lam Kui-shing, put the matter rather precisely when he described Hong Kong people as 'anti-communist Chinese patriots', *SCMP,* 12 September 1987. The demonstrations in support of the democracy movement in China, when it was estimated that over one million Hong Kong people took to the streets, illustrated the point. See also Lau Siu-kai and Kuan Hsin-chi, *The Ethos of the Hong Kong Chinese* (Hong Kong: The Chinese University Press, 1988), p.84 and Norman Miners, *The Government and Politics of Hong Kong,* 5th ed. (Hong Kong: Oxford University Press, 1991), p.23.

34. Report of the Assessment Office, *Arrangements for Testing the Acceptability in Hong Kong of the Draft Agreement on the Future of the Territory* (Hong Kong: Government Printer, 29 November 1984).

35. *Hong Kong Standard,* 22 January 1986.

36. *White Paper: The Further Development of Representative Government in Hong Kong* (Hong Kong: Government Printer, 29 November 1984).

37. See Scott, *Political Change,* Chapter 8.

38. Ibid., p.294.

39. *The Basic Law,* Art. 18.

40. 'Memorandum of Understanding Concerning the Construction of the New Airport in Hong Kong and Related Questions', 4 July 1991 (mimeo).

41. See, for example, Scott, *Political Change,* pp.312-316 and Albert H.Y. Chen, 'Civil Liberties in Hong Kong: Recent Controversies, Evolving Consciousness and Future Legal Protection', *Journal of Chinese Law,* 2, 1(Spring 1989): 137-151.

42. Tsang Tak-shing, 'On Chinese Official Attitudes Towards Legco Election

'91', paper presented at a conference on 'Politics and the 1991 Elections in Hong Kong', City Polytechnic of Hong Kong, 27 October 1991. Presumably the author was excluding candidates from the New Hong Kong Alliance.

43. *Hong Kong Standard,* 7 September 1991.

44. *Hong Kong Standard,* 11 September 1991.

45. *SCMP* and *Ming Pao,* 1 September 1991.

46. There were occasional heated television debates but they were mainly over allegations made about candidates, past support for constitutional reform and attitudes towards China rather than more conventional policy issues. See *Hong Kong Standard,* 4 September 1991.

47. On the origins of political parties in Hong Kong, see Louie Kin-sheun, 'Political parties', in Sun Yun-wing and Lee Ming-kwan, eds., *The Other Hong Kong Report* (Hong Kong: The Chinese University Press, 1991), pp.55-75.

48. The Meeting Point candidate in the by-election in New Territories West in December 1991 was opposed by a candidate from the Association for Democracy and People's Livelihood. Relations between the United Democrats and Meeting Point are much closer than those between the United Democrats and the Association for Democracy and People's Livelihood.

49. The party did win 50 seats out of the 89 contested in the March 1991 District Board elections. However, some of the successful candidates only declared their membership in the Liberal Democratic Federation after the election results had been declared.

50. Lau Siu-kai, 'Public Attitude Towards Political Parties in Hong Kong', paper presented at a conference on 'Politics and the 1991 Elections in Hong Kong', City Polytechnic of Hong Kong, 27 October 1991.

51. Lo Chi-kin, 'Do Parties Matter?', paper presented at a conference on 'Politics and the 1991 Elections in Hong Kong', City Polytechnic of Hong Kong, 27 October 1991.

Part I

Voting Behaviour in Kowloon Central

2

Kowloon Central: The Constituency, the People and the Candidates

Rowena Y.F. Kwok

Kowloon Central, which comprises the administrative districts of Kowloon City and Wong Tai Sin, is one of nine double-seat constituencies which were created for the first direct elections (Map 2.1). It is a largely working-class constituency which forms part of the industrial heartland of Hong Kong. To the east lies Kwun Tong, noted for its factories and high pollution levels; to the west, Mongkok, one of the most densely populated areas in the world. Kowloon Central itself has a population density of just over 41,000 persons per square kilometre, approximately one-third that of Mongkok, but still high enough to make for often cramped living and working conditions.[1] Kai Tak Airport (see Map 2.2) lies on the south-eastern boundary of the constituency and life in Kowloon Central is punctuated throughout the day and much of the night by the sound of aircraft landing and departing. The presence of the airport has meant that the height of buildings has been restricted, discouraging the type of urban renewal which has seen new skyscrapers rise in other parts of Hong Kong. However, there are pockets of middle-class and even upper middle-class housing scattered throughout the constituency. To the south,

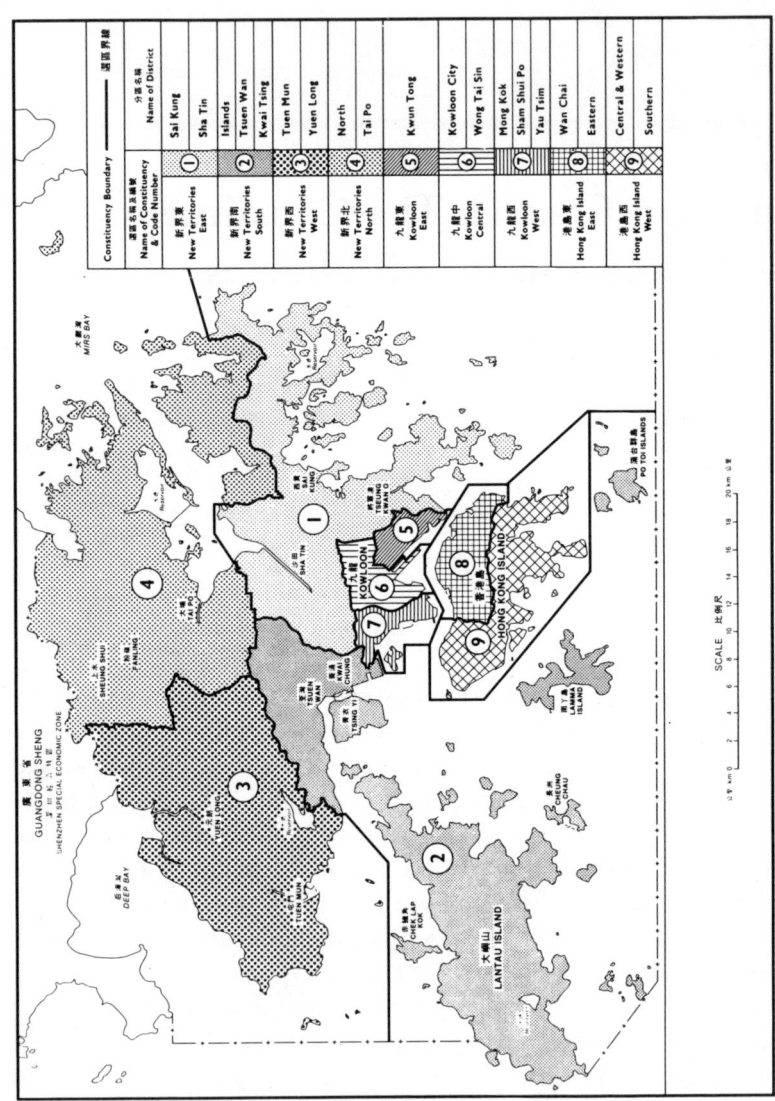

Map 2.1 Legislative Council Electoral Boundaries

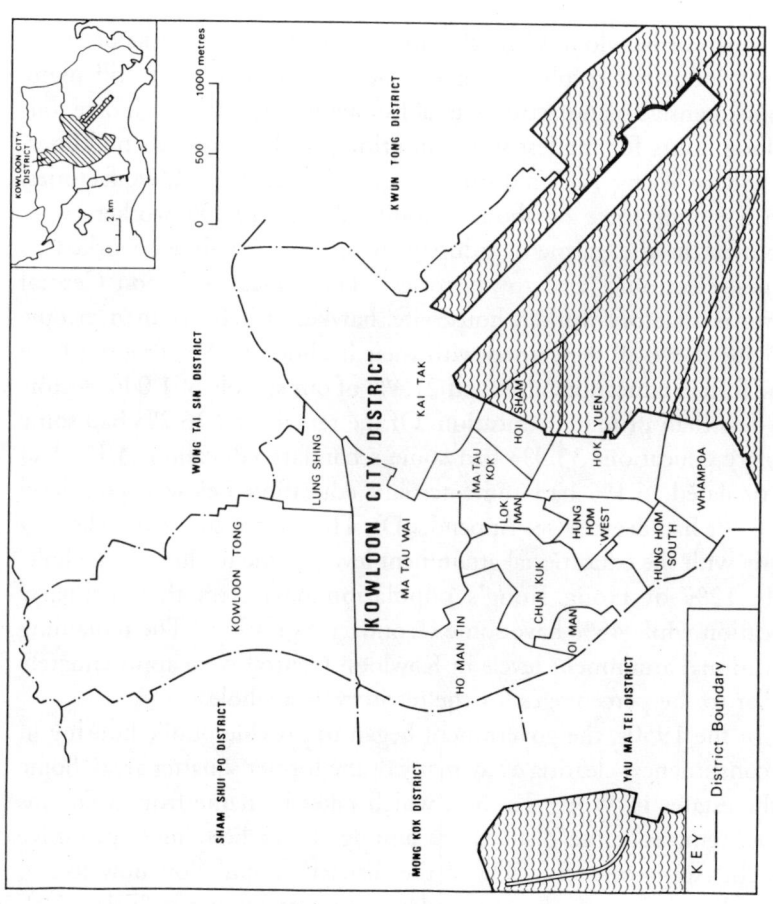

Map 2.2 Kowloon City District

considerable redevelopment has occurred in Hung Hom, Homantin and at Whampoa Gardens, where a middle-class housing estate has sprung up. In the north, the constituency runs through the pleasant middle-class and upper middle-class residential district of Kowloon Tong towards the 'nine dragons' or peaks which give Kowloon its name.

Much of Kowloon Central continues to show the marks of Hong Kong's industrial revolution of the late 1950s. There are still many labour-intensive manufacturing establishments where the workforce toils for long hours for modest wages in grimy, badly ventilated buildings. In 1988, in Wong Tai Sin district (Map 2.3), there were 2,000 factories, with a labour force of about 70,000. Almost 40,000 workers were employed in the garment industry, while the remainder worked in textiles, electronics and toy factories.[2] The typical Kowloon Central elector is a factory worker, housewife, hawker or delivery man, people who are above all concerned with their livelihoods. Most would have some formal education, although 21.4% of our sample of 1,046 electors had 'less than primary' education. Of the remainder, 26.2% had some primary education, 35.9% had some secondary education, 4.1% had matriculated, 6.1% had some tertiary education below degree level and 6.3% had degrees (see Appendix D). The sample compares relatively poorly with the educational attainment levels of the territory as a whole. Only 12% of Hong Kong's population have 'less than primary' education while 45% have some secondary education.[3] The remaining educational attainment levels in Kowloon Central were approximately similar to the percentages for the territory as a whole.

In the 1950s, the government began to provide public housing in the constituency, clearing away many of the former squatter areas. Some of the estates in Wong Tai Sin, which takes its name from a famous Taoist temple in the district, are among the earliest, most primitive models. Approximately 74% of the district's population now live in public housing, with the remainder in private buildings (Table 2.1). In contrast, Kowloon City consists mainly of private buildings, which house about 83% of its inhabitants, 16% of them in public housing estates and the remainder in orphanages, homes for the elderly, rehabilitation centres and temporary housing. Housing is a principal concern in both districts. In 1989, in Kowloon City, for example,

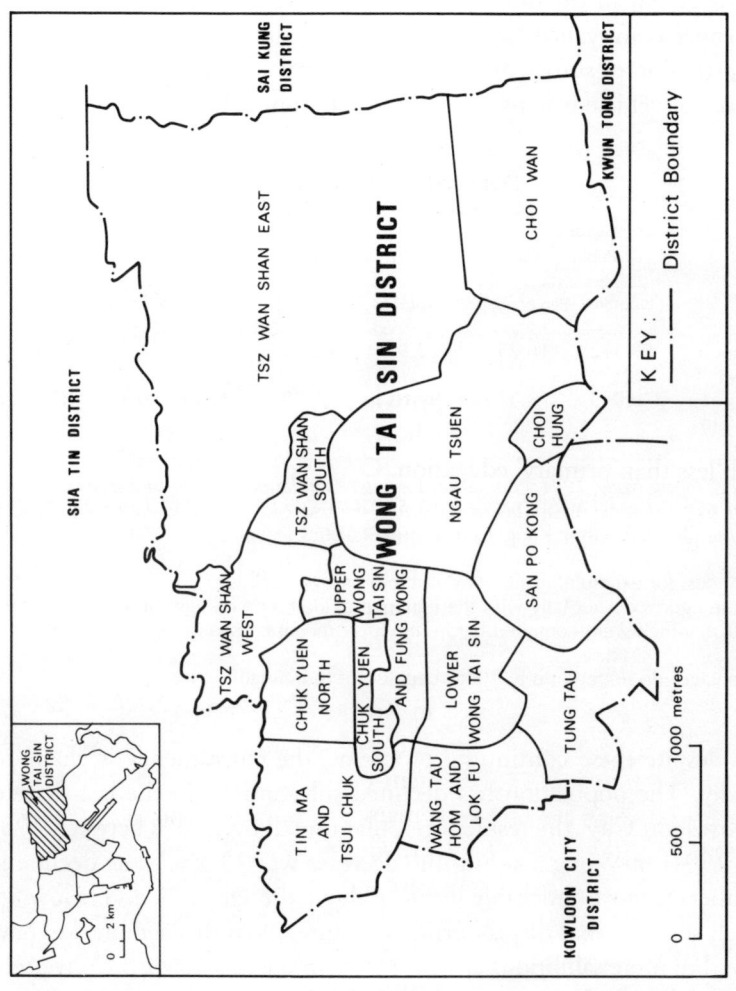

Map 2.3 Wong Tai Sin District

about 31% of complaints to the District Board were about housing while a further 11% each were concerned with social welfare and building management problems.[4] The whole constituency is beset with infrastructural and environmental problems. Needs include the improvement of the drainage system, the installation of underground passenger conveyance facilities, improvements in traffic management, the provision of sufficient parking space and strategies to deal with the impact of vehicle exhaust fumes and environmental pollution.

Table 2.1 Kowloon Central:
distribution of population by housing type

	Public housing		Private housing		Others[a]		Population[b]
	Number	Percentage	Number	Percentage	Number	Percentage	
Kowloon City	63,352	16.25	322,527	82.73	3,960	1	389,839
Wong Tai Sin	279,043	73.87	96,612	25.58	2,081	0.55	377,736

Source: Hong Kong 1991 Population Census: Tabulations for District Board Districts and Constituency Areas: Living Quarters, Households and Population by Type of Living Quarters (Hong Kong: Census and Statistics Department, 1991).

[a] Includes, for example, institutions and temporary housing.
[b] These figures do not tally with the figures provided by the Registration and Electoral Office, which were compiled before the most recent census in March 1991.

Percentages do not add up to 100% because of rounding.

Despite these continuing problems, the constituency is changing rapidly. The population has declined substantially in the last decade. In Kowloon City, the resident population fell by 18.3% between 1981 and 1991; in Wong Tai Sin, the decrease was 23.3%.[5] The decline in numbers is most noticeable in those above the age of 30 and below 55, which suggests that disproportionate numbers in this age bracket have moved to more salubrious environments in the new towns.[6] Conversely, compared with the territory as a whole, the constituency has a slightly higher percentage of young people below the age of 30 and more elderly people above the age of 55. The physical face of the constituency is also changing. The festering sore of the Kowloon Walled City, long a sanctuary for petty criminals, unlicensed medical and dental practitioners and drug addicts, is being demolished and replaced with a park. The airport at Kai Tak will also be closed down when the new airport at Chek Lap Kok is opened in 1997, which will release a further 300 hectares for redevelopment and will help to improve the quality of life in the constituency.

We chose to conduct our surveys in Kowloon Central for two reasons. First, we thought that it would be fruitful to study a constituency in which as many different political interests and groups as possible were represented. In some constituencies — for example, Island East, where Martin Lee Chu-ming, the leader of the United Democrats, was running — it seemed likely that the personal popularity of one candidate would so overshadow the remaining candidates that we would find it difficult to distinguish other factors which influenced vote choice. In Kowloon Central, no single candidate was seen to be in such a strong position that the electoral results were a foregone conclusion. The liberals were strongly represented but so, too, were conservative and pro-China forces. In particular, we thought that it was important to assess the extent and nature of support which a pro-China candidate could mobilize and Kowloon Central was the only constituency in which the pro-China Federation of Trade Unions was represented. Secondly, Kowloon Central presented the chance to ascertain the political views of a largely working-class electorate which supposedly had strong trade union links. There had been previous studies of working-class political attitudes, notably in Kwun Tong,[7] but this was the first opportunity to link those attitudes to voting behaviour in elections which were perceived to be important for the future of the territory. We expected to be able to reach conclusions about the electorate's political orientations and the influence of policy issues and other criteria on the choice of candidate.

Our research findings were derived from the results of three surveys which were conducted on the basis of face-to-face interviews using a structured questionnaire. (For further details and the questionnaire, see Appendices B and C.) The first survey, which was carried out in the week before the elections, elicited 1,046 successful responses. Of the respondents to the pre-election survey, 570 were interviewed again immediately after the elections. The third survey consisted of a further

141 respondents who had not been interviewed prior to the elections. A profile of the respondents is contained in Appendix D.

THE ELECTORATE AND REGISTRATION

For the Legislative Council elections, each constituency was to return two members. Kowloon Central was the second most populous constituency and had the highest number of registered voters (Table 2.2). Of the 287,373 registered voters, 151,231 (52.6%) were male and

Table 2.2 Population and registration by constituency

	Population	Potential electorate	Number and percentage of registered voters
Hong Kong East	794,900	504,178	261,573(51.88)
Hong Kong West	540,700	342,948	171,052(49.88)
Kowloon East	570,300	361,722	217,117(60.02)
Kowloon Central	751,300	476,525	287,373(60.3)
Kowloon West	731,500	463,967	213,345(45.9)
New Territories East	656,100	416,143	197,614(47.4)
New Territories West	647,600	410,751	198,817(48.4)
New Territories South	742,400	470,880	248,045(52.6)
New Territories North	392,400	248,886	121,989(49.0)
Total	5,827,200	3,696,000	1,916,925(51.86)

Source: Compiled from statistics provided by the Registration and Electoral Office of the Hong Kong government.

136,142 (47.4%) were female, close to the territory-wide ratios of 52.85% and 47.15%.[8] The voter registration rate, however, was over 60% of the eligible population, and was the highest among the constituencies, and it was significantly higher than the territory-wide figure of 52%. This may be attributed to efforts by the trade unions to register voters. However, they were not so successful in persuading potential voters to cast their ballots. The turnout in Kowloon Central was, in fact, slightly lower than the territory-wide average. One important variable in explaining turnout is the type of housing. It is clear from Table 2.3, for example, that in all but one previous elections Kowloon City district invariably had a lower turnout rate than Wong

Tai Sin. This may be related to the larger proportion of private sector accommodation in Kowloon City which makes the electorate relatively less susceptible to mass mobilization efforts than the public housing estates in Wong Tai Sin. As a whole, however, Kowloon Central constituency was on a par with the territory average in terms of turnout rates.

Table 2.3 Kowloon Central: voting records (1982-1991)

Election	Numbers and percentage of turnout		
	Kowloon City	Wong Tai Sin	Territory-wide
District Board 1982	28,053(34.8)	33,774(37.5)	342,764(38.9)
Urban Council 1983	17,787(22.0)	13,101(25.8)	127,206(22.4)
District Board 1985	28,666(29.4)	39,878(34.3)	476,558(37.5)
Urban Council 1986	13,234(24.3)	32,215(22.9)	362,107(26.9)
District Board 1988	22,072(22.3)	38,240(29.4)	424,201(30.3)
Urban Council 1989	9,150(16.1)	26,631(18.3)	213,200(17.6)
District Board 1991	25,194(27.5)	30,782(34.8)	423,923(32.5)
Urban Council 1991	23,750(19.1)	17,882(28.5)	393,764(23.1)
Legislative Council 1991	46,603(36.9)	63,440(39.4)	750,467(39.1)

Source: Registration and Electoral Office of the Hong Kong government.

THE ELECTORAL CONTEXT

Kowloon Central is a blue-collar constituency which has had a sufficiently varied political history to suggest that candidates from across the spectrum had chances to win seats. Some thought that the seat was 'red', given the long history of pro-communist forces in the constituency. Some thought that they might be able to turn it 'green', the colour of the United Democrats.[9] And conservative and business groups pointed to their record of control over the Kowloon City District

Board and their belief, as one commentator put it, that 'the old and politically conservative district of Kowloon City does not provide the kind of soil that nourishes the seeds of liberalism'.[10]

Kowloon Central has been called a 'liberated' area because its inhabitants were thought to be supporters of the Chinese government.[11] Organizations sympathetic to Beijing have long been established in the constituency. It is the home of the pro-China Federation of Trade Unions (FTU), which was formed in 1948 and which claims a membership of over 170,000.[12] A vice-chairman of the FTU, Mr Tam Yiu-chung, has been elected unopposed since 1985 as one of two labour functional constituency representatives in the Legislative Council. Since 1988, the FTU has been advocating 'a marriage of the labour movement with the social movement.'[13] Aggressive measures were taken to broaden the base of support for the FTU. Membership of the FTU was computerized on a district basis in 1988 and a chain of shops and a centre for labour education and development were opened. The education centre was meant to hold specially designed courses on the labour movement to groom young union leaders while the shops were run as a service to members. Such measures were seen to be effective in attracting new members and retaining old ones. The emphasis on recruitment was much in line with China's views on the importance of 'cultivating the masses' in the territory. The local director of the New China News Agency, for example, had urged leaders of mass organizations to encourage members to take part in politics and the direct elections.[14] The FTU ran 16 candidates in the March 1991 District Board elections, of whom 12 were elected; six of the 16 candidates ran in Kowloon City.[15]

Kaifong leaders and mutual aid committees also had impressive networks in Kowloon Central. Kaifongs have traditionally provided services such as schools and clinics directly to residents within the district. One important organization located in the constituency is the Hung Hom Sam Yeuk Kaifong Association, which operates temples, schools and clinics. Mutual aid committees were conceived by the Hong Kong government in the 1970s as part of a policy to involve residents of public housing estates in the management of minor environmental matters and law and order issues. Most kaifongs and committees have been conservative and pro-China in their political orientation.

The liberals constituted a third force in the constituency and have been attempting to establish the foundations for electoral success since 1985. In that year, Dr Conrad Lam Kui-shing (hereafter referred to as Lam), later a founding member of the United Democrats and one of their two candidates in the 1991 elections, was elected through the District Board electoral college to the Legislative Council. Three years later, however, Lam was defeated in the electoral college by Cheng Tak-kin, who became Wong Tai Sin's representative in the Legislative Council. Cheng was reported to be closely associated with the influential East Kowloon Residents' Committee and the conservative Progressive Hong Kong Society. The Residents' Committee, which was several thousand strong, was in turn believed to have good 'Beijing connections' which dated back to the 1950s.[16] In previous District Board elections, the liberals had found themselves competing with these peripheral pro-China neighbourhood associations and kaifongs. The liberals had won some seats in those elections but their support was not initially seen to be as strong as the FTU or the conservative and business groups. However, new developments in the constituency gave them some hope. The construction of private housing estates at Whampoa Gardens was expected to dilute the power of the older kaifong groups and bring in a younger middle-class population to Kowloon Central.

THE CANDIDATES

The United Democrats nominated Lam and Lau Chin-shek (hereafter referred to as Lau) as their candidates. Despite Lam's previous service on the District Board and in the legislature and his long-established credentials as a liberal, Lau, who was a prominent labour activist with a high level of name recognition, was seen to be the stronger candidate.[17] He was a committee member of the Hong Kong Alliance, an umbrella organization which was formed in 1989 after the Beijing massacre, and he was widely believed to be one of the pro-democracy activists whom the Chinese government would not tolerate in the post-1997 legislature. Given the Hong Kong people's revulsion against the military suppression of the 1989 pro-democracy movement, Lau's association with the Alliance was expected to be a political asset. Both United Democrats publicized the support given to them by the internationally renowned Chinese dissidents, Professor Fang Lizhi and journalist Liu Bin-yan.[18]

The FTU candidate was Chan Yuen-han (hereafter referred to as Chan), a director of the organization, who had been involved in trade union activities for many years. Both she and Lau claimed to represent the working class. The only major area of difference between them was their respective stances on Sino-Hong Kong relations, although this was also the area in which they were most unlikely to have any

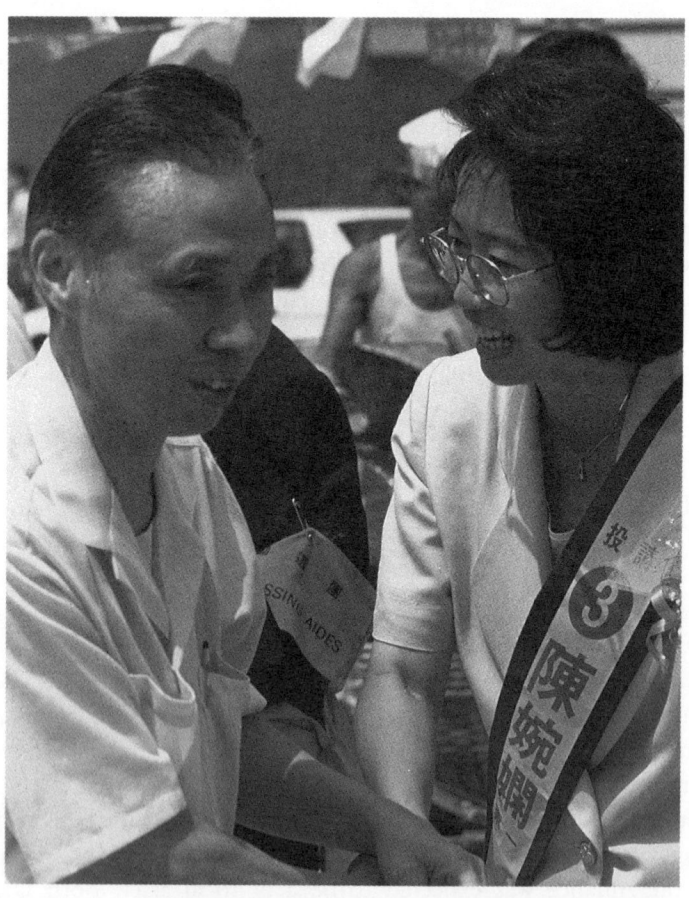

Plate 2 Chan Yuen-han campaigning

real influence. Chan was reportedly backed by a thousand-strong campaign team and had sufficient resources to be able to campaign on a door-to-door basis and to conduct surveys among the electorate on matters of concern.

Apart from the three major candidates, the two oldest political organizations in the territory also chose to field candidates in Kowloon Central. Peter Chan Chi-kwan of the Civic Association and Cecilia Yeung Lai-yin (hereafter referred to as Yeung) of the Reform Club had both been returned from the districts of Kowloon City and Wong Tai Sin to the Urban Council. Peter Chan had served for 22 years before losing his seat in the May 1991 elections. However, he was expected to obtain some support from past loyalists and his record as a legal adviser to the FTU, but he was not explicitly identified with pro-China forces. Yeung had a long association with the kaifongs in the constituency and also had 20 years' service as an Urban Councillor.

The independent candidates, in the face of strong organizational support for their opponents, had to fight an uphill battle to get their message across to the electorate. Mr John Young (hereafter referred to as Young), an independent candidate, attached a huge banner with his name on it to a helicopter which flew over the constituency to try to make an impression on the electorate. He also caused some disquiet when it was reported that he had inserted a discount offer for his academic publications in the promotion materials which the government mailed free of charge on behalf of candidates.[19] Another independent candidate, Mr Justin Cheung Chung-ming (hereafter referred to as Cheung), told us that he had only a fraction of the sanctioned maximum of $200,000 electioneering funds to spend on the campaign and had fewer than 20 friends helping him and even these were not regular helpers. He was so much on his own that he had neither the financial nor the manpower resources to make full use of the government's free delivery of campaign materials. The intensity of the competition and the feeling of being disadvantaged on the part of independent candidates could perhaps be gauged when Young and Cheung threatened to withdraw from the elections when one of the local television stations revealed that it was going to conduct exit polls on polling day but would not promise to keep the findings off the air until polling closed. A profile of the seven candidates is contained in Table 2.4.

Table 2.4 A profile of the candidates in Kowloon Central

Chan Chi-kwan, Peter
55, barrister-at-law. Independent candidate. Former vice-chairman of the Civic Association and legal adviser to the FTU. Former Kowloon City District Board member (1982-1991), and Urban Councillor (1969-1991).
Campaign themes: to keep the government in check and make Hong Kong a stable and prosperous city.

Chan Yuen-han
44, candidate and standing executive committee member of the FTU. Former Hong Kong Island East District Board member (1988-1991) and chairwoman of the Hong Kong and Kowloon Department Store Workers' Association (1989-present).
Campaign themes: to promote democracy, improve people's livelihood and fight for grassroots interests.

Cheung Chung-ming, Justin
37, accounting and tax consultant. Independent candidate. No public service record, a political unknown.
Campaign themes: to push for a peaceful, honest and just social movement to stabilize society; to bargain with the Chinese, British and Hong Kong governments on behalf of the lower to lower-middle classes and small to medium businessmen.

Lam Kui-shing, Conrad
55, medical practitioner. Candidate of the UDHK. Founding committee member and central committee member of UDHK (1990-present). Former Legislative Councillor (1985-1988) and Wong Tai Sin District Board member (1981-present). Also standing committee member of the Hong Kong Alliance (1990-present).
Campaign themes: to fight for grassroots interests and build a democratic Hong Kong.

Lau Chin-shek
46, church worker and high-profile unionist. Candidate of the UDHK. Founding committee member and central committee member of UDHK (1990-present). Director of the Christian Industrial Committee (1980-present) which preaches the Gospel to workers and is active on labour issues. Also Chairman of the Hong Kong Confederation of Trade Unions (1990-current) and standing committee member of the Hong Kong Alliance (1989-present).
Campaign themes: to fight for grassroots interests and build a democratic Hong Kong.

Yeung Lai-yin, Cecilia
60, school supervisor and principal. Independent candidate. Vice-chairwoman of the Reform Club. Wong Tai Sin District Board member (1983-1989, 1991-present) and Urban Councillor (1971-present).
Campaign themes: to reflect grassroots opinions, defend people's livelihood and scrutinize government operations.

Young, John Dragon
42, academic. Independent candidate. Former Shatin District Board member (1988-1991) and former member of the UDHK.
Campaign themes: democracy, human rights and the rule of law.

THE RESULTS

The liberals won the elections in Kowloon Central by a surprisingly large margin (Table 2.5). Their somewhat tenuous base in the constituency was far less important, in the event, than the personal popularity of Lau which, in turn, helped the cause of his running mate, Lam. Chan clearly had support in the constituency but she was not able to overcome the disadvantage of her association with the Chinese government. Peter Chan and Yeung were unable to translate the support which they enjoyed in Urban Council elections to a territory-wide election. The Reform Club and Civic Association do not seem to be organizations which in themselves can generate electoral support and they are unlikely to be significant forces in future territory-wide elections. The independents fared very badly, finding it difficult to convey a message to the electorate which distinguished them sufficiently from the major contestants.

Table 2.5 The election results in Kowloon Central

Candidates	Number of votes[a]	Percentage of the vote in the constituency
Lau Chin-shek (UDHK)[b]	68,489	34.2
Lam Kui-shing, Conrad (UDHK)[b]	56,084	28.0
Chan Yuen-han (FTU)	44,894	22.4
Chan Chi-kwan, Peter (HKCA)	14,145	7.1
Yeung Lai-yin, Cecilia (HKRC)	8,257	4.1
Young, John Dragon (I)	6,273	3.1
Cheung Chung-ming, Justin (I)	2,158	1.1
Turnout	110,043(38.3%)	
Registered electorate	287,373	

Source : Compiled from *The Hong Kong Government Gazette Extraordinary*, 133(41), 20 September 1991, and statistics provided by the Registration and Electoral Office of the Hong Kong government.

[a] Each voter was entitled to two votes.
[b] Elected candidate.

In the following chapters, we examine in more detail the reasons why the electorate in Kowloon Central voted as they did. The most important factor determining the voters' choice for the liberal candidates was their political stance towards the Chinese government. This is analysed at some length in Chapter 3. In Chapter 4, the authors consider the importance of components of the '1997 issue' and the extent to which issue voting was a salient factor in electoral choice. Chapters 5 and 6 examine the criteria used by the electorate in making their choices and the degree to which they were consistent with preferences expressed prior to the elections. The findings suggest that voters were rather more independent, thoughtful and sophisticated than had previously been assumed. Part I concludes with Chapter 7 in which we draw together our conclusions on voting behaviour in Kowloon Central.

NOTES

1. *Hong Kong 1991 Population Census: Summary Results* (Hong Kong: Census and Statistics Department, 1991), p.70.

2. Finance and Standing Committee, Wong Tai Sin District Board, *A Brief Introduction to the Wong Tai Sin District and Wong Tai Sin District Board* (Hong Kong: Government Printer, 1990).

3. *Hong Kong 1991 Population Census: Summary Results,* p.46.

4. Kowloon City District Board, 'Progress Report of the KCDB Members' Meet-the-Public Scheme in 1989', Annex C, KCDB Paper 26/90, February 1990 (mimeo).

5. *Hong Kong 1991 Population Census: Summary Results,* p.69.

6. Calculated from *Hong Kong 1991 Population Census: Summary Results* and *Hong Kong 1991 Population Census: Tabulations for District Board Districts and Constituency Areas: Population by Age and Sex* (Hong Kong: Census and Statistics Department, 1991).

7. See, for example, Ambrose Yeo-chi King, 'The Political Culture of Kwun Tong: A Chinese Community in Hong Kong', in Ambrose Y.C. King and Rance P.L. Lee, eds., *Social Life and Development in Hong Kong* (Hong Kong: The Chinese University Press, 1981), pp.147-168; Lau Siu-kai and Kuan Hsin-chi, *The Ethos of the Hong Kong Chinese* (Hong Kong: The Chinese University Press, 1988).

8. Figures supplied by the Registration and Electoral Office of the Hong Kong government.

9. *SCMP,* 11 September 1991.

10. *Hong Kong Standard,* 26 February 1988.

11. *Far Eastern Economic Review,* 29 August 1991.

12. *SCMP,* 24 February 1991.

13. *Hong Kong Standard,* 19 January 1988.
14. *SCMP,* 21 June 1990.
15. *SCMP,* 24 February 1991.
16. *Hong Kong Standard,* 19 April 1990.
17. In a poll conducted by the Social Sciences Research Centre of The University of Hong Kong from 1 to 6 September 1991 (sponsored by the *SCMP*), Lau had the support of 43.5% of the intended voters while Lam, in second place, obtained 29.9%. These figures were considerably higher than the percentage of the vote actually obtained (see Table 2.5).
18. *Hong Kong Standard,* 11 September 1991.
19. *Ming Pao,* 3 September 1991.

3

Political Orientations: Turnout and Vote Choice

Joan Y. H. Leung

Voting behaviour is affected both by environmental variables such as the political, economic and historical context in which the elections take place and by the socio-economic status and attitudinal dispositions of the electorate. The relative importance of these factors depends on the locality and timing of the elections and whether the electorate believe that critical issues are at stake. The central theme of this chapter is that the turnout and choice of candidates in the 1991 Legislative Council elections were shaped more by Hong Kong's volatile political environment than by the socio-economic attributes of the electorate.

Both environmental variables and personal attributes come together to influence the voter's disposition towards the political world, which consists of cognitive, affective and evaluative perceptions of political reality. According to Milbrath, the political, economic and social setting provides the stimuli from which an individual perceives and formulates his political outlook and perspective which, in turn, are mediated by his personality.[1] Contexts and events in the political world have a role in influencing these dispositions, which are reinforced through cognition or the experienced consequences of behaviour. Political dispositions tend to be stabilized into political orientations, though they may change in response to perceptions of events occurring in the political world. Political orientations, in turn, have considerable implications for voting behaviour because they shape the electorate's attitudes and influence their actions.

This chapter concentrates on the importance of political orientations in the electorate's decision whether to vote or not to vote and the implications for their choice of candidates. We are concerned only with those political orientations which appear to have had a significant impact on vote choice.[2] These were political knowledge, political efficacy and confidence in the government, the perception of Hong Kong's political future and its relationship with China, and attitudes towards the important issues of the provision of welfare by the government and progress towards democracy. There were seven candidates in the Kowloon Central constituency but the discussion is limited to the three major candidates — Lau Chin-shek (hereafter referred to as Lau), Lam Kui-shing (hereafter referred to as Lam) and Chan Yuen-han (hereafter referred to as Chan) — because the numbers of respondents voting for the other candidates were too small to allow firm conclusions to be drawn.[3]

POLITICAL ORIENTATIONS OF THE ELECTORATE

Political Knowledge

The political knowledge of the electorate in Kowloon Central was high. Respondents were well-informed about the date of the elections and the names of the principal candidates and their political stance but were less knowledgeable about the minor candidates and the institutional context in which the elections were taking place. A week before the elections, for example, 79.9% of our respondents could correctly name the date of the elections and 74.7% could identify four or more candidates in the constituency. The number of candidates running in Kowloon Central was among the highest of all constituencies in the 1991 elections, although the contest focused largely on the three main candidates. That a substantial majority of the electorate could identify more than four candidates suggests that there was a high level of cognition in the constituency.

Apart from identifying their names, the electorate also had a good general awareness of candidates' political stance. For example, among those who managed to recognize Lau and Lam, 64.5% and 58.3% respectively identified them as 'liberal' while 34.7% of those who recognized Chan identified her as pro-China (Table 3.1). The fact that as many as 46% were not able to identify Chan's political stance was an interesting finding. This probably reflects her reluctance to be identified as a pro-China candidate, which was clearly seen to be an electoral liability. Nevertheless, a significant proportion of the electorate knew that she had pro-China connections, which again suggests a fairly high level of cognition.

Table 3.1 Respondents' identification of candidates' political stance

Political stance	Lau (%)	Lam (%)	Chan (%)
Liberal	64.5	58.3	6.0
Independent	0.6	1.4	3.7
Conservative/ business	—	0.3	0.9
Pro-China	0.6	0.9	34.7
Others	8.7	5.7	8.8
Don't know/ no answer	25.6	33.3	46.0
Total	100.0%	99.9%	100.1%
(N)	(355)	(348)	(352)

Percentages do not add up to 100% because of rounding.

Our respondents were less well-informed about political groups to which the candidates belonged. Only about one-third of the respondents could correctly name the political organizations to which the candidates were affiliated (Table 3.2). This may be attributed to the short history of the United Democrats, which was only formed in April 1990, and the relatively low profile of the other organizations. The Federation of Trade Unions has a long history in the territory but, because of its opposition to colonial rule, it has avoided any formal contacts with the Hong Kong government. Only after the signing of the Sino-British agreement in 1984 did the FTU begin to support candidates for the

Urban and Regional Councils and District Board elections. Neither the UDHK nor the FTU has yet established the kind of institutional or organizational base associated with political parties in Western countries. The FTU has continually emphasized that it will not become a political party. In view of the institutional histories of the competing organizations, it seems likely that the electorate identified candidates by their political stance based on their past performance rather than by their political group affiliation.

Table 3.2 Respondents' identification of candidates' political affiliation

Political affiliation	Lau (%)	Lam (%)	Chan (%)
UDHK	33.6	35.1	0.3
FTU	2.3	0.6	36.8
Hong Kong Alliance	4.8	4.6	0.9
CIC	2.8	0.3	0.3
LDF	2.5	2.3	—
Independent	0.8	1.4	11.0
Others	5.9	5.2	2.8
Don't know/ no answer	47.2	50.5	47.9
Total	99.9%	100.0%	100.0%
(N)	(354)	(348)	(353)

Percentages do not add up to 100% because of rounding.

Even so, the level of political knowledge of the Hong Kong electorate does not seem to be low when compared with that of electorates in western countries. It has been reported, for example, that in contested elections for the House of Representatives, almost half (46%) of the American electorate knew nothing about the personal attributes of either the Republican or Democrat candidates or their policy positions.[4] One of the reasons for such a low level of candidate awareness was that the American electorate voted on the basis of party identification rather than the candidate's policy position. Similarly, in Britain, in 1987, because the electoral contest was mainly between the Labour Party and the Conservative Party, more than 70% of respondents to a survey were not able to identify whether the Alliance candidate in their constituencies was a Liberal or a Social Democrat.[5] While this particular case may reflect popular confusion over developments in those parties, it is a common finding of electoral studies that most of the electorate pay attention only to that information which enables them to distinguish one party or candidate from another.

The findings from our survey also showed that most of the electorate were less well informed about the institutional context in which the elections were taking place than they were about the contestants. Only a small number of respondents (17.3%), for example, could give the correct number of directly elected seats in the Legislative Council and only about one-third (30.5%) could give the name of their constituency. The constituency had been renamed Kowloon Central for the Legislative Council elections but most of the electorate confused it with the two constituent districts, Kowloon City and Wong Tai Sin. Yet, respondents were well informed about other aspects of the elections. For example, 71.3% of our respondents in the post-election survey conducted in the week following the elections could correctly name the two candidates who were elected in their constituency.

These findings show that the political knowledge of the Kowloon Central electorate is impressive, as this is a working-class constituency in which 51.6% of the respondents had less than secondary education. The electorate on the whole were aware of the electoral activities and the political stance of their candidates and appear to have used this knowledge to decide on their vote choice. The notion that the electorate is ill-informed about political matters, which was used as an argument against the introduction of direct elections to the Legislative Council in 1988 and which surfaced again after the 1991 elections, is simply not supported by the results of this survey.[6]

Political Efficacy

'Political efficacy is the feeling that one is capable of influencing the decision-making process.'[7] Obviously, there is a close relationship between feelings of efficacy and voter turnout; individuals with a high level of political efficacy are more likely to vote.[8] Feelings of efficacy are also strongly correlated with socio-economic status; that is, people with higher educational levels and income believe that they have greater control over their lives and are also more interested in the political process as a means of achieving desired ends.[9]

In Hong Kong, on the contrary, in spite of the relatively high educational levels and economic attainment of the population,[10] studies have suggested that the level of efficacy is low.[11] In a survey conducted in 1988, it was found that as many as 93.3% of respondents believed that they had no influence on government policy.[12] The findings from our survey showed that the level of efficacy of the electorate is higher than that of the general public.[13] Since electoral registration in Hong Kong is not automatic, one would expect that those who take the trouble to register would feel that the act of casting a ballot would have some effect. Yet only 27.1% of our respondents agreed or strongly agreed that they could influence government policies whereas 45% disagreed or strongly disagreed and 27.9% were not sure, saying that they could exert some influence at times. Similarly, in another question related to efficacy, less than one-third of the respondents (32.7%) agreed or strongly agreed that it was useful to complain if they were dissatisfied with government policy; another third (33.4%) felt that it was futile to do so while the remaining third (33.9%) expressed uncertainties about the effectiveness of complaining.

It is possible that the context in which the elections were held may explain this apparent paradox. If voters were well-informed about the candidates and their political stances and cast their ballots despite their belief that their votes would not influence government policies, the vote may have had other meanings. The electorate's lack of trust in both the Hong Kong government and the Chinese government, as supported by the data provided below, and reservations about the various accords on Hong Kong negotiated by the British and Chinese governments[14] may have meant that many voters saw the act of voting as an expression of a lack of confidence in the political future of the territory rather than as a positive way of changing policy.

As mentioned earlier, the level of efficacy is related to the turnout rate. Turnout rates at District Board elections, for example, have been between 30% and 38%.[15] Such low figures, which are usually replicated in local government elections elsewhere, are understandable in view of the limited powers of District Boards. However, our survey findings suggest that the introduction of more representative government at the territory-wide level, in the form of directly elected seats to the Legislative Council, has not yet significantly increased Hong Kong people's feelings of efficacy. In Western democracies, high turnout rates are a feature of elections and are usually taken as a reflection of a high sense of efficacy.

Confidence in the Government

The electorate's attitude towards the Hong Kong government can be described as one of ambivalence. There is a strong sense of mistrust and uncertainty. Nevertheless, there is still more confidence in the present Hong Kong government than in the post-1997 government. Only 30.8% of the respondents believed that the Hong Kong government would protect the interests of the people, 28.2% said it would not, 33.5% were uncertain and 7.6% gave no opinion. Despite this lack of trust, half of the respondents (50.8%) still believed that the Hong Kong government could maintain stability and prosperity during the transitional years. Only 14.6% expressed a clear lack of confidence, 23.6% were uncertain of its ability to do so and 11% gave no opinion. Confidence in the post-1997 government, however, was much lower. Only 35.9% believed that the future government would be able to maintain prosperity and stability after 1997.

The mistrust of the Hong Kong government is probably related to the lack of confidence in the Chinese government and the conciliatory attitude which the Hong Kong and British governments have taken towards China. Yet, relatively speaking, respondents still had more confidence in the present Hong Kong-British government than in the ability of the future government, under the Chinese government's control, to maintain stability and prosperity. This is particularly significant in the Kowloon Central constituency which, prior to the election, was reputed to be an area in which the Chinese government enjoyed considerable support.

The Perception of the Future and Hong Kong's Relationship With China

Mistrust of the Chinese government's ability to maintain stability and prosperity after 1997 has, in turn, led to a very negative reaction to its intervention in Hong Kong's internal affairs. A large majority of our respondents agreed or strongly agreed (76.1%) with the statement that China could make known its views but should not intervene in Hong Kong's internal affairs. Only 8.4% disagreed and 15.5% gave no opinion. To another question which asked whether the first consideration should be to accept China's opinion in cases of Sino-Hong Kong conflict, only 27% said yes, 36.5% said no and as many as 36.5% were uncertain or gave no opinion. Such a high percentage of undecided answers needs to be explained. It appears that, despite their apprehension over future Chinese rule and increasing evidence of Chinese intentions to exert firm control over Hong Kong after 1997, the pragmatism of the undecided respondents reminded them that it would probably be futile to oppose the Chinese government. The large proportion of undecided answers is probably another indication of feelings of inefficacy and the lack of trust in the future government but may, at the same time, represent feelings of uncertainty about the possibility of resisting Chinese rule.

Attitude Towards Welfare

Policy issues also revealed something of the political orientations of the Kowloon Central electorate. Compared with research findings prior to the signing of the Sino-British agreement, there has been a significant drop in people's satisfaction with government performance.[16] The results of our survey showed some evidence of a demand for more and better social welfare policies. Fewer than half of our respondents (40.8%) were satisfied with the Hong Kong government's social policies. None the less, welfare was not the principal concern of the electorate. For example, attitudes towards a more comprehensive social security system were divided. Fewer than half (42.4%) of the respondents supported the idea of more welfare, another 43.5% disagreed with the idea and 14.1% expressed no opinion.

Before discussing the implications of these findings for turnout and vote choice, it is useful to highlight the main features of our respondents' political orientations. In sum, the electorate are, on the whole, politically well-informed but they have a strong sense of inefficacy. In addition, the findings reflect two main concerns of the electorate: a demand for better welfare programmes and a lack of confidence in Hong Kong's political future. Concern about the political future and negative attitudes towards Chinese intervention in Hong Kong affairs, however, were much more strongly expressed than demand for better welfare. Not surprisingly, political orientations of this kind were reflected in the electorate's choice of 'liberal' candidates.

ENVIRONMENTAL VARIABLES AND VOTER TURNOUT

Socio-Economic Variables and Electoral Participation

Most Western studies conclude that modernized and developed societies demonstrate higher levels of political participation than traditional and developing societies.[17] They assert that the amount of political participation is related to the level of economic development. Moreover, it has been widely documented that individuals with a higher socio-economic status are more likely to vote.[18] However, the voter turnout rate in Hong Kong cannot be analysed with reference to the territory's level of modernization and economic development or the socio-economic status of the electorate. There is not a strong correlation between voter turnout and socio-economic variables such as income, occupation and housing type although there is a slight correlation between the educational level and electoral participation (Table 3.3).

An explanation for the low level of electoral participation has to be sought in its historical, political and social experience rather than in the level of economic development or the socio-economic status of the electorate. Previous studies have explained the low level of political participation from historical, institutional, political and sociological perspectives.[19] We suggest one additional and striking factor which affected turnout and vote choice in the 1991 Legislative Council elections: the political environment since the signing of the Sino-British agreement in 1984 and the lack of confidence in Hong Kong's political future.

Table 3.3 Comparison between voters and non-voters: socio-economic status

Socio-economic status	Voters (%)	Non-voters (%)
Monthly household income		
Under $3,000	3.7	6.6
$3,000 – $5,999	9.4	11.0
$6,000 – $9,999	22.7	22.1
$10,000 – $14,999	24.5	23.8
$15,000 – $19,999	10.7	8.8
$20,000 – $49,999	16.7	11.6
$50,000 – $79,999	1.3	1.1
Over $80,000	0.3	0.6
Refuse to answer	10.7	14.4
Total	100.0%	100.0%
(N)	(383)	(181)
Occupation		
Businessman	4.1	2.3
Professional	13.7	9.9
Administrator	4.6	1.7
Clerical	6.6	7.0
Sales	2.7	2.3
Service	4.6	5.2
Production	17.2	14.5
Unclassifiable	1.1	1.2
Not employed (housewife/student retired/unemployed)	45.3	55.8
Total	99.9%	99.9%
(N)	(366)	(172)
Housing type		
Public housing	63.6	62.6
Private housing	23.9	24.7
Home ownership scheme	10.6	11.0
Villa/bungalow	0.5	—
Temporary housing/squatters	0.3	0.5
Others	1.0	1.1
Total	99.9%	99.9%
(N)	(385)	(182)
Education		
Below primary	19.6	32.8
Primary	27.9	27.3
Secondary	34.4	27.9
Matriculation	4.4	3.3
Tertiary: non-degree	5.9	6.0
Tertiary: degree	7.8	2.7
Total	100.0%	100.0%
(N)	(387)	(183)

Percentages do not add up to 100% because of rounding.

The foremost political reality facing Hong Kong is the scheduled transfer of its sovereignty to China in 1997 and the current controversies between the Chinese and Hong Kong governments over issues arising from the transfer of power. The conciliatory attitude displayed by the Hong Kong and British governments towards China during negotiations on the development of representative government (1984-88) and the new airport project has led to a strong sense of disillusionment. The hope for a high degree of autonomy, which was promised in the Sino-British agreement, has been dampened by China's conservative attitude in debates over the Basic Law,[20] the adoption of a limited representative political structure for the future Hong Kong Special Administrative Region and the suppression of the 1989 pro-democracy movement in China. These much-publicized events have enhanced the political cognition of the Hong Kong people, but they have also further increased the already high degree of feelings of powerlessness. Mixed feelings of inefficacy and a lack of trust in the political future continue to persist. For some, electoral participation in the 1991 Legislative Council elections was seen as a last hope for a better future and for the expression of the wishes of the Hong Kong people.

Low Turnout Rate and the Political Environment

Hong Kong does not have a political environment which is conducive to a high voter turnout. There are, for example, no well-established party organizations and it is therefore difficult to contact the electorate. Apart from political parties, there are few kinds of organizational affiliations. In Kowloon Central, for example, which is classified as a working-class district, only 9.4% of the respondents had trade union affiliation; 67.7% of them did not belong to any political, neighbourhood, community or social organization. Studies in other countries show that citizens involved in organizations have a higher level of political interest and participation than uninvolved citizens.[21] If people have a strong sense of inefficacy, it seems unlikely that they would be active in political and community organizations. This low level of involvement circumscribes voter turnout because political and community groups are important agencies in persuading people to vote (see Chapter 8).

In the face of a lack of institutionalized channels, most candidates tried to appeal to the electorate personally, establishing door-to-door contacts and campaigning at bus stations and underground railway stations at rush hours. On Sundays, they concentrated on shopping malls, public parks and crowded areas. Such contacts are very limited, time-consuming, superficial and uninstitutionalized and do not give the electorate a sense of committed participation.

Apart from the lack of institutional linkages, there is also a lack of stimulus from the environment which might encourage electoral participation. The power of the Legislative Council is very limited. Less than one-third (18 out of a total of 60) of the seats in the Legislative Council are directly elected while the rest are appointed or indirectly elected through functional constituencies. There is no need for business and professional élites, who are entrenched within the system, to participate actively in the direct elections because their interests are well protected and guaranteed by the system of functional and appointed seats in the Legislative and Executive Councils. In support of this view, Dahl argues that individuals are unlikely to vote if they believe that the outcome will be satisfactory to them without their involvement.[22]

For the majority of people, the coming assertion of Chinese control, the dominant position of business and bureaucratic élites and the low probability of popular influence on government policies or the political future of Hong Kong mean that the act of voting fails to offer any immediate satisfaction of their urgent and direct needs. It is not surprising, therefore, that many middle-class people might regard pressing concerns for migration more important than voting. They would rather choose 'exit' than 'voice'.[23] For those who do not expect or are unable to migrate, it may be more satisfying to try to meet the imperative needs of daily life than to involve themselves in an activity which is vague and remote from their concrete and direct concerns. Among the non-voters, 48.3% said that they had no time, 13.9% said that they were not interested and 15.6% said that it was futile to vote because of the limited power of the Legislative Council or the China factor (Table 3.4). It may be true that some potential voters really were busy at work and could not find time to vote. For most, however, it was probably an excuse. Downs points out that a rational individual will vote only if the returns outweigh the costs.[24] If the vote is felt to make no difference, it is not surprising that half of the qualified electorate would not bother to register while less than half of those who did register did in fact vote.[25] In view of these factors, a 39.15% turnout rate was a realistic reflection of the various constraints existing in Hong Kong's political environment. Other factors affecting the turnout rate were discussed in Chapter 1.

Table 3.4 Voters' reasons for not going to vote

	Percentage
No time	48.3
Not interested	13.9
No good candidate	5.0
Limited power of the Legislative Council	0.6
Voting no use because of the China factor	15.0
Ignorance/no data on candidate	8.3
Sick/physically immobile	3.3
Polling card/administrative problems	2.8
Out of town	1.1
Others	1.7
Total	100.0%
(N)	(180)

Civic Responsibility: The Most Important Reason to Vote

Those who did turn out to vote in the 1991 elections were citizens who had a strong sense of civic consciousness. Civic duty was the most important reason (52.5%) given by the voters for going to vote and very few (1.5%) said that they voted to influence government policies (Table 3.5). Among the voters, a high percentage (81.1%) had voted in previous District Board and Urban Council elections and only 18.1% were voting for the first time. Moreover, among those who had voted before, 56.9% had voted more than three times previously.[26] Such a large group of habitual voters suggests that a sense of civic responsibility rather than the desire to influence policy issues was the main reason to vote. This proposition is supported by other findings. Among the voters,

55.4% were aware that the Legislative Council had only limited influence; yet they still went to vote because, they said, they wanted to express their views, to fulfil their civic responsibilities, to show support for the first Legislative Council direct elections, to uphold representative government and to express the hope that the number of directly elected seats would be increased in the future. Evidently, voting in the 1991 direct elections was an expressive act to show support for direct elections rather than an instrumental act aimed at influencing government policies.

Table 3.5 Voters' most important reason for going to vote

	Percentage
To support political group	3.8
Civic responsibility	52.5
To influence government policies	1.5
To protect my interest	4.1
To express policy views	9.4
Family influence	1.2
Good candidate	5.6
Neighbour's influence	2.4
Group leader's influence	0.3
Others	19.1
Total	99.9%
(N)	(339)

Note: The results exclude voters who gave more than one reason but failed to rank the most important reason.

Percentages do not add up to 100% because of rounding.

Expressive Rather Than Instrumental Voting: A Comparison of Voters With Non-voters

Other than as a sign of support for direct elections, the 1991 Legislative Council elections could also be seen as a manifestation of people's concerns. In order to gauge these concerns more precisely, it is instructive to compare the views of voters and non-voters. This comparison shows that there is no significant difference in their level of political efficacy. The only differences were the level of trust in the government, the extent of their political cognition, their attitudes towards China's intervention in Hong Kong and attitudes towards social welfare policies (Table 3.6). Relatively speaking, voters had more confidence in the government than non-voters. However, the difference was small and it is important to point out that the level of trust for both groups was low. It is to be expected that voters who have greater political knowledge would be more aware of their rights and interests. They might also be expected to demand more from government than non-voters in the form of more social welfare. However, fewer than 50% of the voters expressed this view (Table 3.6). A more revealing finding was the uncompromising position taken by both voters and non-voters against China's intervention in Hong Kong's internal affairs. A comparison of their responses on this issue with their attitudes towards social welfare shows the different levels of concern expressed by the electorate.

The views of both voters and non-voters on social welfare, in contrast to the issue on China's intervention, were more divided. Among the voters, for example, 45.4% agreed that Hong Kong could afford a more comprehensive social security system; but an almost equal number (42.1%) disagreed with this idea. Yet, on attitudes towards China, as many as 79.5% of the voters and 68.9% of the non-voters agreed that China should not intervene in Hong Kong's internal affairs. Only a very small minority of both voters (7.8%) and non-voters (9.8%) disagreed with this statement. The message, therefore, was not that the views of voters and non-voters were different but rather that Chinese intervention was a central concern for the entire electorate.

Apart from the slight difference between voters' and non-voters' degree of trust in the government, and their attitudes towards China's intervention in Hong Kong affairs, another point of contrast was the voters' more supportive attitude towards working-class interests. Not only did more of them favour a more comprehensive social security system, but they were also opposed to the importation of labour, supported the view that medical charges should not be linked to cost considerations and believed that profit tax should be increased if there was a need for more revenue (Table 3.7). These indicators revealed a concern with quality-of-life issues which are presently subsumed by

Table 3.6 Comparison between voters and non-voters: political orientations

Political efficacy

	Citizen can influence government policy		Useful to make complaints	
	Voters (%)	Non-voters (%)	Voters (%)	Non-voters (%)
Agree	28.7	23.5	33.9	30.1
Disagree	37.3	30.1	31.1	38.3
Uncertain	28.0	27.8	28.8	20.2
Don't know/no opinion	6.0	18.6	6.2	11.4
Total	100.0%	100.0%	100.0%	100.0%
(N)	(386)	(183)	(386)	(183)

Attitude towards China

	Disapproval of China intervening in Hong Kong's internal affairs		Acceptance of China's view in Sino-Hong Kong conflicts	
	Voters (%)	Non-voters (%)	Voters (%)	Non-voters (%)
Agree	79.5	68.9	27.2	26.4
Disagree	7.8	9.8	39.1	30.8
Uncertain	—	—	22.3	19.2
Don't know/no opinion	12.7	21.3	11.4	23.6
Total	100.0%	100.0%	100.0%	100.0%
(N)	(386)	(183)	(386)	(183)

Cognitive level

	Date of the election (%)	Number of directly elected seats (%)	Name of the constituency (%)	Number of candidates in the constituency (%)
Voters (N=386)				
Correct	89.9	21.9	38.9	33.5
Incorrect	3.1	14.0	49.0	39.2
Don't know	7.0	64.0	12.1	27.3
Total	100.0%	99.9%	100.0%	100.0%
Non-voters (N=182)				
Correct	58.8	7.7	12.6	8.9
Incorrect	6.6	10.0	53.9	26.9
Don't know	34.6	82.3	33.5	64.2
Total	100.0%	100.0%	100.0%	100.0%

Trust in government: government protecting citizen's interests

	Voters (%)	Non-voters (%)
Agree	33.5	25.1
Disagree	25.5	33.9
Uncertain	35.3	29.5
Don't know/no opinion	5.7	11.5
Total	100.0%	100.0%
(N)	(385)	(183)

Ability of Hong Kong to afford a more comprehensive social security system

	Voters (%)	Non-voters (%)
Agree	45.4	36.1
Disagree	42.1	46.4
Don't know/no opinion	12.5	17.5
Total	100.0%	100.0%
(N)	(385)	(183)

the more immediate and pressing concern of the prospect of Chinese rule. If it were possible to abstract the 1997 issue from present political debates, it seems probable that such policy issues would constitute central, and perhaps divisive, topics which might affect the choice of candidates.

The survey results do not suggest that there is a strong demand for an accountable government. Nearly half of the voters (48.6%) still believed that it would be better to leave the government to capable leaders than to require constant citizen scrutiny, though more voters (32.5%) than non-voters (22.5%) disagreed or strongly disagreed with the statement (Table 3.8). This political orientation was reflected in their choice of candidates. Because of their feelings of inefficacy, voters may look up to those who have a past record of voicing concern and who might be relied upon to protect popular interests and criticize the government on behalf of the people. It is perhaps not surprising, therefore, that 'willingness to serve the public' was one of the three most important attributes considered by voters in choosing their candidates.

Table 3.7 Comparison between voters and non-voters:
attitudes towards social policies

	Importation of labour (%)	Medical charges should not be linked to cost considerations (%)	Introduction of a profit tax if there were a need for more revenue (%)
Voters (N=386)			
Agree	15.8	72.5	80.9
Disagree	74.7	21.0	11.1
Don't know/no opinion	9.6	6.5	8.0
Total	100.1%	100.0%	100.0%
Non-voters (N=183)			
Agree	18.6	56.8	68.3
Disagree	67.8	29.5	14.2
Don't know/no opinion	13.7	13.7	17.5
Total	100.1%	100.0%	100.0%

Percentages do not add up to 100% because of rounding.

Table 3.8 Preference to leave government to capable leaders
rather than requiring constant citizen scrutiny

	Voters (%)	Non-voters (%)
Agree	48.6	49.5
Disagree	32.5	22.5
Uncertain	7.0	8.8
Don't know/no opinion	11.9	19.2
Total	100%	100%
(N)	(386)	(183)

The 1991 elections were not a contest between political parties to control government. At most, the results can be interpreted only as an expression of the interests and concerns of the more civic-minded citizens. Despite their worries about the political future of Hong Kong, only a minority of the electorate made an effort to air their views. Most believed that their votes would have little effect on present and future circumstances.

IMPLICATIONS FOR THE CHOICE OF CANDIDATES

The Political Stance of Candidates: The Criterion for Vote Choice

Because most political organizations contesting the 1991 elections did not have a record of long-established electoral participation or past performance, it was to be expected that the electorate would tend to identify with the candidates rather than with their political organizations. The distinguishing criterion was the candidates' political stance which, in turn, was based on their past performance and previous stand on policy issues. Candidates were broadly identified as 'liberal', 'conservative/business', 'pro-China' or 'independent'. For example, 64.5% and 58.3% of our respondents in the pre-election survey identified Lau and Lam as 'liberal' and 34.7% identified Chan as 'pro-China' (see Table 3.1). Among our respondents who indicated their intention to vote for Lau and Lam in the pre-election survey, 61.0% and 63.3% respectively said that their votes were based on the candidates' political stance. The majority of those who intended to vote for Chan, however, said that her political stance was not the reason for their choice (Table 3.9). [27] Moreover, most respondents clearly stated that their choice was not based on the groups to which the candidates were affiliated (Table 3.10).

Table 3.9 Intention to vote on the basis of candidates' political stance

	Lau (%)	Lam (%)	Chan (%)
Yes	61.0	63.3	38.4
No	39.0	36.7	61.6
Total	100.0%	100.0%	100.0%
(N)	(312)	(226)	(151)

The political stance of candidates is related to, but different from, policy platforms, which are more concrete and specific proposals on policy issues. The political stance of candidates was more important than their policy platforms in winning support because most of the

Table 3.10 Intention to vote on the basis of candidates'
political group affiliation

	Lau (%)	Lam (%)	Chan (%)
Yes	27.3	30.7	31.2
No	72.7	69.3	68.8
Total	100.0%	100.0%	100.0%
(N)	(308)	(218)	(154)

electorate did not have a good understanding of the platforms of the candidates. This may have been because there was little substantive difference between the candidates' platforms. In an effort to appeal to the majority of the electorate, candidates very often put forward broad objectives without committing themselves to specific policies. It is also possible that some of the electorate were not prepared to spend the time, or did not have the expertise, to evaluate campaign literature or felt that they already knew the relevant facts about the candidates' positions. Whatever the reasons, in our pre-election survey, more than half of the respondents (51.0%) said that they did not understand the platforms of candidates whom they intended to choose and only 20.0% said they had a good understanding of their platforms (Table 3.11).

Table 3.11 Understanding of candidates' platforms

	Percentage
Very good	2.4
Good	17.6
Partial*	29.0
Not very good	39.3
Not good at all	11.7
Total	100.0%
(N)	(290)

* The literal meaning of the Chinese wording in the questionnaire is 'half-half'.

Perception of 'Liberal' Versus 'Pro-China' Candidates

The electorate's lack of understanding of the candidates' policy platforms and their preference for a government by capable leaders raise questions about the respondents' perception of what they understood to be a 'liberal' as opposed to a 'pro-China' candidate.

Their association of 'liberal' candidates with a particular policy stance was probably based on the candidates' past records and previous performance. The main reasons given by those who chose Lau and Lam were 'experience/past performance', 'willingness to serve the public', 'style of work' (the manner in which the candidate conducted public business) and 'policy platform' (see Table 3.12 and Chapter 5). Given the past records and performance of Lau and Lam, it could be inferred that the electorate's perception of 'liberal' candidates was related to the candidates' courageous stance in criticizing government policies

Table 3.12 The most important reasons for the choice of candidates

	Lau (%)	Lam (%)	Chan (%)
Educational attainment	1.7	4.3	0.0
Age	0.9	0.3	0.6
Occupation	0.4	5.6	1.7
Sex	0.0	0.3	1.7
Residence in the district	0.2	0.3	0.6
Membership/support from political or social organizations	10.5	12.6	13.2
Charisma/appearance	0.6	0.0	0.6
Social status/prestige	1.5	2.3	1.7
Style of work	18.9	11.6	12.0
Willingness to serve the public	17.8	13.5	21.1
Policy stance/platform	12.0	14.5	13.1
Past performance/experience	20.8	19.8	9.1
Acquaintance with candidate	0.4	0.3	0.6
Supported by renowned individuals	0.4	2.3	0.6
Family/friend/neighbour influence	1.1	2.0	6.9
Others	12.7	10.2	16.6
Total	99.9%	99.9%	100.1%
(N)	(466)	(303)	(175)

Note: Respondents were asked to name up to three reasons.

Percentages do not add up to 100% because of rounding.

and their explicitly stated position on China. They had challenged the Chinese and Hong Kong authorities on matters relating to Hong Kong's interests, such as support for the introduction of direct elections in 1988, an entirely directly elected legislature for the future Hong Kong Special Administrative Region government, human rights issues in Hong Kong and China, the introduction of a central provident fund and opposition to the importation of foreign labour. The electorate's understanding of candidates was, therefore, probably based on a general image of their past performance and political stance on these issues rather than on any substantive policy platforms for the future. Although these images were vague and impressionistic, they were the factors which determined the voters' choice of candidates.

Attitudes Towards China: The Critical Factor in the 1991 Elections

The candidates' attitudes towards China were the critical factor affecting the electorate's vote choice in the 1991 elections. The majority of those who voted for Lau and Lam explicitly said that their vote was based on the candidates' 'liberal' political stance. Since the majority of the vote for Chan was not based on her political stance, a closer examination of the factors that persuaded voters to cast their ballots for her enables us to consider further the reasons for the choice of candidate. 'Membership or support from political or social organizations' was the second most important reason cited by the voters for choosing Chan. ('Policy platform' was a very close third.) This differed from the criteria used to choose Lau and Lam in which 'membership or support from political or social organizations' was fourth on Lam's list and fifth on Lau's list (Table 3.12).

Chan, out of all the candidates, scored the highest percentage of single votes (53.1%) (Table 3.13) and many of Chan's voters did not vote for a second candidate. However, Lau and Lam, who were both identified by the electorate as 'liberal', received more than half (54.5%) of all the paired votes cast (Table 3.14). From these findings, it can be inferred that some of Chan's voters supported her because of her affiliation to, or their association with, the Federation of Trade Unions, which was pro-China.

Table 3.13 Single votes

Candidates	Votes	Percentage
Lau	17	26.6
Lam	5	7.8
Chan	34	53.1
Chan, Peter	6	9.4
Yeung Lai-yin	1	1.6
Young, John Dragon	0	0.0
Cheung Chung-ming	1	1.6
Total	64	100.1%

Percentages do not add up to 100% because of rounding.

Table 3.14 Paired votes

Candidates	Lau	Lam (%)	Peter Chan (%)	Yeung (%)	Chan (%)	Young (%)	Cheung (%)
Lau	—	54.5	6.2	1.0	13.6	1.0	1.0
Lam		—	2.3	0.7	3.2	0.7	0.7
Chan, Peter			—	1.6	4.5	2.6	0.7
Yeung Lai-yin				—	2.9	0.3	0.3
Chan					—	2.3	0
Young, John Dragon							
Cheung Chung-ming		(N=308)					

Percentages do not add up to 100% because of rounding.

To the extent that our respondents reflect the attitudes of the electorate as a whole, socio-economic status does not seem to be an important variable affecting voter turnout in Hong Kong. Nor was it a factor in the choice of candidates. If it had been a factor, those who voted for Lau and Chan, who are union representatives, should have had a lower socio-economic status than those who voted for Lam. But this was not the case. Those who supported Lau were slightly better off than those who supported Chan (Table 3.15). The socio-economic status of those who supported Lau was even closer to those who voted for Lam, a medical professional. The major common identity between

Table 3.15 Voters' socio-economic status and vote choice

Socio-economic status	Lau (%)	Lam (%)	Chan (%)
Education			
Below primary	18.8	17.0	26.7
Primary	25.9	28.9	31.0
Secondary	34.5	35.6	30.2
Matriculation	4.7	3.6	4.3
Tertiary: non-degree	7.5	6.2	2.6
Tertiary: degree	8.6	8.8	5.2
Total	100.0%	100.1%	100.0%
Household income			
Under $3,000	2.7	3.6	4.5
$3,000 – $5,999	8.2	7.7	11.6
$6,000 – $9,999	23.5	22.7	23.2
$10,000 – $14,999	23.5	25.8	28.6
$15,000 – $19,999	12.2	10.8	10.7
$20,000 – $49,999	18.0	17.5	9.8
$50,000 – $79,999	1.2	1.0	—
Refuse to answer	10.6	10.8	11.6
Total	99.9%	99.9%	100.0%
Housing type			
Public	66.5	63.7	67.2
Private	22.0	22.8	19.8
Home ownership	9.4	11.9	11.2
Villa / bungalow	0.8	1.0	0.9
Others	1.2	0.5	0.9
Total	99.9%	99.9%	100.0%
(N)	(255)	(194)	(116)

Note: Household income rather than occupation is used here because the latter is not a useful indicator of socio-economic status. Occupation divisions in Hong Kong are more fluid than those in western countries.

Percentages do not add up to 100% because of rounding.

Lau and Lam, of course, was their explicit stance in challenging the Chinese authorities on issues related to Hong Kong interests.

In comparing the political orientations of the 'liberal' candidates' supporters and the 'pro-China' candidates' supporters, there was no significant difference in their feelings of political efficacy, confidence

Table 3.16 Voters' political orientations and their choice of candidates

Political orientation	Scale	Lau (%)	Lam (%)	Chan (%)
Political efficacy[a]	Strong	10.2	10.4	5.5
	Medium	46.5	46.0	40.7
	Weak	43.4	43.5	53.9
	Total	100.1%	99.9%	100.1%
Confidence in the Hong Kong government[b]	Strong	19.9	21.0	25.8
	Medium	51.8	53.1	53.9
	Weak	28.2	26.0	20.2
	Total	99.9%	100.1%	99.9%
Disapproval of China's intervention in Hong Kong's affairs[c]	Disagree	4.7	2.4	5.9
	Neutral	19.7	18.8	34.9
	Agree	75.7	78.8	59.3
	Total	100.1%	100%	100.1%
Ability of the future government to maintain stability and prosperity[d]	Strong	29.6	23.0	46.3
	Medium	43.7	47.4	43.0
	Weak	26.8	29.6	10.8
	Total	100.1%	100%	100.1%
Support for welfare programme[e]	Agree	34.4	36.2	34.6
	Neutral	25.3	25.2	24.4
	Disagree	40.4	38.5	41.0
	Total	100.1%	99.9%	100%

[a] The scale on 'political efficacy' is recoded from the aggregated scores on questions 42, 43 and 50 in Appendix C.
[b] The scale on 'confidence in the Hong Kong government' is recoded from the aggregated scores on questions 44, 45 and 47 in Appendix C.
[c] The scale on 'disapproval of China's intervention in Hong Kong affairs' is recoded from the aggregated scores on questions 35 and 48 in Appendix C.
[d] The scale on 'ability of the future government to maintain stability and prosperity' is recoded from the aggregated scores on questions 49 and 51 in Appendix C.
[e] Figures in this table are different from those in Tables 4.4-4.6. For an explanation of this anomaly, see Chapter 7.

Percentages do not add up to 100% because of rounding.

in the Hong Kong government or attitudes towards social welfare policies (Table 3.16). The only major difference among those choosing different candidates was their attitude towards the Chinese government. While over 75% of those who voted for Lau and Lam strongly agreed that China should not intervene in Hong Kong's internal affairs, a lower percentage (59.3%) of those who voted for Chan strongly agreed with this view. Moreover, in contrast to the supporters of Lau and Lam, Chan's supporters were more uncertain of their attitude towards China. A substantial proportion of her supporters (34.9%) were neutral towards China's intervention in Hong Kong's affairs. Furthermore, those who voted for Chan had stronger confidence in the future government's ability to maintain stability and prosperity after 1997 (46.3%) than those who voted for Lau and Lam (29.6% and 23%). These findings further support the thesis that the voters' attitude towards the Chinese government was an important factor for their choice of 'liberal' candidates. While those who voted for Chan did so not because of her 'pro-China' stance but for other reasons, the candidates' attitude towards the Chinese government was still the major issue on the 1991 election agenda.

CONCLUSIONS

Our survey suggested that the Hong Kong electorate are well-informed about electoral activities, political changes and the territory's difficult relationship with China. The low turnout rate was, in part, a reflection of their strong sense of inefficacy and constraints existing in the political environment as well as in the political system. It seems likely that the imminence of Chinese rule, the uncertainties in the political future, a strong sense of powerlessness, the limited number of directly elected seats in the Legislative Council and an unfavourable environment for the development of strong political parties will mean that electoral participation will remain low.

It is clear, however, that the views and concerns of the Hong Kong electorate were adequately expressed in the results of the 1991 direct elections. Our study showed that both voters and non-voters prefer an autonomous Hong Kong and that they have doubts about whether the future government can maintain stability, and prosperity. While voters explicitly made known their concerns in their choice of 'liberal' candidates, non-voters implicitly expressed their uncertainties and powerlessness by abstaining. The majority of people in Hong Kong might therefore be described as behaviourally passive but politically informed. This represents a volatile element in an already volatile situation for an indifferent, but informed, populace may represent a threat to political stability especially in times of economic crisis. It is also likely both to undermine further the legitimacy of the present government and to sustain the prevailing antipathy towards the future government of the Hong Kong Special Administrative Region. The root of the problem lies in the lack of confidence in the future government, which desperately needs the support of the people to cope with future changes. A smooth transition through 1997 would ideally require ruling élites who are acceptable to the Chinese government and political leaders who can command the trust and confidence of the people. Yet, under the present circumstances, this is an impossible prescription. The ruling élites do not enjoy the confidence of the people; those who have the confidence of the people are excluded from power. Voting in elections provides a mandate for those who are elected, but those who were popularly elected in September 1991 have not been invited to take office. A government introducing direct elections but functioning without the support of the elected representatives brings the legitimacy, stability and prosperity of the entire system into question.

NOTES

1. L.W. Milbrath, 'Political Participation and the Citizen', in C.J. Larson and P.C. Wasburn, eds., *Power Participation and Ideology* (New York: David McKay Co., 1969), pp. 178-184.

2. The term 'political orientations' is used in a broad and catch-all sense to include cognitive, affective and evaluative domains. In an article by Jennings and Niemi, for example, political orientations include such categories as interest in public affairs, political efficacy, recognition and understanding of the liberal-conservative dimension, knowledge of political facts, partisanship and electoral behaviour, opinions on public policy issues, political trust and evaluation of government and other socio-political groups. See M. Kent Jennings and Richard G. Niemi, 'The Persistence of Political Orientations: An Over-Time Analysis of Two Generations', *British Journal of Political Science*, 8, 3(1978): 333-363. For further readings on the political attitudes of the Hong Kong Chinese, see

Lau Siu-kai and Kuan Hsin-chi, *The Ethos of the Hong Kong Chinese* (Hong Kong: The Chinese University Press, 1988); Lau Siu-kai, Kuan Hsin-chi and Wan Po-shan, 'Political Attitudes', in Lau Siu-kai *et al.*, eds., *Indicators of Social Development* (Hong Kong: The Chinese University of Hong Kong, Institute of Asia-Pacific Studies, 1991).

3. This study is based on data collected both in a pre-election survey conducted in the week before the elections and in a post-election survey conducted in the week immediately after the elections. Unless otherwise stated, the sample used for the discussion in this chapter is based on the 570 respondents who were successfully interviewed in both the pre-election and the post-election surveys. Among these 570 respondents, there were 387 voters and 183 non-voters. The word 'respondents' or 'electorate', which includes both voters and non-voters, is used whenever the 570 sample is referred to; the words 'voters' and 'non-voters', however, refer to the 387 and 183 sub-samples respectively.

4. Warren E. Miller and Donald E. Stokes, 'Constituency Influence in Congress', *American Political Science Review,* 57 (1963): 45-57.

5. Out of 3,826 respondents, 996 said 'Liberal', 643 said 'Social Democrat' and 2,187 said 'don't know' or 'don't remember'. See A. Heath, 'British Election Study 1987', computer file, University of Essex, Colchester, Economic and Social Research Council (ESRC) data archive, 1989.

6. See, for example, *Public Response to Green Paper: The 1987 Review of Developments in Representative Government; Report of the Survey Office* (Hong Kong: Government Printer, 1987), Part I, p.55; Part II, Appendix III, p.4; Part III, Sample 21, 47; and *SCMP*, 16 September 1991.

7. M. Lal Goel, 'Conventional Political Participation', in D.H. Smith *et al.*, eds., *Participation in Social and Political Activities* (San Francisco: Jossey-Bass Publishers, 1980), p. 127.

8. J. Clotfelter and C.L. Prysby, *Political Choices* (New York: Holt, Rinehart and Winston, 1980), pp. 28-29.

9. See, for example, B.G. Campbell *et al.*, *The American Voter* (New York: Wiley, 1960); R.A. Dahl, *Who Governs?* (New Haven: Yale University Press, 1961); G. Almond and S. Verba, *The Civic Culture* (Princeton: Princeton University Press, 1963); N. H. Nie, G.B. Powell, Jr. and K. Prewitt, 'Social Structure and Political Participation: Development Relationships, Parts I & II', *American Political Science Review,* 63 (1969): 361-378 and 808-832; and S. Verba and N. Nie, *Participation in America: Political Democracy and Social Equality* (New York: Harper and Row, 1972).

10. The Hong Kong population has high educational attainment levels. Among children aged 3-16 years, school attendance is almost universal and 62% of the population have secondary or higher education. The society is also economically prosperous. The median monthly household income in 1991 was $9,964. See *Hong Kong 1991 Population Census: Summary Results* (Hong Kong: Census and Statistics Department, 1991).

11. Ambrose Y.C. King, 'The Political Culture of Kwun Tong: A Chinese Community in Hong Kong', Occasional Paper, Social Research Centre, The Chinese University of Hong Kong, 1972; Lau Siu-kai, *Society and Politics in Hong Kong* (Hong Kong: The Chinese University Press, 1982); and Lau Siu-kai, Kuan Hsin-chi and Wan Po-san, 'Political Attitudes'.

12. Lau Siu-kai, Kuan Hsin-chi and Wan Po-san, 'Political Attitudes'.

13. The sample was drawn from adults aged 18 and over. Ibid., p. 237.

14. In response to the question 'If you were controlling history, what would you most like to happen to Hong Kong in 1997?' only 21% preferred Hong Kong to become part of China. The other replies were: independence (29%); be part of Britain (26%); be part of the Commonwealth (19%) and 'no opinion' (5%). The poll was conducted by Asian Commercial Research and reported in the *Sunday Morning Post* of 30 June 1991.

15. The turnout rates for the various District Board elections were as follows: 38.9% in 1982, 37.5% in 1985, 30.3% in 1988 and 32.5% in 1991. These data were provided by the Registration and Electoral Office of the Hong Kong government.

16. In a research survey conducted in 1982, it was found that over 70% of the respondents said that the government's performance was good or average. Although 'government performance' refers to more general and overall government policies and achievements than 'social policies', the data provide a close reference point and a useful comparison. See Lau Siu-kai and Kuan Hsin-chi, 'The Changing Political Culture of the Hong Kong Chinese', in Joseph Y.S. Cheng, ed., *Hong Kong in Transition* (Hong Kong: Oxford University Press, 1986), p. 29.

17. See, for example, S.M. Lipset, *Political Man* (London: Heinemann, 1969) and Almond and Verba, *The Civic Culture*.

18. See Note 9.

19. See J.S. Hoadley, 'Hong Kong Is the Lifeboat: Notes on Political Culture and Socialization', *Journal of Oriental Studies* 8 (1970): 206-218; Ambrose Y.C. King, 'Administrative Absorption of Politics in Hong Kong', *Asian Survey* 15, 5(1975): 422-439; and Lau Siu-kai, *Society and Politics in Hong Kong* (Hong Kong: The Chinese University Press, 1982).

20. David J. Clark, 'The Basic Law: One Document, Two Systems', in Ming K. Chan and David J. Clark, eds., *The Hong Kong Basic Law* (Hong Kong: Hong Kong University Press, 1991), pp. 36-59.

21. See Note 9.

22. R. Dahl, 'Political Man', in C.J. Larson and P.C. Wasburn, eds., *Power Participation and Ideology* (New York: David McKay Co., 1969), pp. 207-209.

23. Albert O. Hirschman, *Exit, Voice and Loyalty* (Cambridge, Mass.: Harvard University Press, 1970).

24. A. Downs, 'The Causes and Effects of Rational Abstention', in B. Seasholes,

Voting, Interest Groups and Parties (Glenview, Illinois: Scott, Foresman and Co., 1966), pp. 21-27.

25. The potential electorate, based on the 1991 population estimate, was 3,696,000. There were 1,916,925 registered elections, which was 51.9% of the potential electorate. The voter turnout was 750,467 and the voter turnout rate was 39.15%. Voter turnout as a percentage of the total potential electorate was 20.3%.

26. For figures on the frequency of previous voting for the entire sample, see Chapter 1.

27. The data given here are based on the 1,046 sample in the pre-election survey.

4

Issue Voting: Policy Positions and Voting Inclinations

Rowena Y.F. Kwok and Elaine Chan

INTRODUCTION

Issue voting interests political scientists because it links the specific act of voting to broader questions of democratic control and representation. 'Issue voting increases the potential for the reflection of the public will in policy by both making that will clear to decision makers and making responsiveness by decision makers more difficult to avoid.'[1] However, there is no consensus on what issue voting actually is or means. Crudely speaking, it involves voters making a calculated decision about which party or candidate to support on the basis of their policy preferences and assessments of their positions. But views on issue voting are as varied as the research findings on the subject.[2] This diversity presumably results from differences in the contexts of various enquiries, the elections studied, the definition of issue voting and the methodologies employed to study the phenomenon.

On the surface, it would appear that voters do hold generalized images of parties and candidates which are not totally devoid of policy content. In the United Kingdom, for example, the Labour Party is usually associated with such policies as nationalization and pro-trade union legislation while the Conservative Party is generally identified more with privatization and firm law and order policies. It should be emphasized that it is the electorate's perception, not 'objective' truth, which is important. In practice, for example, there may be little difference between the law and order policies of a Conservative or a Labour government.

With these considerations in mind, in this chapter we examine the importance of issue voting in Hong Kong. The 1991 Legislative Council elections were widely perceived to be a contest between liberal and pro-China candidates. We asked two specific questions. First, what were the issues, if any, which concerned the electorate? Secondly, did policy issues have an impact on the electorate's choice of candidate?

To establish that particular policy opinions determine vote choice, it is necessary first to examine both the conditions required for issue voting to occur and the methodological problems which it raises.

Necessary Conditions for Issue Voting

There is no consensus on the conditions necessary for issue voting although there does appear to be a generally consistent view of the most important elements involved:[3]

(a) the issues selected for study must be considered salient by the voters;
(b) voters must have an opinion on the issues;
(c) voters must perceive different parties or candidates as having different stances or policies on the issues;
(d) voters must vote for the party or candidate whose position on the issues is perceived to be closest to their own positions.

Meier and Campbell argue that there is a fifth condition, namely, that for a voter to cast an issue vote, he must accurately perceive the candidates' issue position. Otherwise, the voter's decision cannot properly be termed 'issue voting' because 'the vote would not have the intended effect of promoting a particular policy position'.[4] However, this seems to be beside the point. If one is concerned with the vote as an instrument for promoting a particular policy position, it is perfectly conceivable that factors other than inaccurate perception could similarly neutralize the vote's 'intended effect' , for example, a void ballot. What is the central issue here is the correspondence between the cognitive process and the actual voting act. It is the voter's perception that guides vote choice, assuming for the moment that it is possible to isolate the impact of issue voting from that of other possible influences. Let us suppose that candidates do not actually differ on a certain issue but a voter perceives some differences and decides to vote on that basis in the belief that there are position differences among candidates. Should not this also be considered issue voting? In the words of Mark Franklin, 'The requirement of correct perception is perhaps a little strong. It is ... of the greatest importance that party stances *as perceived* by each voter be employed rather than party stances as perceived by the investigator .... Perceptions could influence voting decisions even though they were incorrect.'[5]

Causal Relationships and Methodological Problems

Even if all four conditions for issue voting are fulfilled, they are not sufficient to demonstrate that it has actually occurred. For issue voting to have taken place, it must be proved that the respondent first established issue preferences and then decided how to vote on the basis of those preferences. Otherwise, disputes might arise over the extent to which issue voting had occurred because the congruence between issue preferences and vote choice could result either from issue voting or from respondents' rationalization of their issue positions in terms of a previously decided vote choice.[6] That is, it is equally plausible for voters to pick a party or candidate first and then adjust their positions to fit the party's or the candidate's policies as for them to select a party or candidate on the basis of their policy preferences. This problem of causation becomes progressively more complex if we allow other variables to come into the reckoning. In order to argue that issue voting has occurred, one must have found not only some correlation between issue position and votes but also that the issue position determined votes, not vice versa. In other words, it is necessary to demonstrate that the issue position was the most important determinant of vote choice as opposed to other possible determinants such as candidates' socio-economic background and political affiliation. The methodological difficulties involved led Denver to conclude that there is 'no simple way of resolving the problem of causal direction empirically. We can demonstrate the extent to which voters fulfil the conditions for issue voting, but ultimately it cannot be proved that issue preferences cause or determine party choice.'[7]

Concomitant with the problem of causation, there is a second methodological difficulty sometimes referred to as the problem of 'decision rules' or 'trade offs'.[8] This essentially asks the question how the issue voter decides which issues will determine his or her vote. In other words, how does a voter 'trade off' a preference for, say, lower taxes against a preference for more environmental protection legislation.

In sum, when one talks about issue voting, there appear to be at least three levels of comprehension and analysis:

(a) Adopting the 'necessary' conditions outlined above, one might attempt to assess the extent to which voters take into consideration issue stances when making their vote decision by measuring the proximity in issue positions between the voter and the chosen party or candidate. At this level, the conclusion which one could at best arrive at would be to say that there is a positive correlation, if indeed there is any, between issue positions and vote choice, and to measure the strength of that correlation. This is not the same as saying that issue voting has occurred. At worst, if no pattern of correlation is found whatsoever between issue positions and votes, then issue voting probably did not happen.

(b) If one were able to overcome the methodological problems associated with establishing causal relationships, then one could presumably demonstrate the existence, or otherwise, of issue voting in a particular context.

(c) One could also try to establish the impact of issue voting on an election result or the extent to which a particular issue affects the election outcome. In this case, one might have to demonstrate the dominant impact of issue voting on the election outcome as against that of a host of other possible factors, for example, party loyalty, personalities, campaigns and so on.

STUDYING ISSUE VOTING IN HONG KONG

As far as the authors are aware, the present survey is the first attempt to study issue voting in the context of Hong Kong. Previous studies on District Board and Municipal Council elections concentrated on the personal attributes of candidates such as public service experience, past performance and educational attainment as the principal voting criteria for selecting candidates (see Chapter 5). That is appropriate because District Boards are only consultative bodies on local, district-level issues and both the Urban and Regional Councils have specific, limited jurisdictions.[9] Elections to these bodies are mostly fought not on the basis of controversial issues but on personalities, experience and the personal style of conducting business.

However, the Legislative Council direct elections were significantly different from previous elections, if only because of the Council's very different constitutional status from the District Boards and the Urban and Regional Councils. The Legislative Council is a central government institution whose formation and functions relate directly to making laws on policy issues and are covered in Hong Kong's 'constitution', namely, the *Letters Patent* and the *Royal Instructions.* The District Boards and the Urban and Regional Councils, on the other hand, are statutory bodies created by ordinance. To run successfully for the Legislative Council elections, it was no longer sufficient to direct electorate attention to public service records and achievements in resolving neighbourhood problems. Rather, candidates had to delineate their positions on substantive policy issues of territory-wide concern, some of which inevitably had great political significance given the imminence of Hong Kong's return to Chinese sovereignty.

The British and Chinese governments signed the Sino-British agreement on the future of Hong Kong in 1984 without much meaningful participation from the people of the territory.[10] The direct elections were the first opportunity for the Hong Kong electorate to pass judgement on the decisions which the two governments had taken for them. As noted in Chapter 1, the 1991 elections could be regarded as a 'referendum' on the Sino-British agreement and its aftermath. In such circumstances, it was anticipated that Sino-Hong Kong relations and 1997-related issues could be important themes on the electoral agenda which might divide the electorate, particularly because some of the candidates had expressed strong views on these matters.

A series of questions in the questionnaire were therefore designed to survey the phenomenon of issue voting and its strength. Essentially, our attempt at this stage is to measure issue voting in terms of the proximity in issue positions between the intended voter and the chosen candidates.

The Absence of Issue Voting

Our questionnaire, which was carefully designed not to impose our opinions on the respondents, used an open-ended question to ascertain what were perceived to be the most salient problems in Hong Kong. In order to look at issue voting, we needed, in addition, to identify the most salient policy issues for the community so that we could assess their relative importance for the voting behaviour of our respondents. Various opinion polls conducted in the months just before the elections found that people were most concerned with problems related to Hong Kong's future, the economy, housing, crime and transport. The Vietnamese boat people, environmental pollution, and the importation of foreign labour were also high on the list.[11] On the basis of these opinion polls, our questionnaire included ten questions gauging the opinions of our respondents on ten different policy areas. These areas included inflation, law and order, the Vietnamese boat people, Sino-Hong Kong relations, foreign labour, housing, social security/welfare, taxation, medical service and environmental protection.

The ten policy areas were expected to cover most of the problems which our respondents would regard as important. Inflation, for instance, hit an alarming 13.9% in April, which subsequently led the Legislative Council to set up an *ad hoc* group to investigate ways in which it could be curbed. Different groups saw different ways of solving the problem. For some, importation of foreign labour was favoured; for others, tighter control of public expenditure and slowing the increases in public utilities fees were endorsed. The suggestion to increase the number of imported labourers fuelled an already heated debate between businessmen and labour unions.[12] Another issue, the future of Hong Kong, has been continually present in the minds of the people of Hong Kong. The uncertain, if not pessimistic, local view of the future can be gathered from the extent of emigration from Hong Kong since the signing of the Sino-British agreement. Another piece of information is quite telling: a recent poll showed that only 21% of the respondents were in favour of returning Hong Kong to China; the majority would like to see Hong Kong stay as part of Britain, become part of the Commonwealth, or declare its independence.[13] The Vietnamese boat people is another frustrating concern. A recent poll found that 88% of respondents wanted to abandon the port of first asylum policy and 70% would still support such a policy even if it led to boat people drowning offshore.[14] The results of these opinion polls, taken in the context of other expressions of concern, lead us to believe that the ten areas which we identified cover the principal policy issues troubling our respondents.

In the survey design, voters were also asked to specify the stance of their intended candidates on the issue which they thought was most salient. In the end, however, many of the respondents named the very broad and vague problem of the '1997 issue' as most salient. As the '1997 issue' could conceivably encompass an unknown number of more specific problems, it was not possible to prepare many relevant position statements in advance. Voters' perception of the candidates' position on this issue was consequently unobtainable. None the less, we did ascertain the issue positions of those voters who named 'Sino-Hong Kong relations' as the most salient problem and the perceived positions of their intended candidates. Sino-Hong Kong relations in this context were measured in terms of Hong Kong's autonomy from China's interference in its internal affairs. As a result of the small number of respondents involved in this case, the issue was incorporated as one of three dimensions constituting the '1997 issue' in the analysis. The other two dimensions were confidence in Hong Kong's future and attitudes towards democratic political development in Hong Kong. In the subsequent analysis, comparisons were made between voters' issue positions as revealed through the survey and candidates' publicly proclaimed positions on the same issue before and during the election campaign.

Despite the double-digit inflation rate, it was the '1997 issue' that preoccupied the minds of our respondents. More than 32% of our respondents reported that '1997' was the most salient issue facing Hong Kong, while 19.4% mentioned inflation. Law and order trailed quite far behind (9.3%), and housing (7.5%) and the Vietnamese boat people (7.4%) had significantly lower percentages (Table 4.1).

Table 4.1 The most salient problem confronting Hong Kong

	Percentage
'1997 issue'	32.1
Inflation	19.4
Law and order	9.3
Housing	7.5
Vietnamese boat people	7.4
The economy	3.7
Social security/welfare	1.2
Medical services	0.9
Foreign labour	0.4
Environmental protection	0.3
Taxation	0.3
Labour relations	0.2
Others	17.4
Total	100.1%
(N)	(679)

Percentages do not add up to 100% because of rounding.

To explore the extent to which issue voting occurred, the following analysis will concentrate on the most frequently mentioned problem — the '1997 issue'. Furthermore, since the competition in Kowloon Central was in essence between the two United Democrats candidates, Lau Chin-shek and Conrad Lam Kui-shing (hereafter referred to as Lau and Lam respectively) and the pro-China candidate from the Federation of Trade Unions, Chan Yuen-han (hereafter referred to as Chan), comparisons among the electorate who intended to vote for these three candidates will be presented.[15] This narrower focus has resulted in a total of 228 cases, with 103 intended supporters for Lau, 75 for Lam, and 50 for Chan. The number of 228 cases exceeds the number of 218 intended voters who cited the '1997 issue' as most salient because each voter was entitled to choose two candidates.

Identifying the issue most salient to the respondents is only the first step in our analysis of issue voting. Before we look at respondents' attitudes to questions related to the '1997 issue', we need to know, on a more basic level, how they looked upon the political orientations of the various candidates. The '1997 issue' is, to a great extent, concerned with the relationship between Hong Kong and China and was the most conspicuous point of contention between liberal and pro-China candidates in the Legislative Council elections. If our respondents did not perceive any difference on this issue between the two liberal candidates and the pro-China candidate in their own constituency, it is quite unlikely that they would cast their votes on the basis of the candidates' positions on issues related to Hong Kong-China relations.

Table 4.2 shows that a predominant number of our respondents put the three candidates into two political camps. Of those who were able to identify Lau as a candidate running in their constituency, 88.3% said that he was a liberal, while the corresponding figure is a little higher in Lam's case (90.5%). Interestingly, the respondents' perception of Chan's political stance was less unitary, 61.5% identifying her as pro-China and 14.4% regarding her as a democrat.

Table 4.2 Candidates' political stance as perceived by respondents

	Lau (%)	Lam (%)	Chan (%)
Liberal	88.3	90.5	14.4
Independent	0.6	1.5	6.7
Conservative/ business	0	0.7	2.9
Pro-China	0	1.5	61.5
Others	11.0	5.8	14.4
Total	99.9%	100.0%	99.9%
(N)	(154)	(137)	(104)

Percentages do not add up to 100% because of rounding.

The perception of the three candidates as belonging to different political camps does not, in itself, entail voting on the basis of political stance. In order to establish the relationship between political stance and intention to vote, we asked our respondents the further question whether they would in fact cast their ballots on the basis of the candidates' political stance. Table 4.3 shows that over 60% of the intending supporters of Lau and Lam gave an affirmative answer (63.0% and 63.9% respectively), while the figure for Chan's intending supporters was substantially lower (44.4%).

Table 4.3 Voting on the basis of the candidate's political stance

	Lau (%)	Lam (%)	Chan (%)
Yes	63.0	63.9	44.4
No	37.0	36.1	55.6
Total	100.0%	100.0%	100.0%
(N)	(100)	(72)	(45)

That a substantial number of intending voters gave their support to Lau and Lam because of their political stance indicates a possibility of issue voting in these two cases. Since the platforms of Lau and Lam were very similar, we would expect the attitudes of their intending supporters on issues concerning Hong Kong-China relations to be similar too. Chan's case, however, complicates the picture. Over half her intending supporters (55.6%) indicated that their choice of Chan had little to do with her political stance. As a result, we cannot determine the views of Chan's intending supporters on Hong Kong-China relations which may not necessarily be different from their counterparts who chose Lau and Lam. We might speculate that the small number of voters (25 cases) who did not vote for Chan on the basis of her political stance might have done so on the basis of her personal attributes, and experience in trade union work. They may have regarded Hong Kong-China relations as the most important issue but their choice of candidate was made according to other considerations. Similar conclusions might be drawn from the minorities who voted for Lau and Lam. Issue voting occurs on the Hong Kong-China issue and seems to be important in a majority of cases, but there is a significant minority of voters who appear to be guided by other considerations.

As mentioned above, the '1997 issue' is a broad term which can be interpreted to encompass a variety of more specific issues. We propose to analyse the issue in terms of three dimensions: (a) the autonomy of the Hong Kong government, (b) confidence in Hong Kong's future and (c) democratic political development. For a clearer case of issue voting to occur, we would expect those who intended to vote along liberal lines to take a more resolute position on issues related to the autonomy of the Hong Kong government and to have been more in favour of having a democratic governmental structure than those who intended to cast a pro-China vote. We would have expected the latter group to have been more confident of the future of Hong Kong than the former group. None the less, our findings might not be as clear-cut as we had expected since they could be complicated by those who did not vote on the basis of political stance.

Our respondents' opinions on the autonomy of the Hong Kong government are presented in Tables 4.4 and 4.5. Table 4.4 contains information on our respondents' opinions about whether China should have a decision-making role in the internal affairs of Hong Kong. None of our respondents, including the pro-China ones, felt strongly that China should have a decision-making role in Hong Kong's affairs. In fact, even among the pro-China voters, only 13.0% said China should

Table 4.4 Acceptance of China playing a decision-making role in the internal affairs of Hong Kong

	Lau (%)	Lam (%)	Chan (%)
Strongly disagree	31.0	32.4	15.2
Disagree	59.0	63.5	71.7
Agree	10.0	4.1	13.0
Strongly agree	0	0	0
Total	100.0%	100.0%	99.9%
(N)	(100)	(74)	(46)

Note: Figures in this table are different from those in Table 3.16. For an explanation, see Chapter 7.

Percentages do not add up to 100% because of rounding.

have a decision-making role. A substantial majority of our respondents, regardless of their political inclinations, thought that China should not have decision-making power in Hong Kong's internal affairs.

Our respondents' views on whether accepting China's opinion should be a first consideration in handling conflicts between Hong Kong and China are presented in Table 4.5. Again, sentiments do not differ much among the intending supporters of the three candidates. While about half of Lau's (52.0%) and Lam's (49.3%) intending supporters did not think that China's opinions in its disputes with Hong Kong were of predominant importance, the proportion of Chan's supporters holding the same position did not lag far behind (46.9%). On the whole, our findings of the views of our respondents on the autonomy of the Hong Kong government suggest that there was little difference between those who intended to choose liberal and pro-China candidates. Neither group was particularly strongly disposed towards accepting China's views.

Table 4.5 The importance of accepting China's views in Sino-Hong Kong disputes

	Lau (%)	Lam (%)	Chan (%)
Strongly agree	1.0	2.8	2.0
Agree	22.0	25.4	24.5
Neutral	25.0	22.5	26.5
Disagree	47.0	46.5	44.9
Strongly disagree	5.0	2.8	2.0
Total	100.0%	100.0%	99.9%
(N)	(100)	(71)	(49)

Note: Figures in this table are different from those in Table 3.16. For an explanation, see Chapter 7.

Percentages do not add up to 100% because of rounding.

Although we had expected pro-China voters to have more confidence in the future of Hong Kong, our findings suggest otherwise. According to Table 4.6, the proportions of intending pro-China and liberal voters who believed that there would be a prosperous and stable Hong Kong after 1997 are very similar. What is more telling, however, is the substantial number of 'neutral' answers (55.3% for Lau's intending supporters, 58.3% for Lam's and 53.7% for Chan's). Since such a large proportion of our respondents had no opinion on this issue, the overall picture suggests that most of our respondents were not certain about the future of Hong Kong.

Table 4.6 Confidence in a stable and prosperous Hong Kong after 1997

	Lau (%)	Lam (%)	Chan (%)
Strongly agree	0	0	2.4
Agree	31.8	26.7	29.3
Neutral	55.3	58.3	53.7
Disagree	11.8	15.0	12.2
Strongly disagree	1.2	0	2.4
Total	100.1%	100.0%	100.0%
(N)	(85)	(60)	(41)

Note: Figures in this table are different from those in Table 3.16. For an explanation, see Chapter 7.

Percentages do not add up to 100% because of rounding.

Whether or not our respondents will leave Hong Kong given the opportunity is another indicator of their confidence in the future of Hong Kong. As shown in Table 4.7, contrary to our expectation, a slightly higher proportion of intending pro-China voters indicated that they would definitely leave Hong Kong (40.4%) than their liberal counterparts (33.7% for Lau's and 36.7% for Lam's supporters respectively).

It appears that, in general, our respondents are ambivalent about the future of Hong Kong but, when opportunity allows, more of the intending pro-China voters, whom we thought would have chosen to stay, indicated that they would leave Hong Kong. Our data showed that a higher proportion of intending liberal voters were of a younger age than intending pro-China voters.[16] Probably the experience of the turbulent years, especially in the latter years of the Mao era, made emigration to a non-communist place a more desirable alternative for the older members of the electorate.

Table 4.7 Intention to emigrate if the opportunity arises

	Lau (%)	Lam (%)	Chan (%)
Strongly agree	7.4	9.9	6.4
Agree	26.3	26.8	34.0
Neutral	14.7	14.1	14.9
Disagree	44.2	39.4	38.3
Strongly disagree	7.4	9.9	6.4
Total	100.0%	100.1%	100.0%
(N)	(95)	(71)	(47)

Percentages do not add up to 100% because of rounding.

The final dimension of the '1997 issue' concerns the voters' views on a democratic governmental structure. We asked the question whether voters would prefer to leave government in the hands of a capable leader on the one hand, or to have citizens constantly scrutinize it on the other. We anticipated that more of the liberal voters would prefer an active citizenry keeping watch over the government to a capable leader. Our findings indicated a slight tendency in this direction (Table 4.8). More of Lau's (38.8%) and Lam's (36.1%) intending supporters indicated their preference for citizens to scrutinize the government than Chan's intending voters (31.9%).

Table 4.8 Preference to leave government to capable leaders rather than requiring constant citizen scrutiny

	Lau (%)	Lam (%)	Chan (%)
Strongly agree	6.1	4.2	14.9
Agree	50.0	52.8	42.5
Neutral	5.1	6.9	10.6
Disagree	24.5	22.2	23.4
Strongly disagree	14.3	13.9	8.5
Total	100.0%	100.0%	100.0%
(N)	(98)	(72)	(47)

To recapitulate our findings, our respondents' opinions regarding the autonomy of the Hong Kong government were quite similar: both intending liberal and pro-China voters favoured a high degree of autonomy. They were, however, rather ambivalent about the future of Hong Kong. Interestingly, a slightly higher proportion of pro-China voters would want to leave Hong Kong if the opportunity arose. Finally, more intending liberal than pro-China voters showed a preference for citizen scrutiny of government.

ISSUE SALIENCY AND VOTING INCLINATIONS

If we were to apply the criteria for issue voting stipulated at the beginning of this chapter, it would be fair to report that this survey was not able to detect unequivocal evidence of issue voting among our respondents. If issue voting is more broadly interpreted as voting in relation to attitudinal inclinations on certain issues, however, our findings do contain some indications of a difference in attitudinal propensity, albeit slight in most cases, between supporters of the two liberal candidates, Lau and Lam, and the pro-China candidate, Chan. Thus, more of the intending supporters of Lau and Lam were opposed to China playing a decision-making role in Hong Kong's internal affairs or attaching priority to China's views when handling Sino-Hong Kong conflicts (Tables 4.4 and 4.5). In the same vein, more of the liberal candidates' supporters than Chan's objected to leaving the job of governing to a capable leader instead of involving the citizenry (Table 4.8).

To some extent, the above findings can be taken as an indication that our respondents picked candidates whose positions on the issue considered most salient were not wildly different from their own. As candidates of the UDHK and active members of the Alliance, both Lau and Lam had a track record of criticizing the Chinese government, especially after the military suppression of the 1989 pro-democracy movement in Beijing. They had also organized protest activities and demonstrations. In addition, both were deeply involved in the movement to press for a quicker pace of democratic reform in Hong Kong.

Following this train of thought, one would have expected the supporters of Chan, who was a FTU candidate, to have voted for her on the basis of her political stance. However, 55.6% of Chan's intending supporters indicated that their choice of Chan had little to do with her political stance. Chan might have won her support from those who regarded her affiliation with the FTU as a social organization. That the FTU has a pro-China political stance is obvious, but whether it is predominantly viewed as a political association by the electorate is still open to question. Among Chan's supporters who said that they were members of organizations, 45.3% had a labour group background. While it is possible that many of those who were affiliated to the FTU did cast their ballots on 'political' grounds, it also seems likely that some of those who had social links with the FTU cast their votes for Chan because of those links.

Notwithstanding these complications, it is the high degree of similarity between the two groups of supporters that is striking and which requires explanation. In the following discussion, we will attempt to account for the lack of a significant divergence between the two groups of supporters in terms of their attitudes on the '1997 issue' when, presumably, they were supporting candidates with very different stances on the issue.

As mentioned in the previous section, the first complication probably results from the fact that, unlike supporters of Lau and Lam, a majority of Chan's intending supporters (55.6%) made it clear that their support for Chan was not based on her political stance. This meant that Chan was chosen for considerations other than her connections with pro-China forces and opened up the possibility that her supporters' political attitudes would be similar to those of the supporters of Lau and Lam.[17]

Another factor which might have mitigated the difference between the two groups of electors was Chan's campaign. Probably mindful that a pro-China label could be an electoral liability, Chan repeatedly sought to put herself across as an independent-thinking candidate, so much so that she avowed her support for revising the Basic Law if there was sufficient demand for that course of action in Hong Kong.[18] Her election slogan was 'to work for Hong Kong as home'.

Investigators of electoral behaviour have been reminded that, in the final analysis, election campaigns are 'a process of political communication' whereby the electorate's levels of conceptualization and comprehension of the issue agenda can be influenced.[19] That a significant 14.4% of Chan's intending supporters could regard her as a 'democrat' (see Table 4.2) is probably a tribute to her success during the campaign to dissociate herself from the image of a hamstrung underling of Chinese forces. As a result, she may have won the votes of some electors who would otherwise have voted for other candidates, though such votes were not numerous enough to win her the election. Alternatively, some voters may have accepted Chan's campaign messages at face value and failed to discern her connections with pro-China forces.

While the respondents under discussion here all named the '1997 issue' as the most salient problem confronting Hong Kong, there is no established wisdom that the actual vote is automatically based on the most salient issue. Rather, as Denver suggests, the vote decision involves considerations of certain 'trade offs'. Even in the case of an issue voter, he or she will have to decide how much a preference for one issue is worth exchanging for another.[20] Rabinowitz *et al.* essentially agree with Denver and argue that, much as the single issue selected as most salient is an important influence on vote choice, 'factors other than salience could well be critical in determining an issue's influence'.[21] Chan's supporters, as discussed above, appear to confirm this hypothesis.

CONCLUSIONS

The common view has been that vote decisions based on policy preferences are superior to choices based on party loyalty or candidate attributes. Issue voters are portrayed as generally more 'rational' than voters who base their vote choice on other considerations.[22] This conventional view has been challenged by Carmines and Stimson who suggest that the lack of issue voting might have resulted from 'inadequacies of choice offered by the political system' rather than inherent limitations of the voters.[23]

In Hong Kong, given its brief experience with electoral politics and a dearth of political skills, the absence of issue voting should not come as a surprise. The newness of the 'party system', coupled with the straitjacket imposed by the Sino-British agreement and the Basic Law on future political development, has meant that the freedom and ability of most political groups and candidates to develop distinctive electoral platforms and dissimilar policy resolutions has been greatly circumscribed. To the extent that our respondents did show a high degree of cognition of political events and personalities around them, however, the potential for issue voting was there.

None the less, the most important indication of political maturity is not whether the electorate are able to engage in issue voting, though this can be one of the measures. It appears to us that the more important concern should be whether political groups or parties and candidates, in presenting differing stances on individual issues, do simultaneously offer different value or ideological frameworks for the electorate. In more advanced democratic countries with established party systems, issue voting is normally consequential upon party identification and loyalty. In the Hong Kong context, however, the process seems to be reversed. Candidates and political groups are located on a political spectrum ranging from 'liberal' to 'conservative' to 'pro-China', depending on their respective stance on the most salient issue which, in our context, was concern over the future of Hong Kong. For the present, however, substantive policy questions have been subsumed by the more central importance of general political orientations towards the future of the territory. Nevertheless, there were indications of an affinity between issue positions and vote choice in the recent elections. To the extent that this trend continues, it is possible that salient policy issues, which have been subsumed by the '1997 issue', will gradually show a greater correlation with vote choice.

NOTES

1. Kenneth J. Meier and James E. Campbell, 'Issue Voting: An Empirical Examination of Individually Necessary and Jointly Sufficient Conditions', *American Politics Quarterly*, 7, 1(January 1979): 21.

2. The diversity of opinion ranges widely. Sarlvik and Crewe claim that policy opinions and assessment of party performance in office affect party choice more than twice as much as the influence of social and economic characteristics taken together. Heath *et al.* and Rose and McAllister, on the other hand, reject altogether the view that issues are an important influence on voting behaviour. Meier and Campbell probably explain the reason for this dichotomy of views when they point out that it is 'difficult to specify the exact conditions that must be met for any particular voter to engage in issue voting ... the conditions necessary for issue voting are idiosyncratic because the involvement of citizens in politics and the circumstances surrounding their vote choice are also idiosyncratic'. See B. Sarlvik and I. Crewe, *Decade of Dealignment* (Cambridge: Cambridge University Press, 1983); A. Heath *et al.*, *Understanding Political Change: The British Voter 1964-87* (Oxford: Pergamon Press, 1991); A. Heath, R. Jowell and J. Curtice, *How Britain Votes* (Oxford: Pergamon, 1985); R. Rose and I. McAllister, *Voters Begin to Choose* (London: Sage, 1986); and Meier and Campbell, 'Issue Voting', pp. 21-50.

3. See Harold D. Clarke *et al.*, 'Voting Behaviour and the Outcome of the 1979 Federal Election: The Impact of Leaders and Issues', *Canadian Journal of Political Science*, 15, 3(September 1982): 517-552; David Denver, *Elections and Voting Behaviour in Britain* (New York: Philip Allan, 1989); Mark N. Franklin, 'Assessing the Rise of Issue Voting in British Elections Since 1964', *Electoral Studies*, 4, 1(1985): 37-56; and Meier and Campbell, 'Issue Voting'.

4. Meier and Campbell, 'Issue Voting', p.24.

5. Franklin, 'Assessing the Rise of Issue Voting', p. 41 (emphasis in original).

6. Richard A. Brody and Benjamin I. Page, 'Comment: The Assessment of Policy Voting', *The American Political Science Review*, 66(1972): 450-458.

7. Denver, *Elections*, p.76.

8. Ibid.

9. For the powers and functions of the District Boards and the municipal councils, see Norman J. Miners, *The Government and Politics of Hong Kong* (Hong Kong: Oxford University Press, 1991), 5th ed., Chapters 11 and 12.

10. *An Agreement Between the Government of the United Kingdom of Great Britain and Northern Ireland and the Government of the People's Republic of China on the Future of Hong Kong* (Hong Kong: Government Printer, 1984).

11. 'Report of an Opinion Poll in March 1991', City and New Territories Administration, April 1991 and 'Report of an Opinion Poll in May 1991', City and New Territories Administration, June 1991. See also *Ming Pao,* 6 July 1991 and *Hong Kong Standard,* 27 August 1991.

12. *SCMP,* 28 April 1991.

13. *SCMP,* 30 June 1991.

14. *SCMP,* 13 January 1991.

15. Our analysis focused on these three candidates for two reasons: first, the '1997 issue' was a major point of contention between the liberal and the pro-China factions and, secondly, the numbers of intended votes for the other four candidates were too small for further analysis. The number of respondents who regarded the '1997 issue' as the most important problem and who intended to vote for Peter Chan Chi-kwan was 16; for Cecilia Yeung Lai-yin, 18; for John Young, 7; and for Cheung Chung-ming, 1.

16. Among Lau's intending supporters 63.1% were between 21 and 39 years old; among Lam's, 60.0%; and among Chan's, 50.0%.

17. Chan's intending supporters gave 'political platform' (17.8%), 'past experience' (14.6%) and her 'willingness to serve the community' (12.4%) as the reasons for voting for her.

18. Chan's profession of independence from the Chinese government's position was conveyed in an interview with the present research team on 3 September 1991 as well as in many electioneering forums.

19. Herbert B. Asher, 'Voting Behavior Research in the 1980s: An Examination of Some Old and New Problem Areas', in Ada W. Finifter, ed., *Political Science: The State of the Discipline* (Washington, D.C.: American Political Science Association, 1983), pp. 339-388.

20. Denver, *Elections.*

21. George Rabinowitz, James W. Prothro and William Jacoby, 'Salience as A Factor in the Impact of Issues on Candidate Evaluation', *The Journal of Politics* 44, (1982): 44.

22. Norman R. Luttbeg and Michael M. Gant, 'The Failure of Liberal/ Conservative Ideology as a Cognitive Structure', *Public Opinion Quarterly,* 49, 1(Spring 1985): 80-93.

23. Edward G. Carmines and James A. Stimson, 'The Two Faces of Issue Voting', *American Political Science Review,* 74(1980): 78-91.

5

Voting Criteria: Ideal and Actual Choices in Candidate Selection

Fred Yeung

Political participation, of which voting is an important component, can be considered an instrumental activity through which citizens communicate their preferences to political actors.[1] In conceptualizing political phenomena, system theorists conceive of voting as input into the political system[2] and pay considerable attention to the message contained in the electoral results. Studies of voting behaviour often concentrate on three distinct features of the process: the decision whether or not to vote, or voter turnout; the choice of a candidate; and the criteria used in choosing the candidate or making a vote choice.

The first two features of the process can be assessed in pre-election public opinion polls which provide simple, testable exercises to predict the outcome of the election. These polls serve to arouse popular interest through the media. In the Legislative Council elections, for instance, many newspapers and television companies sponsored extensive cross-sectional research and sometimes longitudinal research on voting. Their emphases fell predominantly on voter turnout and vote choices.

The neglect of the third feature of the process, voting criteria, may be a consequence of a lack of interest in a deeper understanding of the motivation of voters, but it may also be a consequence of the fact that measurement is more susceptible to methodological uncertainty. Testing the reasons behind a vote choice requires a sophisticated research design to disentangle controversies over, for example, the validity and reliability of the means of measurement. In the United States, even though academics have a long tradition of conducting this kind of research, there is still no universally accepted methodology to study the criteria voters use to choose candidates.[3]

Despite these problems, the study of voting criteria is necessary to understand the underlying, often complex, messages the electorate seeks to convey through the single act of voting. Such studies may also serve to supplement other research on turnout and the choice of candidate and to provide another dimension to understanding voting behaviour. In short, the study of voting criteria enables us to make an additional and deeper assessment of the preferences and feelings of voters. This may be seen as a desirable increase of knowledge on the views of the electorate, especially in those political systems which purport to take the views of the citizen into account.

'RATIONALITY' IN SELECTING CANDIDATES

This study is based on a direct measurement of the voting criteria stated by respondents in pre-election and post-election interviews in the Kowloon Central constituency. Strictly speaking, it is different from studies of the various determinants of vote choice, which investigate attitudinal attributes of the electorate indirectly in order to establish explanatory models of vote choice.[4] These studies construct models which usually focus on three important variables: party identification, issue attitudes and candidate evaluations, which are intertwined by various recursive and non-recursive interrelationships.

We need to be cautious here. Measuring voting criteria directly may produce a higher proportion of 'rational' answers than would have been obtained if we had used other indirect methods.[5] Some voting criteria may be recalled more easily because the respondents perceive them to be more distinct and readily identifiable. Yet, in reality, voters may decide to vote for candidates because of criteria which are not immediately derived from a rational appraisal of the candidates' personal qualities, platform or political affiliation. It is possible, for instance, that community opinion leaders may be influential in persuading some voters to choose particular candidates or that the voter has invariably given his or her support to one political group in past elections. One cannot conclude from this that the voter's behaviour is 'irrational'.[6] It may be that opinion leaders have proved to be adequate guides in complex situations or that loyal support for one political group has been based on a detailed consideration of the group's platform. However, it does mean that the process by which a choice is made does not necessarily accord perfectly with conventional rational models.[7] In this chapter, we attempt to disentangle some of these considerations by identifying the principal voting criteria, both ideal and actual, from which voters claim they would seek to make a choice. We recognize, however, that choice may be mediated by other considerations (see Chapters 3 and 4).

VOTING CRITERIA AND THE HONG KONG ELECTORATE: PREVIOUS RESEARCH

Studies seeking to analyse the voting criteria of the Hong Kong electorate have been conducted since 1985, when the second District Board elections were held. A brief survey of these studies provides the background for our analysis.

Of the eight previous surveys identified,[8] six were studies of District Board elections, while the remainder were studies of Urban and Regional Council elections. Many of them were conducted by local social service centres and focused on one or two constituencies while the others were undertaken by academics studying constituencies which were more widely distributed. Half of the studies used exit polls, which sampled the views of voters who had just left the polling station. The others were pre-election interviews conducted either on a face-to-face basis or by telephone. Only rarely were self-administered questionnaires used. However, despite the diversity in the scale of this election research and the different research methodologies employed, they show some similarities in the ways in which they study voting criteria.

First, they usually ask about the voting criteria used to select candidates generally, not the actual qualities expected of a chosen, particular candidate. It is possible, in consequence, that respondents may offer ideal preferences rather than the actual attributes which have motivated their vote choice.

Secondly, often only a single question is asked to ascertain the voting criteria employed by respondents. This differs from studies conducted elsewhere on determinants of vote choice which have separate questions or even entire research designs which focus on measuring a particular determinant independently. As a result, previous studies of District Board and Urban and Regional Council elections employed catch-all categories to record the possible answers offered by respondents. Many categories used in these studies are similar. They include:

(a) candidates' personal particulars, such as age, educational attainment, occupation and residence in the district;
(b) voters' affective impression of candidates, such as attractiveness of appearance, fame, prestige, capability and willingness to serve the district;
(c) criteria related to candidates' performance, such as platform, service records and experience in the district, past performance as an incumbent;
(d) the support and recommendation of others, for example, recommendation by social and community organizations, friends, neighbours and relatives;
(e) other criteria, such as the candidate's campaign efforts.

Thirdly, putting aside differences in sampling method and research design, respondents are consistently found to identify platform, past performance or experience, and the educational attainments of the candidate as the three most important criteria. Educational attainments generally rank third.[9] While few attempts have been made to interpret these findings, it may be suggested that voters generally prefer candidates who, they believe, can help to improve district administration. Thus, they place emphasis on candidates' platforms when making a choice and consider whether the candidates can fulfil their promises by judging their past performance or experience. Educational attainments are seen as an indicator of ability and capacity to serve the district and may also reflect a traditional trust of those who have high formal educational levels.

THE CONTEXT OF THE 1991 DIRECT ELECTIONS

Before we discuss our survey findings on voting criteria, the contextual setting of the 1991 elections should be noted. The context of the elections can help to explain the pattern of voting criteria identified.[10] In addition, the 1991 direct elections were different from previous elections in a number of respects. These changes in contextual setting may also help to account for discrepancies in the findings between this survey and previous research.

First, candidates for the 1991 Legislative Council elections were seeking a wider mandate than those running in District Board or Urban and Regional Council elections. Although the role and power of the Legislative Council is limited, elected members still provide the most important formal channel for citizens to influence public policies. The Legislative Council is the institution in which legislation and public expenditure are finally approved. It is the apex of the three-tiered representative government in the territory.[11] The selection of Legislative Council members, therefore, might be expected to arouse greater interest among the electorate than District Board or Urban and Regional Council elections. Similarly, voters might have greater expectations of the candidates. Thus, the voting criteria emphasized by respondents in this research may be different from those in previous research which focused on District Board or Urban and Regional Council elections.

Secondly, the constituencies were double-seat, which provided an opportunity for the voter to select not only the best but also the second-best candidate. This contrasts with the Urban and Regional Council elections in which constituencies for elected members are all single-seat.[12] District Board elections comprise both single-seat and double-seat constituencies.[13] Double-seat constituencies may allow voters greater flexibility in selecting candidates. In fact, it is quite possible that the voting criteria used for choosing the first candidate may be different from those for the second candidate.

Thirdly, there were an average of three candidates per seat in the Legislative Council elections, that is, 54 candidates contesting 18 seats. Competition in Kowloon Central was a little more intense, with a ratio of 3.5 candidates per seat. The corresponding ratios for District Board and Urban and Regional Council elections were lower and ratios for both types of elections have declined generally over the years.[14] Differences in the extent of competition for seats may impinge significantly on campaign activities and the interest of voters in the election. In addition, the greater the number of candidates, the more the choice available for selection. This may help voters come closer to finding their ideal candidate.

Fourthly, the size of the constituency for the Legislative Council elections was larger, both geographically and in terms of population, than in previous elections of District Boards, and Urban and Regional Councils. Since the size of the constituency was larger and the number of electors greater than in previous elections, contact between the candidate and the electorate may be more difficult. Again, this might have a significant effect on campaign strategies and electors' perceptions of candidates.

Fifthly, there were altogether three elections in 1991. Each election had a successively higher level of representation than the one which preceded it. It was the first time that this had occurred and it served to create a continuous, stimulating environment for the electorate through extensive media reporting and intensive campaigning. People called 1991 the 'year of elections'.

Sixthly, the level of party activity in the 1991 elections was higher than in previous elections. Campaign activities were more widespread and reached more people. Many candidates were endorsed and supported strategically not only by parties but by quasi-political organizations such as unions.[15] Their effect on voters' attitudes lent a new dimension to electoral behaviour.

Hong Kong has been in a state of turbulence for the last decade.[16] Citizens have become more politically aware as a result of events such as Sino-British negotiations over the future of Hong Kong, attempts to establish a more representative government in the colony, the suppression of the 1989 pro-democracy movement in China, and Sino-Hong Kong conflicts in the transitional period. These events may have had a significant impact on voting behaviour in the 1991 elections and are important in understanding the motivation which led to the voters' choice of candidates.

CRITERIA FOR CANDIDATE SELECTION IN KOWLOON CENTRAL

Taking previous academic work and contextual changes into account, the aim of this chapter is to explore the pattern of voting criteria which respondents say they employ in selecting different candidates. Do respondents employ the same set of voting criteria in selecting candidates? Are there any differences between the ideal attributes of a Legislative Councillor and the actual criteria employed in choosing a particular candidate? Do the criteria employed change before and after elections? What are the substantive criteria at play?

Our information comes from a two-wave panel group of respondents with whom we successfully conducted both a pre-election and a post-election interview. We included a number of questions (see Appendix C) which sought to gauge voting criteria in a similar way to previous research so that we might compare our results with those findings. However, we also took into account methodological inadequacies in previous studies and the need to respond to changes in circumstances which require modification of the old approaches.

In the pre-election survey, we asked respondents to identify the ideal attributes, or the ideal voting criteria, which they would expect of a Legislative Councillor. Next, they were asked to show their preferences for particular candidates. Then, respondents were requested to offer their reasons, or the actual voting criteria, for selecting the particular candidates. By this method, we were able to study possible differences between an ideal and an actual situation after the voters had considered which candidates were running in their constituency. In addition, we were also able to analyse whether the actual criteria used for selecting the two candidates were similar. After the elections, the panel respondents were once again asked for the actual voting criteria which they had used in choosing particular candidates. The results enabled us to gauge possible shifts in their position before and after the elections.

The respondents' answers were recorded in catch-all categories, which included most possible responses. In effect, we followed the method in which the concept of voting criteria was previously investigated in Hong Kong. This provided a simple measurement which served to make the survey easier to administer and enabled comparisons to be made with previous research findings.

In the questions on ideal and actual voting criteria, respondents were free to mention up to a maximum of three most important voting criteria which they had in mind when they selected candidates. However, they were permitted to select fewer than three criteria if they indicated that they had already mentioned the most important ones. Respondents were also allowed to provide different voting criteria for the two candidates chosen. At the end of each question, they were requested to rank the relative importance of the criteria they had mentioned. This enabled us both to identify the single most popular vote criterion and to ascertain the relative significance of different voting criteria for respondents.

The analysis was based on the responses of the panel sample, 570 registered electors in Kowloon Central, whom we interviewed before and after the elections. Since respondents were allowed to mention different voting criteria in selecting each of their two choices, the first objective was to find out if they had in fact done so. If they did, the analysis of voting criteria should probably be based on the individual vote choice mentioned, rather than the individual respondent. Therefore, we measured the level of match of the voting criteria employed to select particular candidates in the pre-election and post-election surveys. For respondents who had indicated two vote choices, we calculated the number of mentions of the same criteria (that is, the count of criteria that are 'matched') for selecting the two candidates against the total number of criteria mentioned.[17] Table 5.1 shows that, in the pre-election survey, the criteria for choosing two candidates were 'fully matched', or entirely the same, for only about a third of our respondents. The level of match of the actual voting criteria employed in the post-election survey was even lower. As a result, the analysis which follows is based on individual vote choices.

In order to assess the relative importance of each criterion, we calculated the total mentions of each voting criterion stated by our respondents by simple aggregation. Then, the total mentions were divided by the number of votes indicated to arrive at the percentage mention for each voting criterion. This provided an overall picture of the pattern of voting criteria of the respondents. As a first step, we

Table 5.1 Pattern of match of the three most important voting criteria employed in choosing two candidates

	Pre-election interview (%)	Post-election interview (%)
Fully matched[a]	33.7	28.1
Partially matched	34.9	31.7
Totally mismatched[b]	31.5	40.2
Total	100.1%	100.0%
(N)	(184)	(281)

[a] Cases where the actual criteria the respondent used in selecting one candidate were entirely the same as those used in selecting the second candidate.
[b] The voting criteria were totally different for the two candidates chosen.

aggregated the three most important voting criteria (Table 5.2). We then focused more closely on the single most important voting criterion mentioned by respondents (Table 5.3).[18] The aggregation of the three most important voting criteria mentioned essentially relaxes the rank order placed on each criterion by the respondents. This provides us with a more general picture of the views of the respondents.

Table 5.2 contains the percentage mentions of the three most important voting criteria stated. The figures for actual voting criteria are based on individual vote choice. The ideal voting criteria, or ideal attributes required of a Legislative Councillor, however, are the respondents' ideal-type considerations and the percentage mentions are based on the individual respondent. On average, respondents offered approximately two criteria for each vote.[19] It is evident that the four most frequently mentioned voting criteria were 'willingness to serve the public', 'policy stance or platform', 'past performance or experience' and 'style of work'. ('Style of work' is a direct translation of the phrase in Chinese which was the operating language of the interviews. It can be interpreted generally to mean the manner in which one conducts business, for example, being efficient, diligent or prudent.) These voting criteria occupy a range from a minimum of 21.5% to a maximum of 44.0% of the total votes mentioned in all the three columns in Table

Table 5.2 Percentage mentions of the three most important voting criteria

Voting criteria	Ideal (pre-election) (%)	Actual (pre-election) (%)	Actual (post-election) (%)
Educational attainment	15.2	5.1	5.4
Age	4.4	4.3	2.8
Occupation	3.6	7.7	5.4
Sex	0	1.3	1.5
Residence in the district	1.7	0.9	0.7
Membership of political group	3.9	8.1	12.3
Membership of social/ community group	1.2	3.2	1.3
Charisma/appearance	1.7	1.3	0.7
Social status/prestige	4.6	6.4	3.5
Style of work	22.5	30.6	26.6
Willingness to serve the public	44.0	32.8	30.1
Policy stance/platform	33.3	21.5	23.5
Past performance/ experience	42.3	39.4	33.2
Acquaintance with candidate	1.5	2.1	0.7
Supported by political group	3.4	3.4	3.8
Supported by social/ community group	1.0	0.4	1.8
Supported by renowned individuals	0.7	1.1	1.3
Family/friend/neighbour influences	4.8	2.6	4.6
Others	16.9	22.1	23.7
Total	206.5%	194.0%	182.9%
(N)	(414)	(470)	(608)

5.2. This pattern is equally clear when we focus only on the single most important voting criterion mentioned (Table 5.3).

A closer examination of the tables also tells us something about the dynamics of candidate selection. From Table 5.2, for example, it is clear that, on average, the respective percentages of emphasis of actual voting criteria in the pre-election and post-election interviews do not differ greatly, with a maximum of 6.2% only on 'past performance or experience'. We can say, therefore, that there is little significant change in emphasis on the actual voting criteria used before and after the

Table 5.3 Percentage mentions of the single most important voting criterion

Voting criteria	Ideal (pre-election) (%)	Actual (pre-election) (%)	Actual (post-election (%)
Educational attainment	3.9	2.1	2.1
Age	0.5	1.1	0.5
Occupation	1.0	2.1	1.0
Sex	0	0.9	0.3
Residence in the district	0.2	0.2	0.3
Membership of a political group	1.5	4.7	7.2
Membership of a social/ community group	1.0	1.7	0.7
Charisma/appearance	0.2	1.3	0.2
Social status/prestige	1.0	2.1	1.6
Style of work	8.0	12.8	13.0
Willingness to serve the public	28.5	18.9	19.1
Policy stance/platform	15.7	12.1	12.3
Past performance/ experience	23.9	21.9	20.1
Acquaintance with candidate	0.7	0.4	0
Supported by political group	0.5	1.5	1.6
Supported by social/ community group	0.2	0	1.2
Supported by renowned individuals	0.2	0.6	0.7
Family/friend/neighbour influences	3.1	1.5	2.8
Others	9.9	14.0	15.3
Total	100%	100%	100%
(N)	(414)	(470)	(608)

elections. However, if we compare the ideal with the actual criteria in the pre-election survey, the differences are more marked. 'Educational attainment' suffers a drop of 10.1% in emphasis if we are evaluating a particular rather than a utopian candidate. 'Willingness to serve the public' also drops by 11.2%. 'Policy stance or platform' encounters a comparable decline of 11.8%. In contrast, 'style of work' rises by 8.1%. In addition, 'membership of a political group' receives more emphasis when we look at the actual criteria being used in selecting candidates. It rises by 4.3% and 8.5% for the pre-election and post-election surveys respectively. The findings reveal that there are differences in emphasis in certain aspects of ideal and actual voting criteria employed by respondents when we consider the three most important criteria mentioned.

A similar conclusion can be derived when we inspect the percentage mentions of the single most important criterion stated (Table 5.3). The difference from the analysis in Table 5.2 is in the intensity of responses. It can be observed that the percentage mentions of actual criteria used before and after the election are even closer, with a maximum difference of only 2.5% on 'membership of a political group'. In addition, the difference between the ideal and actual voting criteria in the pre-election survey differ less dramatically, with the exception of 'willingness to serve the public', which drops by 9.6%.

If we now turn to the results for each question, we can gauge the relative importance of the different criteria mentioned. Two observations can be made. First, we can observe the rank order of the three most important voting criteria mentioned (Table 5.4). Clearly, 'willingness to serve the public' and 'past performance or experience' consistently outweigh 'policy stance or platform' and 'style of work'. Secondly, the spread of these four criteria provides some idea of the size of the

Table 5.4 Rank order of the four major criteria identified

Voting criteria	Ideal (pre-election) (%)	Actual (pre-election) (%)	Actual (post-election) (%)
Style of work	22.5 (4)	30.6 (3)	26.6 (3)
Willingness to serve the public	44.0 (1)	32.8 (2)	30.1 (2)
Policy stance/platform	33.3 (3)	21.5 (4)	23.5 (4)
Past performance/ experience	42.3 (2)	39.4 (1)	33.2 (1)
Spread between the first and fourth criterion	21.5	17.9	9.7

Note: The data are extracted from Table 5.2 on the percentage mentions of the three most important voting criteria. The rank order is arranged in descending order, with (1) referring to the most frequently mentioned voting criterion.

difference in their respective emphasis. Both pre-election questions, ideal and actual, record a spread of about 20%; the post-election study is close to 10%. This suggests that the emphases on the four most important voting criteria are closer and more evenly stressed by respondents after the elections.

From these findings, we can better conceptualize how respondents select candidates. By calculating the variations in respondents' overall percentage mentions of voting criteria, our analysis can reflect the general change in emphasis under different situations between ideal and actual choice, and between pre-election and post-election studies.

Mismatch of Voting Criteria Employed by Respondents in Choosing Two Candidates

We observed great differences in the pattern of voting criteria used for choosing two candidates even during the same interview. This suggests that many respondents made their decisions on criteria which were specific to the candidate. This does not necessarily mean that respondents do not have a clear, consistent and general set of voting criteria for selecting candidates. However, it may suggest that respondents do not demand the same level of satisfaction for choosing two candidates, rather than one. That is to say, a respondent may find a suitable candidate among the contestants and vote for that candidate as the best available choice. However, because the constituency is double-seat, one more candidate can be selected at no additional cost or effort. In that case, the voter may choose the second candidate by relaxing the most important criteria used for selecting the first candidate. The fact that respondents employed two voting criteria on average in evaluating candidates may further lower the level of match in voting criteria. This is because the two criteria employed may differ in importance to respondents. The less important voting criterion may be easier to shift as compared with the more important one, thus lowering the level of match in voting criteria.

Similarly, it may be concluded that the number of candidates restricts the voters' choice. This creates a situation which is recognized by economists where limited resources may limit the achievement of economic satisfaction. To voters, the critical constraint to political satisfaction is not the 'budget' or the number of votes one can cast in an election, but the 'supply of goods' or availability of candidates who can match the standards one is setting. This constraint can be attributed to two factors. The first is the system of elections by constituencies which restricts voters' choice to candidates running within geographically determined areas rather than from the whole pool of candidates running on a single list. The second factor is that the pool of political talents may be limited.[20] Under such circumstances, even if candidates were running on a single list, the electorate might still find it difficult to make an ideal choice.

Irrespective of these constraints, the vote is 'free of charge' and every elector can cast two votes. Therefore, voters tend to exercise their right to choose a second candidate, although they may use different voting criteria in the selection process. This emphasizes the importance of the electoral arrangements in affecting voting behaviour.[21]

Emphasis on Four Major Criteria in Voting

The emergence of four major criteria employed in selecting candidates in the 1991 Legislative Council elections is of importance and the implications behind this should be explored.

'Past performance or experience' is a performance-related criterion which stresses a retrospective approach to evaluation. Respondents using this criterion rely on the candidate's past contribution as a means of measuring what is likely to be achieved in the future. As a result, incumbents may be in a better position than new candidates to appeal to voters on the basis of their public service records and experience. Whether this will favour the 'experienced candidate' depends, however, on the actual contribution the candidate has made in the eyes of voters. A candidate with a long and respectable record of past performance and experience is likely to be a vote-winner, but the determination of whether that record is in fact respectable rests with the voter.

'Willingness to serve the public' is an elusive criterion. It suggests that respondents place emphasis on an affective evaluation of a candidate. A Legislative Councillor has a duty to make public decisions which affect the general population and it is logical that a candidate should be willing to serve the public in order to fulfil this role. Thus, the possession of this quality should be considered a logical necessity rather than a criterion for candidate selection. The emphasis on this criterion, therefore, may suggest that our respondents have a certain mistrust of the candidates. Previous research has indeed indicated that Hong Kong citizens do have little trust in political leaders.[22] Why this is so relates to factors beyond the scope of this chapter but we may note that the context in which the 1991 elections were held might well lead voters to be cautious. Even though discussions of politics have become more common over the past decade, especially since the suppression of the 1989 pro-democracy movement in China and developments towards a more representative government, this does not always appear to have worked to the advantage of candidates running in elections. A candidate's good service record is a considerable asset under such circumstances.

'Policy stance or platform' is considered to be a more specific criterion which takes into account the promises made by the candidate in his platform and his stance on various issues. It is performance-oriented and looks towards future achievement. This is also considered to be a more 'rational' choice in the Downsian sense,[23] especially in an uncertain political environment, since it gives the electorate a clearer idea of the desired results of their choice. A vote choice made in this way is predicated on two pre-conditions. First, there must exist a clear and specific platform provided by the candidate. Secondly, the respondent must trust that the candidate will take the platform seriously should he be elected. Since platforms were not clearly distinguishable in the 1991 elections, we need to consider this criterion more carefully, especially since 'platform' is considered to be one of the three most important voting criteria in previous research. This will be further discussed in the next section.

'Style of work' refers to the manner in which a candidate conducts business. Voters' impressions of a candidate relate to 'the manner in which he performs in order to impress voters'.[24] These impressions are important elements on which an image of a candidate can be built. Social psychologists suggest that voters may use various candidate attributes to form 'image traits' and 'image types' to simplify the process of candidate selection.[25]

Specifically, the 'style of work' of candidates may include voters' judgements of them as, for instance, outspoken, principled, rational, open-minded, prudent and so on. These attributes are subjective evaluations and represent simplified perceptions of candidates to the point where such attributes come to be regarded as more important than issues. Because of its subjective nature, this criterion often takes time to develop and possibly requires specific incidents to influence the voters' judgement. Some of these judgements are, of course, a product of the way in which candidates seek to project themselves to the voters. Respondents using this criterion may perhaps be considered to be more concerned with the candidate's human qualities. None the less, choosing this criterion may also suggest that the respondent does not have a good knowledge of the candidates' platform or service record and hence can only rely on general impressions as the basis for voting.

To make the findings more comprehensive, we can aggregate the voting criteria. The four major voting criteria can be classified as belonging to an 'affective' dimension and a 'performance' dimension.[26] The 'affective' dimension includes 'willingness to serve the public' and 'style of work', which require the voters to make more subjective judgements on the candidates. The 'performance' dimension includes 'past performance or experience' and 'policy stance or platform', which are more concrete in nature and reflect voters' concerns about the candidates' actual performance. If we collapse the other criteria in Table 5.2 into two other dimensions, 'candidates' particulars' and 'supported by others', the predominance of the 'affective' and 'performance' criteria is more evident (Table 5.5).

Overall, our respondents can be considered to be more rigorous in their usage and manipulation of voting criteria than has usually been assumed. They will rely on a sophisticated evaluation of the candidate, which cannot be obtained sufficiently simply by knowing the candidate's personal particulars. The candidate's 'style of work' is particularly relevant in forming and simplifying the image of a candidate. In addition, voters are pragmatic and place great stress on the performance of candidates. As a result, the support and choices of other groups and opinion-formers become relatively unimportant for voters, a finding which is at variance with the traditional wisdom of many campaign planners. Our research suggests a more independent and thoughtful voter than has been recorded in previous studies.

Table 5.5 Percentage mentions of the three most important voting
criteria under reclassified categories

Voting criteria	Ideal (pre-election) (%)	Actual (pre-election) (%)	Actual (post-election) (%)
Candidates' particulars[a]	30.0	30.4	29.4
Affective criteria[b]	74.2	73.2	61.5
Performance criteria[c]	75.6	60.9	56.7
Supported by others[d]	9.9	7.5	11.5
Others	16.9	22.1	23.7
Total	206.5%	194.0%	182.9%
(N)	(414)	(470)	(608)

[a] Includes age, occupation, sex, residence in the district, membership of a political group and of a social or community group.
[b] Includes charisma, appearance, social status, prestige, style of work, willingness to serve the public and acquaintance with the candidate.
[c] Comprises platform, policy stance, experience and past performance.
[d] Consists of support from political, social or community groups, renowned individuals and being influenced by the vote choice of family members, friends or neighbours.

Differences With the Findings of Previous Research

The findings of the Kowloon Central constituency survey display some differences compared with previous research which identified platform, past performance or experience, and educational attainment of the candidate as the three most emphasized criteria mentioned by respondents.[27] While the first two are still important, 'educational attainment' was emphasized in only about 5% of the total votes in selecting a particular candidate in both the pre-election and post-election surveys (see Table 5.2).

The educational backgrounds of the seven candidates in Kowloon Central appeared to offer acceptable differences which could enable voters to choose from amongst the candidates.[28] This qualified 'educational attainment' as a possible and usable criterion which might be employed by our respondents. But the fact that it was rarely mentioned in choosing a particular candidate requires an explanation.

A probable reason is that previous research findings revealed an ideal voting criterion which was reflected in the way the questions were worded. This is supported by the fact that the ideal voting criterion of 'educational attainment' in our research also had a high percentage mention of 15.2%, but suffered a sizable drop of 10.1% and 9.8% in comparison with the actual criteria used for selecting particular candidates in pre-election and post-election surveys respectively (Table 5.2). If this explanation is sound, there is a need to improve the validity of measuring voting criteria by considering carefully the way in which questions are worded.

In addition, given the more important responsibilities of Legislative Councillors compared with those elected to the lower tiers of government, 'good education' alone may not be a sure guarantee of 'good performance'. Therefore, the percentage mentions of the 'educational attainment' for particular candidates, both in pre-election and post-election surveys, are well below the percentage mentions of the four major criteria identified (Table 5.2). This is related to the following point.

The identification of 'style of work' as a major criterion is another difference with previous research. This criterion seldom surfaced in past investigations. It may be that, in past research, this was rarely regarded as an important item. As a result, previous research questionnaires seldom included this criterion as a possible answer. However, it may also reflect contextual changes in which the research is conducted. This may be explained by the differences with previous elections in the roles of the respective councillors.

The Legislative Council has a higher level of representation and is endowed with greater authority to make public decisions affecting more citizens than the District Board and Urban and Regional Councils. In contrast, the authority of the District Board is mainly advisory and is meant only to cope with problems that arise within the delimited district. The Urban and Regional Councils are concerned with the provision of various public facilities and services.[29] Although the Councils discuss various government policies in relation to such public facilities and services, they are normally not expected to arouse much political controversy. Hence, in District Board and Urban and Regional

Council elections, voters may plausibly expect the candidates to be capable persons who are able to accomplish various well-defined tasks once they are elected. But for a Legislative Councillor, this alone is not adequate. In essence, a Legislative Councillor is more 'political' and is required to deal with various issues which might not be defined at the time of the elections. It is not only a question of knowing if the task can be done, but also by what means it is to be accomplished. Voters do not know, and neither can candidates tell, every issue and task an elected Legislative Councillor will be required to undertake. What voters can consider at the moment of elections is how a candidate will perform and how he or she will deal with various social and political issues and conflicts. This consideration probably can be simplified by voters into certain specific requirements on the 'style of work' of candidates. This may make a greater difference to the results and to the satisfaction of the voters than formal educational attainments.

In previous research, 'platform' was considered to be a very important factor affecting a voter's choice. This is also reflected in our survey findings. However, we have some reservations about the substantive difference in the content of candidate platforms, as well as the actual attention given by voters to this aspect of choice. We checked our concern indirectly by asking respondents for their perceptions of the most preferred candidate: 'How much do you understand his general platform?' The result is a contradiction, given the emphasis on 'policy stance or platform' as an important criterion. Many respondents did not understand the candidate's platform very well. Only 19.4% said they understood or understood very well the platform. Another 29% claimed they had some understanding of the platform. Over half (51%) said that they could not understand the platform very well or simply did not understand it at all. Given this inconsistency, the cognitive position of respondents on the use of platform in evaluating candidates is rather interesting. We are not, however, in a position to say that this represents ignorance on the part of the voters. Many platforms were poorly or very briefly stated and were sometimes indistinguishable from those of other candidates. None the less, the relationship between platform and choice of candidates could provide a fruitful focus for further research.

The Match in Patterns of Voting Criteria Between the Pre-election and Post-election Surveys

On the level of the individual respondent, there were considerable changes of voting criteria employed for selecting a particular candidate in the pre-election and post-election surveys (see Chapter 6). However, on the overall level, the patterns of emphasis of voting criteria were found to be very similar before and after the elections. This discrepancy needs to be explained to bridge the gap between these two different levels of analysis. A preliminary concept of 'latent voting criteria' can be suggested.[30] This implies that respondents do have a consistent set of voting criteria in their minds which are probably the four major criteria identified above. However, these criteria are not employed every time a respondent selects candidates. Instead, the way in which these criteria are used in deciding a vote depends specifically on the favourable attributes respondents perceive in individual candidates. Respondents may use one or two of these latent criteria in choosing one candidate, while using the other criteria in selecting another candidate.[31] Even though the voting criteria employed by a respondent may shift, the effect of the shift may be cancelled out by other respondents if we consider the overall percentage mentions. Therefore, it is possible to have overall coherence in the patterns of emphasis of voting criteria before and after the elections while the criteria used by individual respondents may actually be in a state of flux.

The Discrepancy Between Ideal and Actual Responses

The observed discrepancy between the ideal responses, measured in the pre-election survey, and the actual responses, measured in both the pre-election and post-election surveys, suggests that two related, but separate, conceptions of voting criteria are involved. The gap between the ideal and actual voting criteria implies that there are considerable mismatches in certain areas of voting criteria between a utopian, ideal Legislative Councillor and the actual, particular candidate chosen. The difference is readily comprehensible. The use of ideal criteria happens under the most favourable conditions but the practical situation and constraints an elector faces compel him to be more realistic. In fact, voters can perceive the constraints more easily after they have actually cast their votes. This finding signifies that there were mismatches between what the candidates possessed and what the respondents expected, possibly because the choice of candidates was limited and voters were rigorous in assessing the candidates.

In essence, our results suggest that we should be very careful in delineating the different conceptions of voting criteria in future studies of voting behaviour. The assessment of these factors depends very much on the questionnaire design and the exact wording used to obtain the data and this seems to have been overlooked in previous research. This point should be considered and tested continuously to furnish a better means of measurement in future research.[32]

CONCLUSIONS

The study of voting criteria is an important component of voting behaviour studies. It can provide a deeper understanding of the message contained in the act of voting. By analysing the voting criteria, ideal and actual, in our panel group, we reached both methodological and substantive conclusions.

Based on the concern that research design and methodological inadequacies may affect the result of surveys, this study points to the need to refine the concept of voting criteria. One means of doing this is to introduce the concept of latent voting criteria. On the difference in measuring ideal and actual responses, tests should be conducted to establish the validity and reliability of the measurement. Although possible explanations are put forward to account for these findings, they should at present be considered simply as hypotheses, subject to further confirmation and refinement.

Substantively, we observe that the voting criteria used in selecting candidates are specific to the particular candidate chosen. This reflects the influence of the electoral arrangements on voting behaviour and the effect of contextual factors in the election environment. In addition, there are several respects in which findings differ from previous research. The overall emphasis is on certain affective-related and performance-related criteria, which may help to interpret the act of voting. These suggest that the Hong Kong voter is relatively more independent and thoughtful than had previously been realized.

NOTES

1. S. Verba and N.H. Nie, *Participation in America: Political Democracy and Social Equality* (Chicago: University of Chicago Press, 1972), pp.102-121.

2. D. Easton, *A Framework for Political Analysis* (Englewood Cliffs, New Jersey: Prentice-Hall, 1965).

3. H.B. Asher, 'Voting Behaviour Research in the 1980s: An Examination of Some Old and New Problem Areas', in A.W. Finifter, ed., *Political Science: The State of the Discipline* (Washington: American Political Science Association, 1983), p.339.

4. Ibid., pp.341-365.

5. See H.A. Simon, 'Human Nature in Politics: The Dialogue of Psychology with Political Science', *American Political Science Review,* 79, 2(1985): 293-304.

6. For a discussion of the different types of seemingly 'irrational behaviour' in political life, see G. Wallas, *Human Nature in Politics* (London: Constable, 1948), pp.45-80.

7. For example, one prominent model is the Downsian rational voter. See A. Downs, *An Economic Theory of Democracy* (New York: Harper and Row, 1957).

8. A brief survey of previous research in this area includes:

    (a) YWCA Choi Wan Social Service Centre *et al.,* 'A Survey Report on the Voting Behaviour of the 1985 District Board Electorate', 1985. (Original in Chinese)

    (b) Hong Kong Federation of Youth Groups, Cho Yiu Youth Centre *et al.,* 'A Survey Report on the Attitudes of Voters in South Kwai Chung', 1985. (Original in Chinese)

    (c) Hong Kong Federation of Youth Groups, Cho Yiu Youth Centre *et al.,* 'A Report on the Attitudes of the Electorate in Regional Council Elections', 1986. (Original in Chinese)

    (d) Chai Wan Caritas, 'Research on the Voting Behaviour of the Electorate in the 1988 North Chai Wan District Board Elections',1988. (Original in Chinese)

    (e) Meeting Point, Committee on Politics and Law, 'A Survey Report on the Voting Behaviour of the Electorate in the 1985 District Board Elections', 1985. (Original in Chinese)

    (f) C.K. Law, 'A Research Report on the Factors which Influence Electoral Results in the 1985 District Board Elections', The University of Hong Kong, Department of Social Work, 1985. (Original in Chinese)

    (g) W.T. Chui, 'An Exploratory Study on the Voting Behaviour of Hong Kong Citizens in the District Board Elections 1988', City Polytechnic of Hong Kong, Department of Social Administration, 1988 (mimeo).

(h) W.T. Chui, 'A Study of Voting Behaviour of Hong Kong Citizens in the 1989 Urban Council and Regional Council Elections', City Polytechnic of Hong Kong, Department of Applied Social Studies, 1989 (mimeo).

9. For a succinct summary of another five District Board elections studies in 1985, see Law, 'Research Report', p.28.

10. The context of the elections, which includes electoral arrangements, has a significant impact on the voting criteria employed and voter turnout. See T.R. Rochon, 'Electoral Systems and the Basis of the Vote: The Case of Japan', in J.C. Campbell, ed., *Parties, Candidates, and Voters in Japan: Six Quantitative Studies* (Ann Arbor, Michigan: University of Michigan Press, 1981); M.M. Conway, 'The Political Context of Political Behaviour', *Journal of Politics,* 51,1(1989): 3-10; and G.B. Powell, 'American Voter Turnout in Comparative Perspective', *American Political Science Review,* 80, 1(1986): 17-43.

11. The Legislative Council, Urban and Regional Councils, and District Boards are the three tiers of representative government in Hong Kong. They are different in levels of representation because of differences in the size of the population they serve, statutory functions and authority.

12. Hong Kong government, *Hong Kong 1991* (Hong Kong: Government Printer, 1991), p.32. See also *Hong Kong 1983*, p.15; *Hong Kong 1986,* pp.21-22; and *Hong Kong 1989*, p.32.

13. In the 1985 and 1988 District Board elections, the number of double-seat constituencies was about twice the number of single-seat constituencies. However, the situation was reversed in the March 1991 elections. *Hong Kong 1991*, p.32. See also *Hong Kong 1982,* pp.243-244; *Hong Kong 1985,* p.59; and *Hong Kong 1988,* pp.25-26. The ratios of double-seat to single-seat constituencies were 0.09 in 1982, 1.74 in 1985, 2.14 in 1988 and 0.44 in 1991.

14. The candidate-seat ratios for contested constituencies in the Urban and Regional Council elections were: 3.2 in 1983 (*Hong Kong Standard,* 12 February 1983), 3.1 in 1986 (*SCMP,* 1 February 1986), 2.3 in 1989 (*SCMP,* 11 March 1989) and 2.5 in 1991(*Hong Kong Standard,* 26 March 1991). The figure for 1983 refers only to the Urban Council since the first Regional Council elections were held in 1986. The data for District Board elections were calculated from N.J. Miners, *The Government and Politics of Hong Kong* (Hong Kong: Oxford University Press, 1991), 5th ed., p.173. The candidate/seat ratios for contested constituencies were 3.1 in 1982, 2.2 in 1985, 2.0 in 1988 and 2.0 in 1991.

15. For an analysis of the characteristics and the level of involvement of 'parties' and other organizations in the 1991 District Board elections, see K.S. Louie, 'Political Parties', in Y.W. Sung and M.K. Lee, eds., *The Other Hong Kong Report 1991* (Hong Kong: The Chinese University Press, 1991), pp.62-71.

16. I. Scott, 'Policy-making in a Turbulent Environment: The Case of Hong Kong', *International Review of Administrative Science,* 52, 4(1986): 447-470.

17. The analysis included only those voting criteria which could be categorized (that is, excluding 'others') and were ranked clearly by respondents. Almost all respondents could rank their voting criteria without problems.

18. Rochon, 'Electoral Systems', p.3. Rochon aggregates the single most important reason for the vote in order to assess the relative importance of the influence of party, candidate and issue on vote choice.

19. Respondents on average offered 1.94 criteria for choosing a particular candidate in the pre-election study and 1.83 criteria in the post-election study.

20. S.K. Lau, *Decolonization Without Independence and the Poverty of Political Leaders in Hong Kong* (The Chinese University of Hong Kong, Institute of Asia-Pacific Studies, 1990), pp.33-39.

21. See note 10.

22. S.K. Lau, H.C. Kuan, and P.S. Wan, 'Political Attitudes', in S.K. Lau, ed., *Indicators of Social Development: Hong Kong 1988* (The Chinese University of Hong Kong, Institute of Asia-Pacific Studies, 1991), pp.200-202.

23. Downs, *An Economic Theory,* Chapter 11.

24. D. Nimmo and R.L. Savage, *Candidates and Their Images: Concepts, Methods, and Findings* (Pacific Palisades, California: Goodyear, 1976), p.46.

25. Ibid., pp.45-48.

26. This differentiation is in line with some suggestions that the image of a candidate consists of political and stylistic role expectation components, ibid., p.46. It can be considered that they are performance-oriented and affective-oriented respectively.

27. See notes 8 and 9.

28. The educational attainments of the seven candidates were:

    John Young: Ph.D.

    Conrad Lam Kui-shing: university graduate (medical doctor)

    Peter Chan Chi-kwan: university graduate

    Cecilia Yeung Lai-yin: secondary school graduate

    Cheung Chung-ming: secondary school graduate

    Lau Chin-shek: secondary school graduate

    Chan Yuen-han: had not finished secondary school

    See *Ming Pao,* 3,4 and 5 September 1991.

29. Miners, *The Government and Politics of Hong Kong,* pp.158-160, 171-177.

30. The writer is indebted to Dr Law Chi-kwong, Department of Social Work and Social Administration, The University of Hong Kong, for introducing

the idea of a set of latent voting criteria in voters. The test of this concept may be attempted by using the method of 'latent class analysis' which is designed to explore the structure of a latent variable through its influence on a set of observed variables. See A.L. McCutcheon, *Latent Class Analysis* (Newbury Park, California: Sage, 1987).

31. See note 19.

32. J.M. Converse and S. Presser, *Survey Questions: Handcrafting the Standardized Questionnaire* (Newbury Park, California: Sage, 1986), pp.41-47.

6

Voter Consistency: Turnout, Choice and Criteria

Elaine Chan and Fred Yeung

It is common practice in the study of voting behaviour to examine party identification, the characteristics of the candidates and the importance of issue voting. These three factors have been found to structure voters' preferences in such a way that their choice cannot easily be swayed. If such a set of structured considerations for candidate selection does exist, the voter who is influenced by these factors will, in principle, be more consistent in his or her choice of candidate than the one who is not affected by these influences. Since Hong Kong has neither a long electoral history nor a tradition of political parties, whether or not preferences were structured in this way in the Legislative Council elections raises important questions. This chapter is an attempt to address one aspect of this topic through the concept of 'voter consistency'.

'Voter consistency' refers to the correspondence between stated intentions before the elections and reported behaviour after the elections. We will consider three dimensions of consistency: the electorate's intention to vote, their criteria for making vote choices and their intended choice of candidates before and after the elections. The focus of our analysis is to compare data collected in two independent samples of the registered electorate in Kowloon Central. One sample, the panel group, was interviewed twice, once before and once after election day. The other sample is made up of respondents who were interviewed only after election day.

In addition to the substantive concern of whether a set of selection criteria exists, studying voter consistency can influence future voting behaviour research. The Legislative Council direct elections precipitated a series of opinion polls, most of which were one-shot cross-sectional studies conducted prior to polling day. The utility of pre-election polls is based on the assumption that intention corresponds closely with actual behaviour. If the majority of the respondents who indicated that they would vote did not in fact do so, these studies would lose their value. Whether this assumption is valid in Hong Kong has not been tested but studies in other countries have shown that intention and behaviour do not always concur. The reasons why people do not do what they said they would do are varied: they may want to 'look good' to interviewers; they may simply forget what they said before; or other more immediate considerations, such as bad weather, may prevent them from carrying out their stated intentions. Whatever the reasons, it is important to assess the extent to which respondents' intentions match their behaviour.

The substantial gap between the rate of voting intention reported by various polls and the actual turnout rate in the Legislative Council elections indicates that our concern is legitimate. When voters were asked in July whether or not they intended to vote in the elections, 56.7% gave an affirmative answer. [1] In a poll conducted between 5 and 7 September by the Hong Kong Institute of Asia-Pacific Studies of the Chinese University of Hong Kong, 77% of the respondents said that they would vote. [2] In another poll conducted between 11 and 13 September by the Social Sciences Research Centre of The University of Hong Kong, the corresponding figure was 72.5%. [3] These figures are all much higher than the actual voter turnout of 39.15%. The sizeable gap between voting intention and actual turnout calls for an explanation.

The aim of this chapter is not to find out the set of criteria for candidate selection but rather to ascertain the consistency of our electorate. The objective is twofold: first, to make suggestions for future electoral behaviour research and, secondly, to indicate the extent to which the preferences of the voters are structured.

DIMENSIONS OF ELECTORAL CONSISTENCY

To find out the degree of consistency between data obtained from pre-election polls and actual behaviour, we have concentrated on three dimensions: voter turnout, vote choice and criteria for selecting candidates. Our panel group consisted of 570 respondents, with whom we successfully conducted both a pre-election and a post-election interview. In addition, we also used data from a second sample of respondents who had not been interviewed during the pre-election survey. This second group contained 141 successful responses.

In the following analysis of voters' consistency in vote choice and voting criteria, only those who indicated their intentions to vote (63%) in the elections were included. The group who decided not to vote (20%) and those who were not sure whether they would vote (17%) were excluded from the analysis. The 'undecided' respondents were excluded because their pattern of voting behaviour might be different from those who had decided to vote and because they might be more vulnerable to influences in a period of intensive campaigning. We are aware that the exclusion of the 'undecided' electorate will boost the level of consistency in our analysis. However, a change of mind among the already 'decided' electorate, whom we thought would have been less vulnerable to situational influences, would be a more forceful indicator of the fluidity of stated intentions. In other words, a high level of voter inconsistency would refute the view that voters' preferences are structured.

Consistency in Voter Turnout

When respondents said that they would cast their votes on polling day, did they in fact do so? Table 6.1 shows that, among those who claimed that they had already made up their minds whether they would vote at the time of the interview, there was a very high degree of consistency between intention to vote and actual turnout. In principle, it is quite reliable to predict voter turnout on the basis of committed respondents' intentions. Among the undecided potential voters, however, the turnout rate was about half (46.4%), and it was consequently more difficult to predict their turnout rates.

Table 6.1 Consistency of voting intentions and turnout

Actual turnout	Intend to vote (%)	Do not intend to vote (%)
Voted	88.6	21.1
Did not vote	11.4	78.9
Total	100.0%	100.0%
(N)	(359)	(114)

Note: The figures presented here exclude the group of respondents who had not decided whether or not to vote in the pre-election survey. This group constituted 17% of our sample.

Chi-square = 197.02, significant at 0.01 level.

If respondents' stated voting intentions correspond closely with their actual behaviour, then voting intentions should reflect the actual turnout in the Kowloon Central constituency. However, this is not the case. The rates of voting intention and actual voter turnout were quite different. As Table 6.2 shows, the voting intention of the panel group was 63.0%, which was higher than the actual turnout rates in Hong Kong as a whole (39.15%), and in Kowloon Central (38.29%). As the results show, the discrepancy between intention and actual voting was in fact quite substantial. Thus, although our respondents did cast their ballots, as they said they would, making voter turnout predictions on the basis of voting intentions overestimates the actual turnout rate.

Table 6.2 Voting intentions and actual turnout rates

	Panel group		Post-election survey only (%)	Turnout in Kowloon Central (%)	Turnout in Hong Kong as a whole (%)
	Intend to vote (%)	Actual turnout (%)			
	63.0	67.9	55.3	38.29	39.15
(N)	(570)	(570)	(141)	(287,373)	(1,916,925)

It has been argued that the official turnout rate does not reflect the actual turnout rate because the electoral roll contains inaccurate and invalid names and addresses (see Chapter 9). If these names and addresses are taken into consideration, the estimated actual turnout rate would have been an average of 48.04% for the whole territory and 47.0% for Kowloon Central.[4] However, even when the adjusted figures are used for comparison with the actual turnout of our panel group, the latter (67.9%) was still significantly higher than the estimated turnout rate (47.0%) of the constituency. The discrepancies between various figures in Table 6.2 will be discussed later in the chapter.

In sum, among those who told us that they were going to vote, most did actually cast their ballots. However, there is a considerable gap between intention to vote and the actual turnout rate in the Kowloon Central constituency. Making voter turnout predictions on the basis of intention therefore risks producing an overestimation of actual behaviour.

Consistency in Vote Choice

If the data on the voter turnout of the panel group reflect a high degree of consistency between intention and behaviour, the results of their consistency in vote choices seem to be equally impressive. This may be illustrated by looking at how 'consistent' a voter is (voter consistency) or, alternatively, by looking at how consistently a vote is given (vote consistency). We look at both measures of consistency because voters had a choice of voting for one or two candidates. It is therefore possible that they might change their minds on one or both of their intended vote choices when they actually cast their vote.

The first measure, 'voter consistency', takes the individual respondent as the base and is made up of three categories. 'All matched' means the respondent did vote for the candidate(s) selected in the pre-election interview. 'All mismatched' refers to a situation where the intended vote, regardless of whether one or two names were given, does not match actual choice. 'Partially matched' occurs when only one intended vote is consistent with the actual vote choice while the other is not. The second measure, 'vote consistency', assesses whether the intended vote for a particular candidate did eventually go to that candidate. Since the basis of comparison is the vote, it is either 'matched' or 'mismatched'; the category 'partially matched' does not apply to this 'vote consistency' dimension.

In addition, since our respondents could choose one or two candidates, there could be four types of consistency or inconsistency based on vote intention and actual vote. We have broken down our respondents on the basis of these four combinations. Type I respondents refer to those who intended to choose one candidate and did indeed vote for one candidate. Type II refers to the group who intended to choose one candidate but voted for two. Type III refers to the group who intended to choose two candidates but in the end only voted for one. Type IV are those who intended to vote for two candidates and did actually vote for two candidates. Since Types I and II respondents intended to cast only one vote, by definition they are either 'all matched' or 'all mismatched'. Similarly, since Type III respondents intended to cast two votes but actually only cast one, they cannot, by default, be included in the 'all matched' category.

The results of respondent consistency are presented in Table 6.3. This contains the data of the respondents who indicated their intentions to vote and had decided on their choice of candidate. In total, about three-quarters of our respondents were fully consistent in their vote choices. The intended vote(s) of about 8% of respondents were entirely different from their choices in the pre-election interview. The remaining 18. 3% changed their minds on one candidate: they either voted for another candidate or did not cast a second vote.

In terms of vote consistency, we find that 83.0% of the 405 intended vote choices 'matched' with post-election data, while the remaining 17.0% were 'mismatched' (Table 6.4). The two figures suggest that using the preference of respondents in pre-election interviews to predict how many votes a candidate would get, even within a week of election day, may not be as accurate as one might think. It is interesting to note that 17.3% (N=70) of the total votes are in the Type II and III categories. This figure indicates a degree of fluidity in vote choice since a considerable number of our respondents changed their minds from choosing one candidate to two and vice versa.

Table 6.3 Consistency of pre-election and post-election vote choices by respondents

	Type I (%)	Type II (%)	Type III (%)	Type IV (%)	Total (%)
All matched	76.0	86.0	—	74.2	73.6
Partially matched	—	—	100	21.9	18.3
All mismatched	24.0	14.0	0	3.9	7.9
Percentage of total (N)	10.4% (25)	20.8% (50)	4.2% (10)	64.6% (155)	100% (240)

Note
Type I   : 1 intended vote and 1 actual vote
Type II : 1 intended vote and 2 actual votes
Type III : 2 intended votes and 1 actual vote
Type IV : 2 intended votes and 2 actual votes

The analysis includes only respondents who indicated an intention to vote in the pre-election survey.

Table 6.4 Consistency of pre-election and post-election vote choices by vote

	Type I (%)	Type II (%)	Type III (%)	Type IV (%)	Total (%)
Matched	76.0	86.0	50	85.2	83.0
Mismatched	24.0	14.0	50	14.8	17.0
Percentage of total (N)	6.2% (25)	12.4% (50)	4.9% (20)	76.5% (310)	100% (405)

Note
Type I   : 1 intended vote and 1 actual vote
Type II : 1 intended vote and 2 actual votes
Type III : 2 intended votes and 1 actual vote
Type IV : 2 intended votes and 2 actual votes

The analysis includes only respondents who indicated an intention to vote in the pre-election survey.

Consistency in Candidate Selection Criteria

The third and final dimension of consistency we will look at is concerned with respondents' purported criteria for vote choice before and after the elections. Since our findings show that there are some changes in vote choice, the following comparisons will focus on matching the set of criteria cited for choosing a particular candidate.[5] For example, we will only compare the criteria mentioned for a respondent who had intended to choose and had actually voted for candidate A.

Two measures were employed to find out whether our respondents had used the same set of criteria to evaluate a particular candidate over time. The first compared the most important criterion our respondents told us they had used in making their choice for a particular candidate. The second measure was based on the three most important criteria they had used in their selection of a particular candidate. The set of criteria was then compared with the corresponding set of criteria obtained in the post-election study. The relative rankings of the items in the two sets of criteria were ignored.

The first measure shows that the most important criterion in candidate selection was, in most cases, not the same in the pre- and post-election interviews. When we compare the most important criterion used in making a vote choice, there is a low level of consistency. Only 24.8% of our 159 respondents cited the same criterion for their choice of the same candidate, while 75.2% cited different criteria.

The low degree of consistency might reflect a situation in which two or three criteria are consistently used but are not always consistently ranked in the same way. Thus, it is entirely possible for a respondent to cite 'past experience' as the most important criterion and 'platform' as the second most important criterion for selecting candidate A in the pre-election interview while giving the same two reasons but in reverse order of importance in the post-election interview. In fact, if our respondents were not strongly committed to a particular criterion, this situation could be quite common. Taking this possibility into consideration, we employed the second measure which relaxes the ranking requirement and combines the three most important criteria cited for choosing a particular candidate. This combined set of criteria was then matched with the corresponding data obtained in the post-election interviews. The results are presented in Table 6.5.

The value in Table 6.5 can be interpreted as a scale, ranging from zero indicating a total mismatch, to one, signifying total match. It shows that, although none of our respondents used an entirely different set of criteria in selecting a candidate, only about one-fifth of them used the same criteria. We know, however, that on average at least 65% of our respondents cited two of the same criteria out of the three mentioned for choosing a particular candidate in their pre-election and post-election answers. Thus, our respondents were not entirely random in their evaluation standards. However, it is likely that the order of importance of these standards changed between the pre-election and post-election interviews.

Table 6.5 Consistency in the three most important candidate selection criteria in the pre-election and post-election surveys

Proportion of matched criteria (%)	Corresponding percentage (%)
0	0
33	3.8
40	10.6
50	20.6
67	33.8
80	10.6
100	20.6
(N)	(160)

Note: '0%' corresponds to the situation where the vote criteria are totally mismatched, while '100%' refers to the condition where all vote criteria mentioned are matched. The analysis includes only respondents who indicated an intention to vote in the pre-election survey.

IMPLICATIONS AND EXPLANATIONS OF THE CONSISTENT ELECTORATE

Consistency in Voter Turnout

Our results on voter turnout demonstrated, first, that there was a high degree of agreement between respondents' voting intentions and their actual turnout and, secondly, that there was a large gap between the voting intentions of our panel group and the actual turnout of the Kowloon Central constituency. To recapitulate, 63.0% of our respondents intended to vote; their actual turnout was 67.9% compared with an estimated 47% for the Kowloon Central constituency.

The discrepancy between voting intentions and estimated turnout for the Kowloon Central constituency was 16%. This substantial gap warns against turnout predictions made solely on the basis of voting intentions. Some kind of adjustment should certainly be made. One researcher made this adjustment on the basis of respondents' past voting records and predicted a turnout of 61% from a 69% voting intention rate for the whole of Hong Kong. [6] This adjusted figure, as we have seen, is still much higher than the estimated turnout rate (48.04%). As will be discussed later, this discrepancy can in part be explained by a response bias in our respondents.

As far as actual voter turnout rates are concerned, there is a gap of 20.9% between our respondents' turnout (67.9%) and the estimated turnout in our constituency (47.0%). Such a substantial gap calls for explanation. It has been suggested that the higher turnout rate of the interviewed group compared to the actual voter turnout is a result of interview effect. Interview effect refers to changes in respondents' behaviour and perceptions due to interviewer-respondent interaction. The interview 'stimulated' the respondent's interest in the elections, heightened the saliency of politics and 'awakened his citizen conscience'.[7] All these factors contributed positively to the likelihood of the respondent casting a vote on election day. Generally speaking, there is agreement on the existence of the interview effect or, more precisely, turnout enhancement effect. The disagreement centres on the process by which turnout enhancement effect occurs and how persistent the effect is. While some suggest that it is short-term and confined to the immediate election,[8] others hold that the effect is long-lasting. [9]

The results from our panel group point to the possibility of a turnout enhancement effect. Our second group of respondents were not subject to the pre-election interview. They are, so to speak, our control group. If a turnout enhancement effect was at work, the turnout rate of the control group should be lower than the panel group and should reflect the turnout of the constituency. As shown in Table 6.1, the turnout of the control group was 55. 3%, 12.6% lower than the turnout of the panel group but 8.3% higher than that of the estimated turnout, which was 47.0%. The 12.6% difference is, we would suggest, partly due to the turnout enhancement effect. The 8.3% difference between the turnout of the control group and the estimated turnout may be a result of a response bias. The bias reflects a selection process in which those who agreed to be interviewed were more interested in politics. Consequently, the likelihood of this group casting their votes was higher than the group who refused to be interviewed.

In view of these factors, it seems that both the voting enhancement effect and the response bias may lead to an overestimation of voter turnout on the basis of vote intention. Adjustment made on the basis of past voting records is, therefore, desirable. In fact, we were able to establish that respondents with voting experience were more likely to go to vote. Some 81.1% of voters alleged that they had voted before but only 44.3% of non-voters said that they had previously done so.

What is worth noting, in addition to past voting records, is the extent of the undecided electorate. As shown in various surveys, the percentage of undecided respondents was quite high. A telephone survey conducted between 5 and 7 September found that 17.5% of those interviewed were not sure whether they would vote[10] while another survey between 11 and 13 September revealed an even higher 20.4%.[11] Our own face-to-face interviews indicated a 17.0% undecided response. Most of the turnout predictions in this election were made without entering this group into their calculations. Since our results indicate that about half of this group did turn out to vote, entering them into the turnout prediction formula, with appropriate adjustment, should improve the accuracy of the prediction. [12]

Consistency in Vote Choice and Criteria for Candidate Selection

As far as vote choice is concerned, we found that, although the majority of our respondents voted for the candidates they told us they would vote for in the pre-election study, there was still some room for manoeuvring. Even among those who were able to tell us for whom they would vote, one-quarter changed their minds in one way or another. If we look at the vote, 17% of all votes were 'mismatched' in the pre- and post-election interviews. We do not want to play down the high degree of consistency in our respondents' vote choices. However, changes in vote choice still took place up to election day. Our data show that 49.6% of all votes were decided within one week of the elections; some 20.9% indicated that they only decided on election day. If seven-tenths of all votes were decided within a week of election day, we can conclude that the possibility of change is quite high, especially in a relatively close campaign. Unless a candidate is leading the second placed candidate by a clear margin, one should be cautious in making predictions.

If there are prospects for changing vote choice right up to election day, it may be a good idea to ask respondents in future to rate various candidates. This might help to overcome the problem found in conventional methods which solicit the names of the candidates for whom the respondents intend to vote. Making predictions based on rating is an indirect method, which should normally be avoided, but it has some advantages over the conventional one. [13] The most obvious advantage is that rating provides information on how much more one candidate is favoured over the other candidates. This additional information indicates how substantial a lead the most favoured candidate has and is particularly useful in a close race. Rating also seems to be relevant in a double-seat constituency context. Predicting a pair of winning candidates is much more difficult than predicting the winning candidate in a single-seat constituency system. A double-seat constituency system thus makes the knowledge of how well a candidate fares over the other candidates much more important in the prediction of which two candidates will get elected.

If consistency in vote choice is in general quite high, then consistency in voting criteria is less so. When we asked our respondents to tell us the most important criterion they had used when choosing a particular candidate, only one-quarter of them reported using the same criterion in the post-election interview. Our respondents therefore seemed to be wavering between different criteria in candidate selection. However, although the most important criterion changed frequently, the consistency in a set of criteria mentioned for choosing a particular candidate was much higher. Close to two-thirds of our candidates mentioned the same two criteria out of the three in their choice of a particular candidate in the pre- and post-election interviews.

The low degree of consistency in the most important vote choice criterion indicates that our electorate could have been led by a candidate's campaign to emphasize a particular criterion while using a second criterion to judge another candidate. The effect a campaign has on the electorate partially explains the fluidity of voting criteria. This effect is often described as a process of building a relationship between campaign message and candidate image. [14] Since situational factors affect the reasons why the voter chooses one candidate over others, we believe it is more effective to tap the set of criteria used rather than the most important criterion. The degree of consistency in the set of criteria used to select a candidate is much higher than that of the most important voting criterion used.

The Consistent Electorate in a Period of Political Transition

On the whole, our survey of respondents in Kowloon Central suggests that the electorate is consistent on all three dimensions: turnout, [15] vote choice and candidate selection criteria. Of all the measures, only the most important criterion in candidate selection revealed a high degree of fluidity.

In the light of the context in which the elections took place, this constituency is a little surprising. Until recently, the government has discouraged political participation. The process of building a representative government has frequently been stalled. Civic education has received attention only in the last few years. Respect for human rights and a faster pace of democratization gained wider societal support only in the wake of the 1989 pro-democracy movement in Beijing. All these institutional, historical and circumstantial factors have been anything but conducive to the development of political consciousness. Yet, the consistency of the voters suggests that, to some extent, preferences have already been structured. There might be an emerging set of values or criteria which a majority of voters consistently use to evaluate candidates. Albeit a minority, the 'inconsistent' electorate is also an interesting group. In the following paragraphs, we try to establish whether there is any difference between the consistent and the inconsistent electorate and to suggest reasons for the inconsistency.

With regard to the voter turnout dimension, it appears that the consistent electorate did not have a special set of attributes which were distinct from the inconsistent electorate. There was no difference between the two groups in terms of age, sex, level of education, income or housing type. Nor could we separate the two groups by their identification with Hong Kong society. The only significant variable was whether the respondent had voted three or more times previously. The proportion of the consistent electorate who had voted three or more times was 90.1%, compared with 81.3% of their counterparts who had voted less than three times. To be sure, people changed their minds for various reasons. But it is possible that the experience of voting has made voting part of people's lives in such a way that, when they say they will vote, they will normally do so unless some unexpected event takes place.

The low degree of consistency in the single most important voting criterion is not surprising. In established Western democracies, party identification, issue voting and candidate characteristics have always been found to be the three most salient considerations in vote choice.[16] In the context of Hong Kong, the phenomenon of the political party is too new to have a significant impact on a large part of the electorate. In past District Board, Urban Council and Regional Council elections, candidates' party affiliations were virtually irrelevant in winning votes.[17] The same thing can be said about issue voting. Even in the Legislative Council elections, where the issues involved were very different from other elections, issue voting did not occur (see Chapter 4). If party identification and issue voting played a minor role in vote choice, then candidate characteristics and perhaps other short-term and situational factors were at play. Factors such as image-setting, last-minute campaigning and mass media exposure might well affect a voter's decision.

Findings from past District Board and Urban and Regional Council elections have shown that the candidate's personal particulars are important in candidate selection. Hence, aside from emphasizing platforms, personal backgrounds and suitability, candidates also tried to project a favourable image of themselves. It was reported, for example, that UDHK hired an image consultant to advise their candidates.[18] Projecting a good image of oneself was particularly important because of extensive television coverage. A poll conducted in mid-August found that more than 60% of the electorate came to know the candidates running in their constituency through the mass media.[19]

In the absence of a party tradition, reliance on candidates' personal background and the influence of situational factors in candidate selection are to be expected. Thus, it is not surprising that a number of our respondents were not sure if they would vote or for whom they would vote, even within a week of election day. Without putting the figure into proper context, 17.0% of 'vote mismatch' might be high. But taking into consideration the historical background and the political situation in Hong Kong, the percentage is lower than we expected. Although about three-quarters of the most important criterion for candidate selection were mismatched in the pre-election and post-election interviews, the proportion of mismatch in the three most important criteria used was substantially lower. Since this was the first major attempt by political parties to exercise their influence on candidate selection, our respondents were consistent in the sense that, once they had decided, they were not easily swayed.

CONCLUSIONS

To summarize, this chapter suggests, first, that prediction of voter turnout on the basis of voting intention will have to be adjusted downwards to take into account turnout enhancement effect and response bias. We also recommend that the group of undecided voters be taken into consideration in future research. Secondly, there is still a substantial amount of vote fluctuation and too many 'late deciders' to warrant a clear prediction of the winning candidates, unless they lead by a comfortable margin. In addition, predicting which two candidates will win based on the ratings they get is suggested as an alternative to the conventional method. Lastly, the high degree of change in the most important criterion for candidate selection indicates that it may be more reliable to look at a set of criteria instead.

In addition to a high level of agreement between voting intentions and actual turnout, our respondents revealed quite a high degree of consistency in their vote choice and the set of selection criteria. Indeed, these results can be treated as an indication that the preferences of our voters were, to some extent, structured. On what basis those preferences were structured is beyond the domain of this chapter. However, as political parties take shape and establish themselves, we would expect the degree of consistency in vote choice, as well as in selection criteria, to be even higher in the next election.

NOTES

1. See *SCMP,* 17 July 1991. The poll was conducted by the Social Sciences Research Centre, The University of Hong Kong.

2. See *Hong Kong Economic Times,* 10 September 1991.

3. Social Sciences Research Centre, The University of Hong Kong, 'Public Opinion Programme', 11-13 September 1991, sponsored by Asia Television Limited (mimeo).

4. Robert Chung, 'What Went Wrong With the Turnout Rate?' (unpublished manuscript, mimeo).

5. This is done because it has been shown that voting criteria are, to a large extent, candidate-specific (see Chapter 5).

6. Li Pang-kwong. See *Hong Kong Standard,* 26 August 1991.

7. A. R. Clausen, 'Response Validity: Vote Report', *Public Opinion Quarterly,* 32 (1968): 588-606.

8. Ibid. ; R. F. Yalch, 'Pre-election Interview Effects on Voter Turnout', *Public Opinion Quarterly,* 40, 3(1976): 331-336; and M. W. Traugott and J. P. Katosh, 'Response Validity in Surveys of Voting Behaviour', *Public Opinion Quarterly,* 43, 3(1979): 359-377.

9. R. E. Kraut and J. B. McConahay, 'How Being Interviewed Affects Voting: An Experiment', *Public Opinion Quarterly,* 40, 3(1976): 398-406.

10. See *Hong Kong Economic Times,* 10 September 1991.

11. See note 3.

12. In the history of election polls, to anticipate how the undecided will vote is one of the five important factors in producing an accurate estimate of how people vote. See P. Perry, 'Certain Problems in Election Survey Methodology', *Public Opinion Quarterly,* 43, 3(1979): pp. 312-325.

13. For a discussion of the advantages of candidate rating and how to use ratings, see George Rabinowitz, James W. Prothro and William Jacoby, 'Salience as a Factor in the Impact of Issues on Candidate Evaluation', *The Journal of Politics,* 44 (1982): 41-63.

14. K. E. Boulding, *The Image* (Ann Arbor, Michigan: University of Michigan Press, 1956); and D. Nimmo, *Candidates and Their Images: Concepts, Methods, and Findings* (Pacific Palisades, California: Goodyear, 1976).

15. We realize, of course, that the voter turnout rate of our respondents is higher than the general turnout rate as a result of the stimulation effect as discussed. But even when we take into account this effect, the level of consistency in voter turnout is still very impressive.

16. H. B. Asher, 'Voting Behaviour Research in the 1980s: An Examination of Some Old and New Problem Areas', in A. W. Finifter, ed. , *Political Science: The State of the Discipline* (Washington: American Political Science Association, 1983), p. 339.

17. That candidate's party affiliation is irrelevant can be inferred from the

lack of this information in past research. In the few cases where the effect of party affiliation was gauged, it was found to be insignificant in candidate selection. This finding is reasonable for elections prior to 1991 because political organizations had rarely staged themselves in as prominent a position as they did in the 1991 elections.

18. *SCMP,* 20 July 1991.

19. *Sing Tao Daily,* 26 August 1991.

7

Summary Findings and Implications

Joan Y.H. Leung

In this chapter, we attempt to bring together the findings of Chapters 3 to 6 to present an overview of voting behaviour in Kowloon Central and to consider briefly its wider implications.

Our survey shows that the electorate were well-informed about the date of the elections, who was running in the constituency, the political stance of the principal candidates and the successful contestants. Yet, despite this high level of political cognition, there were indications that the elections were not seen as an important catalyst. This may be attributed, in part, to the electorate's strong sense of inefficacy, their mistrust of the Hong Kong government, their lack of confidence in the Chinese government and the restricted powers of elected Legislative Councillors. Many of those who voted, and most of those who did not, had limited expectations about the power of the electoral process to bring about significant changes in their lives.

Our survey results confirm that the political future of Hong Kong was the main issue on the 1991 electoral agenda. A substantial majority of the electorate, irrespective of whether they voted for liberals or the pro-China candidate, felt that China should not have a decision-making role in Hong Kong's internal affairs. Most of our respondents were uncertain of the ability of the future Hong Kong Special Administrative

Region government to maintain stability and prosperity after 1997. In addition, a majority of those who chose liberals explicitly stated that their choice of candidates was based on political stance. When we examine the political orientations of the electorate, we find that there is a significant relationship between the voters' attitude towards the Chinese government and their choice of candidates. However, when we attempt to assess whether issue voting occurred, it is difficult to conclude that specific attitudes on particular issues were the cause of these voting patterns. We would have expected a crude divide between liberal voters, who were concerned about the future and voted accordingly, and pro-China voters, who were not concerned about future Chinese intervention. Yet, there were no major differences between the supporters of the two liberal candidates and the supporters of the pro-China candidate in their attitude towards China playing a decision-making role in Hong Kong's affairs; nor were there major differences in their confidence in the future of the territory. Both sets of voters were almost equally opposed to Chinese intervention in Hong Kong affairs and equally supportive of autonomy.

There seem to be two reasons for this apparent anomaly. First, while the conclusion that votes were cast on the basis of the candidates' political stance is firmly established as a general political orientation of the electorate who voted for liberal candidates, when we ask about specific issues there may well be 'trade-offs' at work on particular aspects of the '1997 issue'. It is conceivable, for example, that some voters who voted for the pro-China candidate may have done so for reasons other than her identification with China. A single act of voting carries with it a multiplicity of messages. The absence of issue voting may simply reflect countervailing concerns which, for a majority of voters, are, in the event, aggregated into a decision to vote on the basis of the political stance of the candidate.

A second, methodological, consideration may also help to explain the absence of voting patterns based on particular aspects of the '1997 issue'. The analysis of political orientations (see Chapter 3) is based on those respondents who were successfully interviewed in both the pre-election and the post-election surveys. However, the analysis of issue voting (see Chapter 4) was based only on those respondents who thought that '1997' was the most important issue facing Hong Kong.

In addition, when we analysed the relationship between voters' attitudes towards China and their choice of candidate in Chapter 3, we used the actual choices made by voters. In the analysis of issue voting in Chapter 4, however, intending voters were used for analysis because we wanted to obtain as many cases as possible. The picture is further complicated because a substantial portion of the electorate (46%) failed to identify the pro-China candidate's political stance; she had made some effort to disassociate herself from China during the campaign. Given these various factors, it is perhaps not surprising that issue voting did not occur. What we can reiterate is that 1997 was perceived to be the most salient policy issue facing Hong Kong; that the vote for the liberals was on the basis of the candidate's political stance; and that there were major objections from all quarters to China's intervention in Hong Kong affairs and reservations about the ability of the Hong Kong Special Administrative Region government to maintain stability and prosperity after 1997.

Our survey results also confirm that political parties in Hong Kong, which are still at an embryonic stage of development, have yet to make a significant impact on the electorate. As many as 70% of our respondents said that their vote choice was not based on the candidates' political group affiliation. If neither issue voting nor political groups were significant factors affecting the voting behaviour of the electorate, then candidate characteristics and perhaps other short-term or situational factors may have been at play. Chapters 5 and 6 attempt to explore these factors further and to discuss the methodological issues which affect the measurement of voting criteria and the concept of voter consistency.

Voters made their decisions on criteria which were particular to the candidate chosen and not on the basis of the ideal attributes of candidates as suggested in previous research on Hong Kong elections (see Chapter 5). Our findings show that there were discrepancies between the ideal and the actual criteria employed in choosing a particular candidate after voters had considered who was actually running in their constituency. In addition, our respondents expressed differences in the voting criteria they used in choosing each of the two candidates standing in the constituency, even within the same interview. There is some evidence from other constituencies of a 'coat-tails' effect where association with a strongly preferred 'best' candidate works to the advantage of his running mate. This was also a factor in Kowloon Central. However, there is still support from the survey results for the view that voters thought carefully before casting their second ballots. The single votes which went to the pro-China candidate illustrate the point and the presence of other voting criteria mentioned by respondents indicates perhaps that, as their actual choices narrowed following the selection of the first candidate, other voting criteria came into consideration. The other obvious conclusion is that the electoral arrangements made a difference to the process of candidate selection. The double-seat constituencies permitted a free choice (in the sense that there was no cost) for the second candidate and allowed for the relaxation of the more rigorous criteria applied to the first choice. Clearly, this would not have occurred if the constituencies had been single-seat.

Another important finding of our survey, which differs from previous research, is the changes in the substantive criteria which voters used in selecting their candidates. As pointed out in Chapter 5, previous studies of District Board elections consistently identified platform, past performance and experience, and the educational attainments of the candidate as the three most important criteria used by the electorate in choosing their candidates. We also found that 'style of work' (the manner in which the candidate is perceived to conduct public business) and 'willingness to serve the public' were important factors. Given the relatively weak voter identification with political parties, the absence of issue voting, the inefficacy of the electorate and the lack of confidence in the present and future governments, it is not surprising that voters favoured candidates who were perceived as defenders of the public interest.

Educational attainment as a criterion for candidate selection was not as important as in previous studies. This highlights a distinction between ideal and actual choices. Previous research focused principally on the ideal attributes which voters would expect in candidates. Faced with an actual choice, however, the criterion may become relatively less important, especially if most candidates have relatively high formal educational attainments or if the context of the election means that other qualities are more highly regarded. 'Past performance' and 'platform', however, continued to be important voting criteria, even though many voters said that they did not have a very good understanding of the candidates' platforms. This may simply reflect an objective assessment of the situation: many candidates' platforms were not very detailed and could not be easily distinguished from those of their rivals.

Our findings suggest that voters were politically well informed and relatively independent and thoughtful in making their choices. They tended to use more refined standards in evaluating candidates' abilities and performance for the Legislative Council elections than had perhaps previously been used in District Board elections, where candidates' personal attributes, education and occupation appeared to have been more important. For the Legislative Council elections, more sophisticated affective criteria, such as 'willingness to serve the public' and 'style of work' and relatively substantive performance criteria, such as 'past performance and experience' and 'platform or policy stance', were the most important yardsticks used in assessing candidates.

In addition, by comparing the degree of correspondence between voting intention and actual vote choice in the pre- and post-election data (see Chapter 6), we may conclude that the electorate is quite consistent in its vote choices. The agreement between intention and behaviour was high, which suggests the possibility that voter preferences may be structured over longer periods of time, a finding which needs to be tested in the next Legislative Council elections in 1995.

The Kowloon Central survey is a first step towards obtaining a more detailed picture of the attitudes and behaviour of the Hong Kong electorate. It is evident that we need such a picture for, even from our study of this single constituency, it is clear that some cherished beliefs about political attitudes are incorrect. The Hong Kong electorate is not ignorant. Voters are neither fools nor puppets. Most voters make their choices carefully and they know why they make them. Both those who voted for the liberals and those who voted for the pro-China candidate want a future in which the territory is free from Chinese intervention in its domestic affairs; but there is great scepticism about whether this can be achieved and considerable doubt about whether the actions of Hong Kong people, such as voting, can significantly affect the outcome. This is political inefficacy, not political apathy, and it is moderated by the support which the electorate is prepared to give to leaders who seek to bring about change on their behalf. The answer to the electorate's concerns is not necessarily only more civic education to encourage a higher turnout rate or a more 'informed' voter but also a more responsive political system which will reflect more adequately the expressed wishes of the population.

Part II

Catholic Voting Behaviour

8

The Catholic Voter

Beatrice Leung

Religious people have generally been found to hold political values close to those of the moral teachings of their own denominations.[1] It would seem to follow that the political act of voting would reflect the orientations of the religion, but this begs an important question. Does the voter adopt political values from the religious group? Or does the religious group simply reinforce values which are acquired from life experiences outside the religion? Is socio-economic status a significant intervening variable affecting the electoral choices of members of the religion? Is the age of the voter an important factor? This chapter investigates these questions by focusing on the Catholic Church's role in political socialization and by examining the voting behaviour of Catholics of different social backgrounds. The discussion is based on 952 responses to a questionnaire distributed simultaneously in four Catholic parishes with different socio-economic profiles.

THE CATHOLIC CHURCH IN HONG KONG

Both Roman Catholic and other Christian Churches arrived in Hong Kong shortly after the occupation of the territory in 1841. Church-state relations developed quickly and smoothly and, by 1843, the

Churches were involved in catering for the community in such fields as social services, education and medical care.[2] Until the Second Vatican Council (1963-1965), the Catholic Church in Hong Kong tended to take its stance towards the state from the more traditional or conservative school of thought on church-state relations. This view of legitimate political authority is based on St Paul's epistle to the Romans (Romans 13:1-2). 'Since all government comes from God' therefore Christians 'must obey the governing authorities'. This tradition was taken as orthodoxy for hundreds of years until the emergence of the progressive or radical school in Latin American countries in the 1950s. The Theology of Liberation draws its inspiration from the teachings of Exodus, where God frees His chosen people from the oppression of the Egyptians.

> I have seen how cruelly my people are being treated in Egypt. I have heard them cry out to be rescued from their slave-drivers. I know all about their sufferings and so I have come down to bring them out of Egypt ... (Exodus 3:7-10)

Although the Hong Kong government is a colonial government, the Catholic Church has not criticized it, from a Theology of Liberation perspective, in the same way that it has criticized the actions of authoritarian or semi-authoritarian governments in South America, the Philippines, Korea and Poland. There seem to be two principal reasons why this has been so. First, although the Hong Kong government is not democratic, it is not authoritarian or repressive either. The degree of political freedom prevailing in the territory has made it a haven for political and economic refugees from China for the past 150 years. The Church played an important role in providing relief services for refugees in the 1950s and subsequently expanded into socio-educational work in the 1960s and 1970s and to socio-political involvement in the 1980s. Secondly, Catholics are well integrated into the territory's power structure and support the prevailing non-repressive ethos. Ha has estimated that, although there are only 253,000 practising Catholics in Hong Kong, about one-quarter of the entire primary and secondary school population attends Catholic schools.[3] The quality of Catholic education is highly respected and graduates of these schools often make their way to local universities and eventually to prestigious positions in government and the private sector. The socio-economic status and formal educational levels of Catholics are generally perceived to be higher than those of the population at large, an impression which is reflected in the educational levels of our sample.[4]

Politically, the Church in Hong Kong now takes the middle way, derived from the Second Vatican Council, between the traditional orthodoxy and the Theology of Liberation. This places emphasis on the well-being of man rather than on the paramountcy of political systems and stresses the intimate relationship between the Church and mankind. The Church declares:

> The joys and the hopes, the griefs and the anxieties of the men of this age, especially those who are poor or in any way afflicted, these too are the joys and hopes, the griefs and anxieties of the followers of Christ ... That is why this community realizes that it is truly and intimately linked with mankind and its history.[5]

In a recently issued encyclical, *Centesimus Annus* (1991), Pope John Paul II claims that 'man is the way of the Church' and that 'the Church's social doctrine focuses especially on man as he is involved in a complex network of relationships within modern societies'.

After the signing of the Sino-British agreement in 1984, the Church in Hong Kong began to play a more prominent political role. The Catholic Institute for Religion and Society was established in 1986 with the aim of developing social consciousness in adherents according to Christian principles and religious values. Three years later, following the rise of democratic movements in China, the Church set up the Catholic Alliance in Support of Democratic Movements in China. These developments were generally aimed at preparing Catholics to face the challenge of a Chinese takeover and to commit themselves to participation in public affairs.[6] They were reinforced in a pastoral exhortation, 'March into the Bright Decade', from Cardinal John Baptist Wu, the prelate of Hong Kong, and in the celebration of the 150th anniversary of the founding of the Hong Kong Catholic Diocese which expressed solidarity with the Hong Kong people in its theme 'Hand in Hand Towards the Future'.[7] Civic education programmes on the 1991 elections were systematically organized. Church groups held seminars and forums on the elections and information on the candidates was printed and distributed. Many Church premises were turned into centres for the registration of voters and prayers for the success of elections were repeatedly said in religious services. Colourful banners were hung on church buildings to remind churchgoers to vote.[8] Priests and pastoral workers were instructed by the Church authorities to encourage Catholics to cast their ballots and Cardinal Wu issued pastoral letters reminding the congregation to participate actively in the elections. Sermons from the pulpit became a channel for the Church's social teachings.[9]

The political values which were emphasized in these publications, seminars, forums, celebrations and religious observations essentially sought to reinforce Catholic preferences for democracy and autonomy after 1997. Yet, despite the unprecedented involvement of the Church in the 1991 elections, its authorities were careful to avoid partisan

Plate 3 Registration of voters in a Catholic church. The banner is exhorting people to register and vote.

commitments. This stemmed from a tradition, dating from the nineteenth century, in which the Church was willing to support governments provided that they were just and to the common advantage. Elections were a means of choosing the government preferred by the people but this did not imply a commitment on the part of the Church. The Church made it clear, therefore, that it would not openly support any candidate. Church premises were available for the election campaign but not exclusively for any particular candidate. Instruction was given to the clergy in the diocese that, according to the Canon Law, they were not permitted to take up public office and therefore were not entitled to run as candidates in the elections.[10] (Annex 8.1 reproduces the letter sent by the Chancellor of the Catholic Diocese to Catholic leaders giving guidelines on the participation of parishes, Catholic schools and diocesan institutions in election activities.) In short, the Church's policy on political participation was based on social teaching: concern for the society and its political development and willingness to take responsibility in these matters, together with other Hong Kong citizens. This permitted the Church to encourage intensive political participation from the Catholic laity and to suggest moral values in their socio-political activities; but it prevented direct participation in the political process by the Church itself.

A SURVEY OF FOUR CATHOLIC PARISHES

We may consider these values in the context of political socialization and of the findings from the survey research in four Catholic parishes (hereafter referred to as the 1991 survey). Merelman has argued that political socialization is a process by which people acquire political orientations.[11] In acquiring these orientations, groups can exert important influences which may be further reflected in the decision whether or not to vote and in the way in which voters cast their ballots. The difficulty, however, lies in separating this influence from values and attitudes acquired in the wider social and home environments. Groups may mediate or reinforce political values as well as provide them in the first instance. It is important to bear in mind also that the Church itself has changed its political stance since the Sino-British agreement. It is conceivable, in consequence, that different value messages, and hence perhaps orientations, can be communicated through the same organization over time. These factors, together with socio-economic status, are taken into account in our survey of four Catholic parishes.

The parishes chosen for this study are located on Hong Kong island and in Kowloon. The first, St Jude's Church in North Point, is a very traditional Catholic parish with a long history, located on Hong Kong island. The parish covers the busy commercial area of King's Road and is associated with nearby high-rise residential buildings which were built in the 1950s and 1960s. Further up the hills of this district, people in higher income brackets have moved into newer apartment buildings in the past decade. As a result, the parish has a mixed population of low- and high-income Catholics.

The second sample came from a sub-parish which is located in the big private housing estate of Taikoo Shing on Hong Kong island. The parishioners form a homogeneous middle-class group and are mainly professionals and business people.

The third parish is St Bonaventure's Church, covering a large residential area in Tze Wan Shan, Kowloon, which was developed in the late 1960s as a new district with both private and public housing estates. In the past ten years, this parish has been under the leadership of a priest who is known to be very conservative in his religious and socio-political outlook. Church members generally fall into the lower-middle and low-income brackets. The parish might be said to take a strong Durkheimian approach to religion, viewing socio-political activities as 'profane' matters which have little to do with the Church, which is perceived by the congregation to exist mainly for 'sacred' religious activities.[12]

The fourth parish is located in the heart of the public housing estate of Shun Lee Estate on Kowloon peninsula. It is composed mainly of low-income and lower-middle-income Catholics who have been under the leadership of a succession of parish priests from a foreign missionary society in Belgium. In Catholic circles, these priests are regarded as very liberal in their religious and socio-political outlook.

The survey was designed to employ necessary quantitatively oriented measures, such as cross-tabulation, to count the Catholic voting rates and to identify sources of political influence. Several questions were designed for T-test and chi-square test with a factor-based scale to measure: (a) the respondents' acceptance of political parties, direct elections and preference for candidates and (b) the relationships between their political orientation, political participation and social background. Each item for which we intended to test was scored on a five-point ordinal scale ranging from 1 = very conservative/never, through 3 = moderate/neutral, to 5 = very liberal/intensive. (Conservative/liberal relates to political orientation; never/ intensive relates to political participation.)

Table 8.1 Distribution of respondents by parish

	St Jude's Church (North Point)	Delia Memorial School (Taikoo Shing)	St Bonaventure's Church (Tze Wan Shan)	Our Lady Queen of Mass Centre (Shun Lee Estate)
Number of Catholics	13,389	4,000	3,231	2,934
Number of questionnaires distributed	587	205	246	120
Number of valid questionnaires	522	142	188	100
Number of valid questionnaires as a percentage of parish membership	3.90	3.55	5.82	3.41
Return rate (%)	88.93	77.17	90.38	83.33

Source: 1991 survey.
Note: The overall return rate was 86.62%.

The questionnaire (see Annex 8.2) was distributed in the four parishes shortly after the election was held. Respondents were requested to complete the form during the last part of the Sunday mass held at 9.30 a.m. on 29 September 1991. The sample consisted, therefore, of practising Catholics who were, to some extent, a captive population. This explains the high average rate of return of over 86%. Table 8.1 shows the distribution between parishes. Although the percentage of respondents is low compared with the registered figure for all Catholics given by their parish offices, the sample is representative of the views of active Catholics and provides interesting indications of the political values and attitudes, levels of political participation and factors governing the choice of candidate of these committed Catholics. There are also some findings which suggest lines of analysis which might be pursued in the field of political socialization.

Prior to this survey, the Catholic Institute for Religion and Society conducted a small-scale, pre-election survey in the Taikoo Shing and Shun Lee Estate parishes in 1990. This survey was designed to study Catholic political participation at a time when the diocese was considering launching a programme to promote civic responsibility towards the society. A total of 367 valid questionnaires were returned and these can be used as a comparative measure to assess the 1991 findings.

THE CATHOLIC VOTING RATE

Respondents to the 1991 survey claimed a very high voting rate of 86% in the Legislative Council elections, which compares very favourably with the overall territory-wide rate of 39.15% (Table 8.2). However, the comparison has to be treated with some caution. The effective territory-wide voting rate was probably significantly higher than the official figures (see Chapter 1). There is also the possibility that respondents to the 1991 survey felt a need to answer positively the question whether or not they had voted. None the less, there is other evidence which supports the view that Catholics turned out to vote in significantly higher numbers than the general population and that the percentage intending to vote increased rapidly in the year before the election. In the 1990 survey, 66.5% and 52.6% of the registered Catholic voters in Taikoo Shing and Shun Lee Estate respectively expressed their intention to vote in the 1991 Legislative Council elections. In our 1991 survey, 86.4% of the respondents in Taikoo Shing and 85.5% in Shun Lee Estate said that they had voted. In other words, the disparity between the intention to vote and the actual vote had increased markedly within a single year (Table 8.3). The surprising finding in Tze Wan Shan is that the turnout rate in this traditional Catholic parish was so high, given the generally low turnout in the constituency and the value orientations of Catholics in this parish.

Table 8.2 Catholic voting rates in the 1991 elections

	Catholic voting rate (%)	General voting rate (%)	Difference (%)
Legislative Council elections	86.6(492)	39.1	47.5
District Board elections	63.5(337)	32.5	31
Municipal Council elections	54.4(256)	23.1	31.3

Source: 1991 survey.
Note: Respondents were asked: 'Have you voted in the following elections held this year?' The number of respondents is given in brackets.

Table 8.3 Voting rates in four Catholic parishes in the Legislative Council elections, 1991

	North Point (%)	Taikoo Shing (%)	Tze Wan Shan (%)	Shun Lee Estate (%)
General voting rate	38.5	46.1	33.9	38.6
Catholic voting rate	86.5(303)	86.4(88)	88.1(101)	85.5(76)
Catholics who in 1990 had expressed the intention to vote in the 1991 election		66.5		52.6
Growth of the expressed intention to vote rate between 1990 and 1991		19.9		32.9

Source: Registration and Electoral Office of the Hong Kong government, the 1990 survey of two Catholic parishes and the 1991 survey.
Note: The number of respondents is given in brackets.

There is further evidence of high Catholic voting rates in surveys on voting behaviour in the Urban Council elections. The overall voting rate in the 1989 Urban Council elections was 17.6% while the turnout rates in Taikoo Shing and Shun Lee Estate were 15.5% and 13.7% respectively (Table 8.4). In the 1990 survey, 38.9% and 52.6% of the respondents respectively said that they had voted. In the Urban Council elections held in 1991, Catholics also seem to have voted in greater numbers than the general population and to have shown a significant increase in turnout over 1989 (Table 8.5). Additional evidence of high Catholic turnout comes from the 1991 District Board elections, where the overall voting rate was 32.5% but the reported Catholic turnout, at 63.5%, was nearly double the response from the general public (Table 8.2). Finally, the Kowloon Central constituency survey shows that members of religious groups do tend to turn out to vote in larger numbers than non-members.

Table 8.4 Voting rates in two Catholic parishes in the Urban Council elections, 1989

	Taikoo Shing (%)	Shun Lee Estate (%)
General voting rate	15.5	13.7
Catholic voting rate	38.9	52.6
Difference	23.4	38.9

Source: Registration and Electoral Office of the Hong Kong government and the 1990 survey.

Table 8.5 Reported Catholic voting rates in Urban Council elections,1989 and 1991

	Taikoo Shing (%)	Shun Lee Estate (%)
Catholic voting rate, 1989	38.9	52.6
Catholic voting rate, 1991	61(47)	69.8(44)

Source: 1990 and 1991 surveys.
Note: The number of respondents is given in brackets.

Another important indication of Catholic political participation is the percentage who registered as voters. Since registration was largely left to the individual's initiative and was not conducted by government canvassing teams, a comparison of Catholic registration levels with general registration levels is instructive. Of the 903 respondents who answered the question on voter registration, 646 (71.5%) claimed that they had registered as voters. The breakdown by parish shows that the lowest registration rate was in Tze Wan Shan, a finding which is consistent with the value orientation of political avoidance among Catholics in that parish. Conversely, the registration rate among the 'activists' in Shun Lee Estate was highest. A comparison between Catholic registered voters and the general registration of voters is shown in Table 8.6.

Table 8.6 Comparison of Catholic registered voters with general registration rates

	North Point (%)	Taikoo Shing (%)	Tze Wan Shan (%)	Shun Lee Estate (%)	Territory-wide average (%)
Registration of voters by district	54.3	54.3	69.6	60	50.2
Catholic registered voters	71.1(350)	75.6(102)	65(117)	80.2(77)	71.5(646)

Source: Registration and Electoral Office of the Hong Kong government and the 1991 survey.
Note: The number of registered voters in the sample is given in brackets.

What explains the high level of Catholic political participation? It seems evident that political participation is influenced by many factors and that it is difficult to assign a particular weight to any single factor. First, the role of the Church in the 1991 elections was not dissimilar to that of the Hong Kong government. Both stressed the importance of registration, voting, the development of representative government and the need for orderly and responsible behaviour. Potential Catholic voters, however, were receiving this message from the Church as well as from the government. Since attendance at mass can be taken as one important indication of commitment to the institution, one can at least make the assumption that injunctions to register and to vote were taken seriously by the congregations who made up this sample. For the Church itself, a political reason for supporting the election was that this is part of its strategy for survival after 1997. The political experience of the Church in China and in other communist countries does not suggest that future interactions will be as comfortable as the traditional working relationship with the outgoing Hong Kong government. It is in the Church's best interests to try to help to secure the autonomy and the development of representative government which were promised in the Sino-British agreement but which are increasingly under threat from China.

For the Catholic voter, the message from the Church may have reinforced political values which had already been received and accepted from other sources. The average income of our respondents revealed that many of them belong to the middle class; 60% of our sample had a personal income of over $10,000 per month. Many of these respondents would be Western-educated and probably sceptical of the promises of the Chinese communist government. Further, the voters as a whole had strong preferences for an autonomous Hong Kong, which was essentially congruent with the message being put out by the Church.

None the less, the Catholic turnout probably owes something to the commitment of the Church to promoting the 1991 elections. The increase in voting rates in Taikoo Shing (61% in 1991, 38.9% in 1989) and Shun Lee Estate (68.9% in 1991, 52.6% in 1989) in the Urban Council elections can possibly be explained in part by the greater effort made by the Church to encourage voting in the period between the elections (see Table 8.5). The Church did not, however, indicate a preference for candidates and it is apparent that Catholic voters made their choice of candidate principally on the basis of personal judgement (see Table 8.7). Priests and nuns, by comparison, did not exert great influence on the voters' choice of candidates.

Finally, differences between the parishes in registration and voter turnout rates need some explanation. The Shun Lee Estate Catholics had very high registration rates, which may be attributed in part to the legacy of their liberal parish priests over the past decade. By contrast, the conservative Tze Wan Shan Catholics were less eager to register; their value orientations stressed avoidance of political affairs. However, when the Church authorities stressed that involvement in the elections

Table 8.7 Rank order of influence on Catholic voters' choice of candidate

Source of influence	Mean	Standard deviation	Number of cases
Integrity and capability of the candidate	4.4711	0.9451	433
Platform of the candidate	4.0767	1.1783	417
Association with political group	3.9313	1.2218	393
Mass media	3.4198	1.3671	374
Family members	2.6123	1.5695	374
Community leaders	2.6030	1.3931	335
Peer group	2.4355	1.4018	349
Priest or nun	2.1024	1.3714	332
Church community	2.0923	1.3645	325
School teacher	1.8874	1.3155	293

Source: 1991 survey.
Note: Respondents were asked: 'To what extent did the following factors affect your choice of candidates for the direct elections in 1991?' They were asked to mark a scale ranging from 1 = no influence, through 3 = moderate influence, to 5 = very influential.

was desirable, Catholics in Tze Wan Shan began to register in greater numbers. Although, compared with other parishes, the registration rate still remained low, voters in Tze Wan Shan turned out in even greater numbers relative to the registration rate than their fellow Catholics in other parishes. It may be inferred that the Church was able to instil a commitment not simply to register but also to vote. These examples also suggest that real political differences between parishes may be partly attributed to the different stances taken by the priests historically; but it would be wrong to draw this conclusion too strongly for the evidence is still too slight to be definitive.

SOURCES OF INFLUENCE ON THE CATHOLIC VOTER

At the risk of overgeneralizing, we can say that the major sources of influence on Catholics' voting behaviour come from the socio-political environment rather than the Church. In this respect, we consider four possible dimensions of influence on vote choice and attempt to derive a profile of the Catholic voter from our assessment of those influences. First, knowledge of Church literature relating to social and political matters was not high among our sample, although there was considerably greater awareness of local literature than of the encyclicals and the Second Vatican Council document. Secondly, although Catholic groups did not seem to be important sources of socialization, participation in the activities of some groups was closely correlated with reported voting patterns, leaving open the question of whether it is self-selecting behaviour or the influence of the group which affects the predisposition to vote. Thirdly, the choice of the candidate seemed to be influenced principally by secular rather than religious considerations. Priests and nuns ranked relatively low on the list of opinion-formers while the mass media and the personal attributes of candidates seemed to be more important influences on vote choice. There is some evidence, as might be expected, that younger voters exercise greater personal judgement than their elders who are more reliant on family members and the Church in forming political opinions. Finally, all respondents were very positive towards the introduction of direct elections and the development of representative government. We consider these various potential sources of influence in turn.

Knowledge of the Church's Social Teaching

A majority of respondents in our Legislative Council elections sample — 73.3% of the voters and 89.9% of the non-voters (in total, 380 cases) — claimed that they had never read the Papal encyclicals on social teaching. Only 4.1% and 1.4% (19 cases) of voters and non-voters respectively said that they had read the papal document carefully. The remainder (104 cases) claimed various degrees of understanding of the encyclicals. Knowledge of the Second Vatican Council document was scarcely better. Some 71.2% of voters and 82.6% of non-voters respectively (or 362 of 497 respondents) claimed that they had never read this document, which is the foundation of Catholic socio-political teaching. Only 4.9% of voters and 1.4% of non-voters said that they had studied the document intensively.

Simplified religious literature on social teaching was better received. Some 44% of the whole sample said that they had some knowledge of the Church's social teaching. However, just over 46% of voters and

55% of non-voters had never read even the simplified religious literature on social teaching. At the other extreme, 9% of voters and 7.2% of non-voters claimed to have studied this literature intensively. The pastoral letters of Hong Kong's Catholic Bishop, Cardinal John Baptist Wu, which discussed socio-political issues, had been read carefully by 12% of the voters and almost 6% of the non-voters. Over 40% of the voters and 60% of the non-voters had never read the pastoral letters. About 46% of the whole sample had some degree of awareness of the contents of pastoral letters.

There are two related conclusions which may be drawn from these findings. The first is the significant difference between voters and non-voters. On every score, voters were more informed of the Church's social teaching than non-voters. That does not mean to say that voters drew specific instructions from the Church on how to vote. The pastoral letter focused on the desirability of participation and did not express support for particular candidates. It may be that the individual's decision to vote came from secular sources and that Church teaching simply reinforced that decision. Certainly, for a majority of Catholic voters, the direct sources of influence on the specific choice of candidates were much more likely to be secular. None the less, as a second related conclusion, it is conceivable that, for the minority of Catholic voters who had read Church literature carefully, the Church may have provided broad contextual guidance both on the desirability of voting and on the way in which the ballot should be cast. It could hardly have escaped the notice of devout Catholics, for example, that Cardinal Wu, together with all the Hong Kong Catholic clergy, concelebrated a high requiem mass to mourn the victims of the June 4th massacre. If this event had been related to teachings in the pastoral letters or sermons, it might well have led a committed Catholic voter to select a particular candidate.

The Influence of Catholic Groups

As mentioned previously, the Church responded to the post-1984 political situation by creating two groups, the Catholic Institute for Religion and Society and the Catholic Alliance in Support of Democratic Movements in China. The main objective of the Catholic

Institute for Religion and Society is to promote human social development in accordance with Catholic principles. Developing democratic and political awareness is, consequently, one means of attaining its objective. The Catholic Alliance in Support of Democratic Movements in China was created to support the student movement in China in May-June 1989. However, there were also older Catholic groups, the Catholic Justice and Peace Commission, the Hong Kong Federation of Catholic Students and the Catholic Youth Council, which played a role in propagating the Church's social and political views. The Catholic Justice and Peace Commission is better known than the other two for its views on critical socio-political issues. Its principal purpose is to promote human rights and to improve the quality of human life in the light of the gospel and the social teachings of the Church. All five groups have a reputation for being politically liberal and socially aware. The voter turnouts for three of the five groups were higher than the claimed turnout of the respondents to the whole survey which, as we have seen, was already significantly higher than the average turnout of voters. The two groups in which participation was not correlated with high turnouts, the Federation of Catholic Students and the Catholic Youth Council, possibly did not have the same impact as the other groups because their activities focused to a greater extent on youth who were not voters.

There are very significant relationships between membership in the other three organizations and political participation in terms of voting. Of 458 respondents, only 60 had taken part in the activities of the Catholic Justice and Peace Commission but, of these, 59 claimed to have voted. Similarly, only 68 respondents had participated in the activities of the Catholic Institute for Religion and Society but 67 of them claimed to have voted. The Catholic Alliance in Support of Democratic Movements in China is of particular interest because we would expect that membership in this body would be closely correlated with predispositions to vote for liberal groups associated with the territory-wide alliance in support of democracy in China. Catholic groups were originally part of the wider alliance but the Church subsequently ordered official Catholic organizations to withdraw from the alliance. Ha has observed that this was intended 'to show that the Catholic diocese as such did not wish to be involved in politically sensitive organizations'.[13] None the less, of the 481 respondents in the sample, 145 had taken part at least once in the activities of the Catholic Alliance. Of these, 135 were voters and ten were non-voters. There were also positive correlations between participation in the Federation of Catholic Students and the Catholic Youth Council but the relationship was not quite as strong as that for the other groups.

We have expressed this relationship in the positive sense that participation in a Catholic group tended to mean that the participant would be much more likely to vote than the average respondent. We might also express the relationship negatively, observing that non-voters were far less likely to belong to a Catholic group or to participate in its activities. While these findings are interesting, they are not conclusive evidence that these organizations play a strong socializing role. It is possible that participation or membership is self-selective: that is, that the organization reflects views which the member had already acquired. In this sense, Catholic groups would simply provide reinforcement for political and social values which had been drawn from the wider environment.

Secular and Religious Influences on Catholic Vote Choice

Table 8.7 shows the rank order of influence on Catholic vote choice. It is apparent that secular influences are generally more significant than religious factors but there are some variations if the findings are related to the disaggregated results by age, income and parish sub-groups. The personal judgement of the voter is reflected in each of the first three criteria chosen, 'integrity and capability of the candidate', 'platform of the candidate' and 'background of the political group'. Tables 8.8 and 8.9, which show the relationship between age and income and sources of influence, indicate that there are no significant differences between sub-groups. Some of the high scores among poorer sub-groups may, however, reflect the views of new immigrants from China who have suffered as a result of Sino-Vatican disputes. These new immigrants have incomes which are well below average and are generally more politically sensitive as a result of their experiences. It may also be true that older Catholics had themselves been persecuted or have friends or relatives who were persecuted in the 1950s and 1960s. These observations are drawn largely from experience in those Catholic communities. The high scores on the 'political platform of the candidate' criterion tend to support this observation but the number of cases is small and it is difficult to distinguish the views of members of the sub-group more precisely.

Table 8.8 Age and sources of influence

Sources of influence	Age				
	21-29 years	30-39 years	40-49 years	50-59 years	60 years or above
Integrity of candidate	4.61 (68)	4.56 (129)	4.50 (112)	4.63 (33)	4.50 (8)
Platform of candidate	4.01 (66)	4.04 (126)	4.33 (110)	4.28 (28)	4.66 (9)
Association with a political group	4.00 (65)	4.08 (127)	4.02 (96)	3.86 (29)	3.66 (3)
Mass media	3.46 (63)	3.44 (118)	3.43 (86)	3.61 (26)	3.25 (4)
Community leaders	2.51 (58)	2.42 (109)	2.65 (76)	2.55 (20)	3.25 (4)
Family members	2.46 (63)	2.15 (112)	2.92 (89)	3.23 (26)	4.57 (7)
Peer group	2.62 (64)	2.03 (107)	2.66 (86)	2.65 (20)	2.66 (3)
Church community	1.94 (57)	2.08 (107)	2.19 (76)	2.21 (19)	2.00 (3)
Priest or nun	1.72 (54)	2.04 (108)	2.23 (78)	2.42 (21)	2.50 (4)

Source: 1991 survey.

Note: Respondents were asked: 'To what extent did the following factors affect your choice of candidates for the direct elections in 1991?' They were asked to mark a scale ranging from 1 = no influence, through 3 = moderate influence, to 5 = very influential. Responses were averaged.

Table 8.9 Income and sources of influence

Sources of influence	Income (HK$ per month)						
	Nil	Below $3,000	$3,000 to $5,999	$6,000 to $9,999	$10,000 to $19,000	$20,000 to $39,999	$40,000 or above
Integrity of candidate	4.23 (43)	5.00 (4)	4.66 (18)	4.57 (52)	4.48 (126)	4.73 (76)	4.55 (20)
Platform of candidate	4.12 (40)	4.60 (5)	4.10 (19)	4.21 (51)	4.18 (120)	4.09 (76)	4.00 (19)
Association with a political group	3.77 (35)	4.66 (3)	4.23 (17)	4.09 (44)	4.00 (118)	4.17 (78)	3.16 (18)
Mass media	3.27 (36)	4.33 (2)	3.23 (13)	3.79 (43)	3.30 (110)	3.62 (72)	3.12 (16)
Community leaders	2.70 (31)	4.00 (2)	2.57 (14)	2.97 (36)	2.30 (100)	2.51 (64)	2.06 (15)
Family members	3.17 (41)	2.00 (2)	2.70 (17)	2.21 (42)	2.61 (108)	2.40 (65)	2.18 (16)
Peer group	2.53 (32)	1.50 (2)	2.62 (16)	2.20 (40)	2.60 (106)	2.14 (63)	2.31 (16)
Church community	1.92 (28)	2.50 (2)	2.69 (13)	2.29 (37)	2.06 (101)	1.96 (62)	1.73 (15)
Priest or nun	1.96 (29)	1.00 (2)	3.00 (14)	2.34 (38)	3.04 (99)	1.90 (63)	1.68 (16)

Source: 1991 survey.

Note: Respondents were asked: 'To what extent did the following factors affect your choice of candidates for the direct elections in 1991?' They were asked to mark a scale ranging from 1 = no influence, through 3 = moderate influence, to 5 = very influential. Responses were averaged.

The selection of the first three criteria, which reflect personal judgements, leaves open the question how these political orientations were formed. 'Mass media' ranks fourth on the list and appears to have been particularly important for those whose income falls below $3,000 per month (mean = 4.33). The wealthier Catholics rely on the mass media to a far lesser extent (mean = 3.12) as a source of influence on their vote choice. While this would appear to accord with common sense — wealthier Catholics probably have readier access to other information — it is again necessary to be cautious because the number of cases is small.

Other sources of influence, both secular and religious, appear to have less impact on vote choice. Older Catholics were more likely to rely on the advice of family members and of priests and nuns. Younger Catholics said that they made independent judgements and did not base their vote choice to any great extent on the views of family members, the Church community or priests or nuns. There are some differences in this respect between the Catholic parishes. The Church community and priests or nuns were more important sources of influence in North Point and Tze Wan Shan than in Taikoo Shing and Shun Lee Estate.[14] This may be attributed to the traditional role played by the Church in these areas. Priests and nuns have long been active as opinion-formers in North Point while Tze Wan Shan is a conservative parish whose members might be expected to follow the lead of Church authorities. In Shun Lee Estate, by contrast, the emphasis has tended to be placed on personal responsibility for decisions and on informed social awareness. In all parishes, however, it is clear that family and religious influences are not, in most cases, the primary determinants of vote choice. The circumstantial evidence supports the view that most Catholics voted for liberal groups, with younger voters showing considerable independence from established family, community and religious organizations in making their choices.

General Orientations Towards the Election and Political Development

We sought to test the views of our respondents on two critical issues relating to the present and future political development of Hong Kong. Many Catholics are in favour of direct elections and developments towards a representative government. To support these aims a Joint Meeting of the Catholic Bodies Concerned for the Development of the Hong Kong Government System was set up in 1987.[15] A total of 765 signatures were collected in August and September 1987 in various parishes to support the introduction of direct elections in 1988. The same Catholic group sent out 2,374 questionnaires to seek opinion on the introduction of direct elections in 1988. A total of 1,705 respondents favoured direct elections in 1988 while 326 were opposed to the idea and 342 had no opinion. These results are supported by the answers to our questions. First, we asked whether the election would have a positive or negative impact in promoting the autonomy of Hong Kong. Secondly, we enquired whether the emergence of political parties would have a positive or negative impact on the future development of Hong Kong. (For the precise questions asked, see questions 10 and 11 in Annex 8.2). A scale ranging from 2 = very negative (conservative) to 10 = very positive (liberal) was used to ascertain respondents' views. The results are summarized in Table 8.10.

Table 8.10 Catholic orientations towards the election and future political development by parish

	Mean	Standard deviation	Cases
All respondents	7.9334	1.7	736
North Point	7.9296	1.8	396
Taikoo Shing	7.8585	1.9	106
Tze Wan Shan	7.9272	1.7	151
Shun Lee Estate	8.0617	1.5	81

Source: 1991 survey.

It is clear that the general response to the election and political development was positive and that there were few significant differences between parishes. However, if we look at these results in terms of the reactions of voters and non-voters, the differences were rather more pronounced. Voters had a mean of 8.1017 while non-voters dropped to a mean of 7.6337. While this suggests that both groups were positive towards political developments, it may be that some of the non-voters regarded those developments as negative and chose not to exercise their franchise as a consequence. The results show, too, that there were some variations between those in different income sub-groups, with wealthier Catholics proving less positive (mean = 7.6190) towards the election and political development than poorer Catholics. Age, however, appears to make relatively little difference. Younger voters aged between 21 and 29 years (mean = 8.1857) were the most positive while those over 60 (mean = 7.9048) were the most negative.

172   *Beatrice Leung*

If we test for participation in Catholic groups, the respondents who had taken part in their social affairs activities were very positive in their attitudes towards the election and political development, as Table 8.11 shows.

Table 8.11 Orientations towards the election and political development by participation in Catholic groups' activities

Catholic groups	Never	Once	Twice	Three or more times
Justice and Peace Commission	8.0302	8.2222	8.6250	8.7
Catholic Institute for Religion and Society	8.0249	8.3514	8.2727	8.5
Catholic Alliance in Support of Democratic Movements in China	7.8821	8.3134	8.6429	8.65

Source: 1991 survey.
Note: On a scale where 2 = very negative towards the election and the political party and 10 = very positive.

It is evident that those who had participated three or more times in the activities of these Catholic groups were most inclined to view the elections and political development positively. Since these are essentially liberal, rather than conservative, attitudes in Hong Kong's present political climate, it may be assumed that respondents generally represented an informed group of Catholics who probably voted mainly for liberal groups. It appears that they acquired their political attitudes from the society rather than the Church but that the Church played a supportive role in arguing, through its social teaching, for democracy, political participation and human rights. Although the participants in these Catholic organizations are the most positive of all sub-groups, it should be reiterated that Catholic respondents as a whole were very positive towards the election and future political development.

CONCLUSIONS

This study has enabled us to formulate some conclusions about the Catholic voter and to suggest certain future directions for research in political socialization.

First, we may observe that the Catholic voter turnout rate was very much higher than the average rate, even if we assume that some respondents sought to please the researchers by claiming to have voted. We may attribute this high voting rate to such variables as formal education — our sample was much better educated than the average population[16] — and to exposure to environmental influences such as the mass media. However, we cannot rule out the fact that the Church itself played an important reinforcing role by stressing the moral desirability of participation in the election and by providing the institutional means for emphasizing that message.

Secondly, it is clear that participation in Catholic groups which seek to increase political and social awareness is strongly correlated with voting behaviour and with affirmative attitudes towards the election and political development. Cause and effect relationships are difficult to distinguish in this context. It is possible that individuals who participated in these groups chose to do so because they reflected views which they already held. Or it may be the case that Catholic organizations helped to formulate those attitudes. This is an important area for the study of political socialization. Further research is required to delineate more precisely how these political attitudes are acquired; the present study can serve simply to identify membership and participation in these groups as an important variable.

Thirdly, the study suggests a profile of the Catholic voter. Vote choice is influenced principally, it seems, by secular sources. Young voters especially are informed of developments through the mass media and make choices independently of the views of their family, Church members or priests or nuns. The Church does not reinforce choices in this respect for it does not support individual candidates. Some vote choices may, however, derive from the Church's social teaching or from the actions of prominent Church figures.

Finally, although the division of this study by parish does not suggest that there are great differences among Catholics' political attitudes and voting behaviour, it is clear that different traditions, whether liberal or conservative, do have an impact on such issues as the influence of priests or nuns and on registering to vote. In general, however, the Catholic vote in the 1991 elections may be characterized as being apprehensive of future communist rule, highly participative and very supportive of future democratic political developments.

NOTES

1. See David Leege, Joel Lieske and Kenneth Wald, 'Towards Cultural Theories of American Political Behaviour: Religion, Ethnicity and Race, and Class Outlook', in William Crotty, ed., *Political Science: Looking to the Future*, vol.3 (Evanston: Northwestern University Press, 1991) pp.1-65 and Michael Welch and David Leege, 'Dual Reference Groups and Political Orientations: An Examination of Evangelically Oriented Catholics', *American Journal of Political Science*, 35,1(1991): 28-56.

2. See the chronology of events in the *Hong Kong Catholic Directory, 1991,* Catholic Truth Society, 1991.

3. Louis Ha, 'Catholicism in Hong Kong', in Sung Yun-wing and Lee Ming-kwan, eds., *The Other Hong Kong Report 1991* (Hong Kong: The Chinese University Press, 1991), pp.529 and 532.

4. In our sample, 49% had completed secondary education, 11.2% had matriculated and 37.3% had tertiary-level education.

5. 'Gaudium et Spes', in Walter W. Abbot, ed., *The Documents of Vatican II* (New York: Guild Press, 1966), pp.199-200.

6. See *SCMP*, 27 December 1990 and *Kung Kao Po,* 16 November 1990.

7. See *Kung Kao Po,* 10 November 1989 and 7, 14 and 21 December 1990; and *SCMP,* 27 December 1990.

8. *Ming Pao,* 25 July 1991; *Economic News* 15 April 1991; and *Kung Kao Po,* 5 July 1991.

9. *Kung Kao Po,* 9 March 1991. The prelate's pastoral letters were reprinted in the parishes. Outlines of sermons and prayers for the faithful were distributed by the Diocesan Liturgical Committee to the Catholic parishes and focused on praying for the success of the elections and on the encouragement of the Catholic participation in the elections.

10. *The Code of Canon Law: An English Translation,* prepared by the Canon Law Society of Great Britain and Northern Ireland (London: Collins, 1984), Art. 285(3).

11. Richard Merelman, 'Revitalizing Political Socialization', in Margaret Hermann, ed., *Political Psychology* (San Francisco: Jossey-Bass, 1986), pp.279-319.

12. See W.S.F. Pickering, *Durkheim on Religion* (London: Routledge and Kegan Paul, 1973), pp.95-96.

13. Ha, 'Catholicism in Hong Kong', p.536.

14. This is shown from disaggregated information from Table 8.7.

15. Report of the Survey Office, *Public Responses to Green Paper: The 1987 Review of Developments in Representative Government,* Part II (Appendices) (Hong Kong: Government Printer, 1987). Submission by the Joint Meeting of the Catholic Bodies Concerned for the Development of the Hong Kong Government System (Annex 3, Appendix 7).

16. See note 4.

ANNEX 8.1

Letter from the Chancellor, Catholic Diocese to Catholic leaders on participation in elections, 25 July 1988

To : All diocesan clergy/heads of Catholic schools/religious superiors and communities

Dear Rev. Father/Rev. Sister/Sir/Madam,

Re: Guidelines on participation of parishes, Catholic schools and diocesan institutions in election activities

To assist parishes, Catholic schools and diocesan institutions in taking part in the activities leading to the Legislative Council elections in September, Cardinal John B. Wu, in consultation with the Council of Priests, has decided that the following guidelines are to be observed:

1. Following the teachings of Vatican II, parishes, schools and diocesan institutions should actively undertake the formation of the faithful, so that they can fulfil the civic obligation of taking part in voting.

2. In order to be fair and impartial, parishes, Catholic schools and diocesan institutions may not do propaganda for individual candidates, take sides, or support specific groups.

3. Clerics and religious *[sic.]* in the Diocese, like all citizens, have a right to choose personal options. However, they may not in their own names publicly give support to or recommend a specific candidate, lest their personal option should appear to the faithful to be the only legitimate one or become a cause of division among the faithful. [Cf. the 1971 Synod of Bishops, document on 'The Ministerial Priesthood', Part Two, I, n.2b, AAS 63 (1971) 912-913.]

4. In principle, churches are reserved for worship and liturgical functions. However, if there are justifying reasons, they may be used for other purposes, with prior permission of the Bishop. [Cf. canon 1210.]

5. If there is a genuine need, the premises of parishes or diocesan institutions may be used for election activities, on condition that they are made available to all candidates in the same district, with due regard for the exception mentioned in n.(6) below.

6. If a candidate's platform is contrary to Christian ethical values or the spirit of the Gospel, then he/she may not be allowed to organize election activities in any Church or diocesan institution.

7. In parishes, Catholic schools and diocesan institutions, only the posters printed by the Government, as well as all (but not just some specially selected) posters regarding individual candidates, may be displayed.

The above guidelines also apply to other election activities organized by the Government. It is understood that these guidelines of a restrictive nature are not sufficient by themselves. For this reason positive recommendations on social concern and participation in election activities are being drafted jointly by the three Vicariates and the Council of Priests. Hopefully such recommendations will serve to make the faithful more well prepared for the coming elections of the Urban Council and the Regional Council in March 1989.

Yours sincerely in Christ

Fr. Lawrence Lee
Chancellor
Catholic Diocese of Hong Kong

ANNEX 8.2

Questionnaire on the political attitudes and participation of Catholic voters in the 1991 Legislative Council elections*

Dear brothers and sisters in Christ,

Our parish is holding a survey in co-operation with the Catholic Institute for Religion and Society and Sister Beatrice Leung from The University of Hong Kong. The purpose of this survey is to understand the views of Catholics aged twenty-one or above towards the elections and political participation. All personal data will be kept confidential and will be destroyed upon completion of analysis. Thanks for your co-operation.

Political Attitudes and Participation of Catholic Voters

Please put a tick inside the box of the appropriate answer.

1. Which of the following member(s) of your family is/are Catholic(s)?
   1 [ ]   Myself
   2 [ ]   Father/mother
   3 [ ]   Sibling(s)
   4 [ ]   Spouse
   5 [ ]   Son(s)/daughter(s)
   6 [ ]   I am not a Catholic

2. How many years has elapsed since you were baptized?
   1 [ ]   Less than five years
   2 [ ]   Between five and ten years
   3 [ ]   More than ten years
   4 [ ]   Not applicable

3. Have you ever studied in the following educational institution?
   A. Catholic/Christian primary school: 1 [ ] Yes   2 [ ] No
   B. Catholic/Christian secondary school: 1 [ ] Yes   2 [ ] No

*The distributed questionnaire was in Chinese.

4. A. Are you a member of any association of the laity?
    1 [ ] Yes   2 [ ] No
    B. Are you employed by a Catholic institute?
    1 [ ] Yes   2 [ ] No

5. In your opinion, what is the degree of social awareness of the following person(s)/group(s)? Please circle the correct number.

	Very concerned	Not concerned
A. The religious group to which you are most committed	1 2 3 4 5	
B. Atmosphere of the parish as a whole	1 2 3 4 5	
C. Pastoral priest	1 2 3 4 5	

6. How well do you know the following book(s)/document? Please circle the correct number.

	Intensively studied	Never read
A. Relevant encyclical letters	1 2 3 4 5	
B. Relevant chapters in Vatican II	1 2 3 4 5	
C. General reading on social affairs for Christians (e.g. pamphlets published by the Hong Kong Diocese)	1 2 3 4 5	
D. Pastoral letters from Cardinal Wu concerning social affairs	1 2 3 4 5	

7. If the government initiates a bill which you consider to be unjust or unfavourable to yourself, what would you do? Please tick one choice only.
    1 [ ] Nothing
    2 [ ] Contact District Board
    3 [ ] Contact government department
    4 [ ] Contact Exco or Legco
    5 [ ] Contact influential person(s)
    6 [ ] Contact mass media
    7 [ ] Participate in petition

8 [ ]   Participation in demonstration

9 [ ]   Depends on situation

10 [ ]   Do not know

11 [ ]   Others (Please specify: _____)

8. To what extent have you participated in the social affairs activities held by the following group(s)? Please circle the correct number.

	Never	Once	Twice	Three times or more
A. Justice and Peace Commission of the Diocese	1	2	3	4
B. Catholic Institute for Religion and Society	1	2	3	4
C. Catholic Alliance in Support of Democratic Movements in China	1	2	3	4
D. Catholic Youth Council	1	2	3	4
E. Hong Kong Federation of Catholic Students	1	2	3	4
F. Others	1	2	3	4

(Please specify: _____)

9. Which of the following ways have you ever adopted to show concern for social affairs? You can tick more than one choice.

1 [ ]   Discuss with family members

2 [ ]   Discuss with friends outside Church

3 [ ]   Discuss with priests/friends within Church

4 [ ]   Participate in forums to know more about the issues

5 [ ]   Express opinions through the mass media

6 [ ]   Keep informed through the mass media

7 [ ]   Petition

8 [ ]   Take part in signature campaigns

9 [ ]   Demonstrations

10 [ ]   Pray (group)

11 [ ]   Pray (personal)

12 [ ]   Others (Please specify: _____)

10. Do you think direct elections to the Legislative Council will have a positive or negative impact on the future autonomy of Hong Kong?

| Highly | Highly |
| positive | negative |

1 2 3 4 5

11. Do you think the emergence of political parties will have a positive or negative impact on the future development of Hong Kong as a whole?

| Highly | Highly |
| positive | negative |

1 2 3 4 5

12. If a friend invites you to join a political group whose direction you agree with, would you consider doing so?

1 [ ]   Have already joined

2 [ ]   Would definitely join

3 [ ]   Would consider joining

4 [ ]   Would definitely not join

5 [ ]   No opinion

13. Are you a registered voter?

1 [ ]   Yes (Please go to question 15)

2 [ ]   No

14. Why did you not register as a voter? You can tick more than one choice.

1 [ ]   No time

2 [ ]   No interest

3 [ ]   No suitable candidate

4 [ ]   Voting is not an effective instrument in influencing government policies

5 [ ]   Don't believe China will allow Hong Kong to develop democracy

6 [ ]   Others (Please specify: _____)

15. Have you voted in the following elections held this year?
    Please tick the appropriate boxes.

	Yes	No	Not applicable (Seats uncontested)
A. District Board	[ ]	[ ]	[ ]
B. Urban Council/ Regional Council	[ ]	[ ]	[ ]
C. Legislative Council	[ ]	[ ]	[ ]

16. If you have not voted in the Legco elections, what is the most important reason? Please tick one choice only; those who have voted do not need to answer this question.

    1 [ ] No time

    2 [ ] No interest

    3 [ ] The quality of candidates is too poor

    4 [ ] Voting is not an effective instrument in influencing government policies

    5 [ ] Don't believe China will allow Hong Kong to develop democracy

    6 [ ] Platforms of candidates are almost the same and it is hard to make decision

    7 [ ] Others (Please specify: _____)

17. To what extent did the following factors affect your choice of candidates for the direct elections in 1991? Please circle the correct number.

	Very influential				No influence
A. Family member(s)	1	2	3	4	5
B. Peers	1	2	3	4	5
C. Priest(s)/nun(s)	1	2	3	4	5
D. Church community to which you belong	1	2	3	4	5
E. School teacher	1	2	3	4	5
F. Mass media	1	2	3	4	5
G. Recommendation by community leaders	1	2	3	4	5

H. Association with political group   1 2 3 4 5

I. Platform of the candidate   1 2 3 4 5

J. Integrity and capability of the   1 2 3 4 5
candidate

K. Others   1 2 3 4 5

(Please specify: _____)

18. Please go through the following statements and circle the number which most appropriately reflects your opinions.

	Strongly agree	Strongly disagree
A. The integrity of the candidate is not important, what is important is his/her fame.	1 2 3 4 5	
B. 'Readiness to speak for the poor' is not required of the candidate, what is important is his/her capability and knowledge.	1 2 3 4 5	
C. Being accepted by the PRC is not required of the candidate, what is important is that the candidate insists on upholding human rights.	1 2 3 4 5	
D. Voting is a civic responsibility and it is not a requirement of our faith.	1 2 3 4 5	
E. Church leaders should be concerned with saving souls and should not be involved in politics.	1 2 3 4 5	
F. The Church should be neutral between the rich and the poor. No priority should be given to the poor.	1 2 3 4 5	
G. Defending human rights is good but it is not a requirement of our faith.	1 2 3 4 5	

19. Regarding emigration, your present status is:

1 [ ]   Holding foreign passport

2 [ ]   Intend to emigrate before 1997

3 [ ]   Intend to return to Hong Kong after acquiring a foreign passport

4 [ ] Intend to stay with no consideration of getting a foreign passport

5 [ ] Do not meet requirements to emigrate and have no choice

6 [ ] No plans yet

7 [ ] Others (Please specify: _____)

20. What is your age?
   1 [ ] 21-29 years
   2 [ ] 30-39 years
   3 [ ] 40-49 years
   4 [ ] 50-59 years
   5 [ ] 60 years or above

21. Sex: 1 [ ] Male 2 [ ] Female

22. What is your marital status?
   1 [ ] Single
   2 [ ] Married
   3 [ ] Married, with spouse deceased or out of touch
   4 [ ] Divorced/separated

23. What is your occupation?
   1 [ ] Teacher
   2 [ ] Social worker
   3 [ ] Health care worker
   4 [ ] Other professions
   5 [ ] Administrator/executive/manager (including senior government administrator)
   6 [ ] Entrepreneur/businessman
   7 [ ] White collar worker
   8 [ ] Self-employed
   9 [ ] Production worker/transport equipment operator/labourer
   10 [ ] Sales worker
   11 [ ] Service worker
   12 [ ] Agricultural worker/fisherman

13 [ ]   Housewife
14 [ ]   Student
15 [ ]   Unemployed
16 [ ]   Retired
17 [ ]   Others (Please specify: _____)

24. What is your education level?
    1 [ ]   No formal education received
    2 [ ]   Primary school
    3 [ ]   Secondary school
    4 [ ]   Matriculated
    5 [ ]   Tertiary institution: non-degree course
    6 [ ]   Tertiary institution: degree/masters degree/Ph.D.

25. What is your personal monthly income?
    1 [ ]   Nil
    2 [ ]   Below $3,000
    3 [ ] $3,000 to $5,999
    4 [ ] $6,000 to $9,999
    5 [ ] $10,000 to $19,999
    6 [ ] $20,000 to $39,999
    7 [ ] $40,000 and above

Part III

The Electoral Process

9

Government and the Electoral Process: The Need for Review

Rowena Y.F. Kwok

An essential component of a representative and democratic system is an electoral process which is seen to be managed in a fair and equitable manner. A successful election requires that the details of electoral administration, such as whether the register of voters is accurately compiled, whether the polling procedures are truly secret and whether vote counting is conducted honestly, should be carefully scrutinized to ensure that the results are a proper reflection of voters' preferences. This, in turn, means that the integrity of the registration officers, polling clerks and returning officers who operate the system must be above suspicion. There are many ways in which the administrative machinery may fail and, in so doing, undermine the public's confidence in representative government.[1]

The task of organizing elections in such a way that the results are not open to challenge is particularly difficult when there is no previous experience on which the administration can rely. The Hong Kong government had successfully run District Board and Municipal Council elections for some years before September 1991 and it had administered the functional constituency elections to the Legislative Council in 1985 and 1988; but it had no prior experience in making electoral arrangements for direct elections to the Legislative Council under a universal franchise. Under the circumstances, it is perhaps not surprising that the government chose to apply provisions used in past elections to the 1991 direct elections rather than to examine afresh the question of electoral administration. Thus, voter registration, constituency delimitation and public education, the three principal areas with which this chapter is concerned, were all largely based on previous practice. It says something of the government's success in administering the elections that the results were generally agreed to be fair and accurate, that there were few complaints about voting procedures or counting and that the entire election passed smoothly. The only incident of major significance was the charge that a bribe had been offered in the closely contested Regional Council functional constituency which has only 36 voters.[2] In general, however, there were few public or academic comments on the administrative aspects of organizing the elections, a sign perhaps that the process was widely accepted as impartial and legitimate.[3]

None the less, the direct elections did throw into relief areas of major concern in the management of the electoral administration system. It will be argued that experience with previous elections was not an entirely reliable guide when it came to trying to encourage a large number of people to register and vote, to delimit constituencies and to provide information about the elections. The system of registration, which was based on the existing register, was seriously flawed. The constituencies varied enormously in size because of the government's commitment to constituency delimitation on the basis of the district boundaries. And public education was at once offensively paternalistic and lacking the detailed information that voters required to cast their ballots.

In the following sections, the system of electoral administration is described, its weaknesses are examined and recommendations are made for improvement.

THE ELECTORAL ADMINISTRATION SYSTEM

Electoral administration in Hong Kong is mainly the task of the

Registration and Electoral Office (REO), a division within the Constitutional Affairs Branch. Established in 1982 in preparation for the first popular elections at the district level, the office is responsible for:

(a) registering electors for the General Electoral Roll for District Board, Municipal Council and Legislative Council elections, and the Functional Constituency Roll for Legislative Council indirect elections;[4]

(b) holding District Board, Municipal Council and Legislative Council ordinary elections and by-elections;

(c) updating the electoral rolls through annual vettings;

(d) formulating and reviewing electoral and registration procedures and arrangements;

(e) reviewing electoral boundaries and polling stations;

(f) undertaking research and preparing and collating electoral statistics and proposals pertaining to constitutional and electoral matters for use in policy and legislative reviews.[5]

Headed by a Principal Executive Officer, the office has an establishment strength of about 60 people (Fig. 9.1). Depending on the workload at different times, however, the size of the actual workforce fluctuates. Seconded and temporary staff may swell numbers to over 100 during registration exercises. The duties of the office staff are also flexible in accordance with the demands of the moment. Generally, however, they are focused on three major areas: vetting and updating the General Electoral Roll for the direct elections, vetting and updating the electoral roll for the Legislative Council's indirect elections and providing general and administrative support for the office. In 1991, the office was allocated provisional expenditure of HK$13.3 million for operational costs and HK$14.8 for publicity for the District Board, Municipal Council and Legislative Council elections.[6]

Provisions for electoral preparations and arrangements in Hong Kong are contained in the Electoral Provisions Ordinance (EPO) (Cap 367) and the Legislative Council (Electoral Provisions) Ordinance (LEPO) (Cap 381). These stipulate the electoral franchise, qualifications for candidature, delimitation of constituency boundaries and the method of conducting the elections. Procedures for the registration of electors and arrangements for the actual conduct of elections are set out in four sets of subsidiary legislation. These are the Electoral Provisions (Registration of Electors) Regulations (EPRE) (Cap 367), the Electoral Provisions (Procedure) Regulations (EPP) (Cap 367), the Legislative Council (Electoral Provisions) (Registration of Electors and Appointment of Authorised Representatives) Regulations (LREAAR) (Cap 381) and the Legislative Council (Electoral Provisions) (Procedure) Regulations (LEPP) (Cap 381). In addition, the Corrupt and Illegal Practices Ordinance (CIPO) (Cap 288) is intended to ensure fair and honest elections and to prevent such irregular electoral practices as bribery, intimidation, cheating and misleading publicity.

Registration of Electors

A Hong Kong permanent resident who is 21 years of age or over and is ordinarily resident in Hong Kong or anyone who has been resident in Hong Kong for the preceding seven years is eligible for registration as a voter in the constituency in which he or she lives.[7] There is no compulsory or automatic registration of electors in Hong Kong. Registration is voluntary and dependent upon the individual completing a form. The REO enters new applications and corrected particulars every year and the electoral register is rolled over from year to year. A provisional register is published before 22 June each year to allow for public inspection and objection. A final register is published before 8 August and it stays in force until it is replaced.[8]

One of the issues in relation to registration which has aroused much public debate is whether the voting age should be lowered from 21 to 18. In June 1990, it was announced that the age of majority would be reduced to 18 from October 1990.[9] However, the government has refused to make the same change for the voting age. At one stage, the Secretary for Home Affairs allegedly argued that certain candidates would be disadvantaged by the inclusion of teenage students in the franchise because they were likely to be better organized and inclined to vote in a bloc.[10] This specious reasoning has been criticized[11] but official opinion has not changed its mind and the minimum voting age remains a controversial issue on the electoral reform agenda.

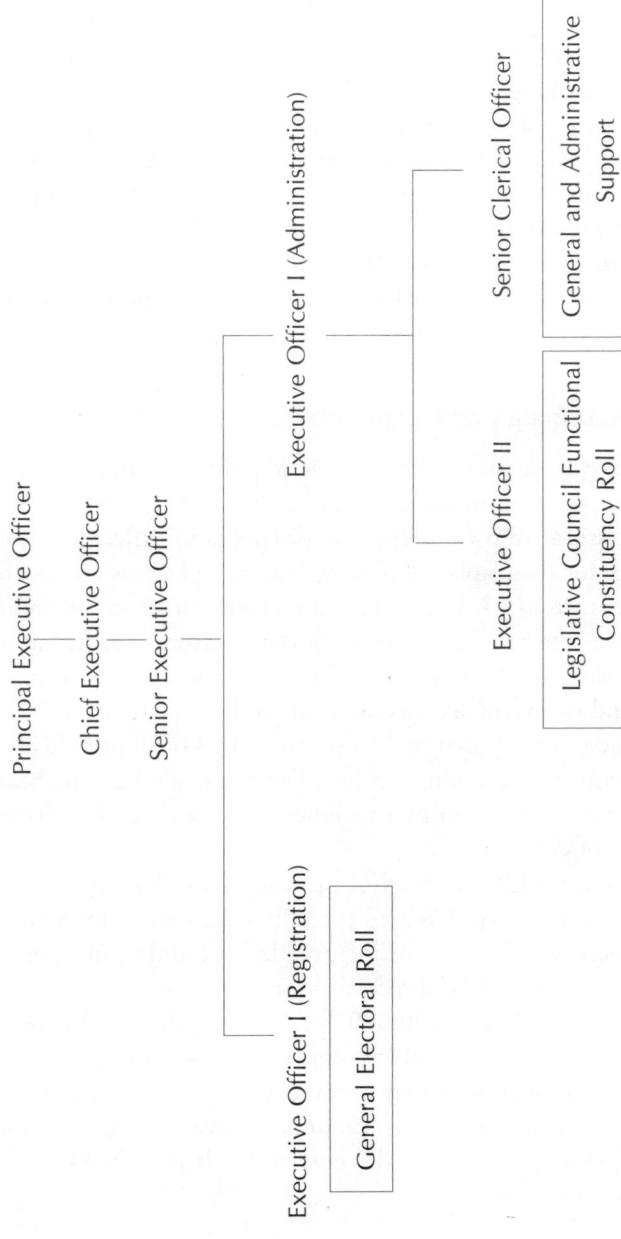

Source: Registration and Electoral Office of the Hong Kong government.

Figure 9.1 The Registration and Electoral Office: Organizational Chart

Nomination

Any person may stand as a candidate in the direct elections in any constituency as long as he or she is a registered elector and has been resident in Hong Kong for ten years or more preceding the date of nomination.[12] An elector cannot stand as a candidate for more than one constituency in any one election nor simultaneously as a candidate in a functional constituency.[13] Completed nomination papers have to be submitted to the returning officers in person by a candidate or the candidate's proposer or seconder with an election deposit being placed with the Director of Accounting Services.[14]

Electoral Campaign and Expenses[15]

Provisions are made for candidates to hold public meetings for election purposes but the Commissioner of Police has to be given prior notice. With permission from the respective district land officers, candidates may arrange for the display of posters, banners, placards and boards in public areas such as roads, streets and highway structures. Candidates may not advertise or electioneer using the electronic media, although they may participate in public affairs and other programmes on television and radio which are conducted on the 'equal time' principle.[16]

A candidate is required to deposit two copies of all printed election materials with the returning officer. The materials have to bear the name and address of the printer together with the date of printing and the number of copies printed.

Under section 13(1) of the Corrupt and Illegal Practices Ordinance (1987), the Governor-in-Council prescribes the maximum amount of election expenses which may be incurred by a candidate in an election. For the September 1991 direct elections, the maximum campaign amount permitted was $200,000 for each candidate. There is no statutory stipulation about what comprises election expenses or when the counting of such expenses commences. Within 30 days of the publication of an election result, candidates have to submit a return of election expenses.[17] Breach of the regulations is punishable by a fine and imprisonment.

Voting

Voting is in person and by secret ballot.[18] The 'first past the post' system applies, based on a relative majority of votes. Polling days are on Sundays in the belief that more electors will turn out to vote on a rest day and that the atmosphere will be better than on a working day. Polling hours are long; the polls open at 7.30 a.m. and do not close until 10.30 p.m.

Counting of Votes

The ballot boxes are transported to a single counting station in each district and are counted immediately after the poll closes. A ballot paper is considered void and not counted if:

(a) votes are cast for more candidates than there are vacancies;
(b) no vote has been marked on it;
(c) the voter's intention is not clear;
(d) it is marked in a way by which the voter can be identified;
(e) it is substantially mutilated;
(f) it is endorsed on the front with the word 'Tendered'.[19]

After the results of all elections are decided, ballot papers — counted, unused, spoilt and rejected — are sealed and handed over to the registration officer for safe-keeping.[20] Except by the order of the High Court on the basis of investigating an offence in relation to ballot papers or for the purpose of an election petition, no person is allowed to inspect any ballot papers in the custody of the registration officer.[21] Such ballot papers and all documents related to an election are retained for six months after which they are destroyed.[22]

This description of the electoral process has concentrated principally on the work of the Registration and Electoral Office. It does not cover the wider involvement of government in such sensitive issues as the delineation of constituency boundaries or its efforts to educate the public about proper electoral procedures. However, these elements are also components of the electoral process and, together with voter registration, were three aspects of the process which caused considerable public concern. The following discussion focuses on these areas.

Plate 4   A returning officer emptying one of the ballot boxes

VOTER TURNOUT AND THE ELECTORAL REGISTER

The turnout rate of 39.15% for Hong Kong's first direct elections to the legislature confounded all pre-election predictions and expectations. At one stage, opinion poll results suggested that over 70% of registered voters intended to vote.[23] In the event, even the government's more conservative expectation of a 50% turnout proved to be over-optimistic.[24] There were various reasons for the discrepancy, some methodological.[25] A flawed electoral register, however, was certainly one of the most prominent reasons for the low turnout.

An initial question was whether the Hong Kong government was committed to devising satisfactory procedures and to providing resources to meet its stated objective of registering as many eligible electors as possible. Under current electoral laws, voter registration in Hong Kong is voluntary. Eligible electors register once and their names remain on the register. Unlike the United Kingdom, where under the Representation of the People Act, electoral registration officers have a statutory duty to conduct 'house to house or other sufficient inquiry... as to the persons entitled to be registered',[26] the onus in Hong Kong is on the elector to make sure, either in person or by post, that his or her name and other required information are correctly included in the final register. In 1991, 1.9 million of an estimated potential electorate of 3.7 million registered, yielding a voter registration rate of 51.9%.[27]

A voluntary registration system assumes a conscientious and motivated electorate and will almost inevitably result in reduced electoral participation because apathy or lack of time or numerous other concerns prevent the less energetic or less public-spirited citizens from taking advantage of their opportunity to register. These individuals, however, may or may not vote if their names have been automatically entered in the electoral roll. Furthermore, since interest in elections is normally higher nearer polling day, there is always the chance that some people will want to vote but are prohibited from doing so because they have not registered in time. The last Legislative Council elections were held on 15 September 1991. However, closing date for voter registration was 1 July, fully ten weeks before polling day and almost one month before the nomination of candidates. It is not surprising that some qualified electors did not feel any incentive to register before the early closing date. A voluntary system therefore tends to suppress electoral participation.

A matter of equal concern is the question how the electoral register can be kept as accurate as possible. No electoral register will ever be completely up to date given the high rate of mobility in modern societies and the enormous resource implications of trying to keep it so. Permanent registration in a voluntary system such as Hong Kong's is, however, almost certain to lead to a progressively more inaccurate register over time. Although there is an exhortation in the voter registration form for people to inform the REO of subsequent changes in residential address, this is once more making assumptions of a dutiful electorate. Perhaps what is worse is that there do not seem to be attempts to facilitate the reporting process. People are asked to notify the REO when changing address, but the place that one has to contact is not an easy-to-remember post box number or telephone number; rather it is an address consisting of seven lines as it appears on the registration form. Nor is the telephone number a simple one.

The anomalies of a permanent voluntary registration system were amply demonstrated in the last Legislative Council elections. One potential candidate, Mr Lai King-tim of Kowloon East, had his nomination declared invalid because his name had been taken off the electoral roll.[28] It later transpired that this happened because the public housing block in which the candidate lived was due for demolition before polling day. As the REO did not hear from the candidate about his change of address, his name was removed from the register.[29] A further 35,000 voters had, under similar circumstances, been purged from the electoral roll. The Executive Council had to be recalled from its summer recess to authorize an amendment to the electoral laws to reopen the register for the disenfranchised.[30] The amendment restored the right of the candidate to contest the polls though he finally pulled out of the race, claiming that the incident had adversely affected the morale of his campaign team and delayed fund-raising plans.[31] In another instance, voters were reported to have turned up at polling stations only to discover that their names were not on the roll.[32]

These incidents are cited to illustrate the impediments that a permanent voluntary system puts in the path of voters and the difficulties that electoral administration officials face. It is a system which essentially contradicts the stated objective of the Hong Kong government which was to encourage as much participation as possible. The electoral roll, first compiled in 1981, has never been thoroughly updated. The REO does use a variety of sources to check the continual validity of the register's entries, including records on drivers' licences and public housing residents respectively.[33] These have been found to be inadequate. A majority of Hong Kong's population do not possess driving licences and about half of them live in private accommodation. Some elected legislative councillors claimed that they had found that at least 10% of addresses in their constituencies were inaccurate when they were canvassing door to door.[34] As one commentator put it, the government concentrated on enlarging the electorate without taking care to ensure that the records obtained were correct. This resulted in a reduced voter turnout rate.[35] Taking errors in the register into account, it has been estimated that the effective turnout was more likely to have been around 48%.[36]

Even if the electoral register had been reasonably accurate, the lower-than-expected voter turnout was not entirely surprising given the electoral arrangements. In recent years, Hong Kong people have travelled a great deal. Census statistics show that, at any one time, over 150,000 of the territory's residents may be abroad.[37] In the absence of provisions for postal or proxy voting, this means that a substantial number of possibly registered voters are effectively disenfranchised. While their names may stay on the register, they are not in a position to exercise their right to vote.

There is also the problem of civil servants on duty in polling stations on polling day. A total of 6,000 civil servants were assigned to man 354 polling stations and handle election-related duties in the September elections, several hundred of whom were presiding officers. Presiding officers were responsible for what happened in a polling station and had to be there to respond to contingencies. They were not expected to be absent from their respective polling stations for any extended period of time. To ensure fair play, however, they were normally assigned to polling stations outside the district in which they resided. Because of their official duties, these officers were effectively disenfranchised, whether they were registered voters or not, because no special arrangements were made for them to cast their ballots. Similarly, while presiding officers were encouraged to release their station staff during voting hours so that the latter could vote, no special arrangements were made for that purpose.[38]

If the 150,000 residents abroad and the 6,000 civil servants on duty on polling day were all eligible and registered voters but had not been able to vote, this amounted to the disenfranchisement of over 8% of a registered electorate of 1.9 million. In terms of the turnout rate, this represents a possible reduction of 3.5% if all of the eligible electors in these sub-groups had voted.

If existing practices are found to be wanting, the next logical step is to look for reform or improvements. Various systems of registration and managing the electoral register obviously have different advantages and disadvantages. In the following section, several varieties of automatic registration are examined, as opposed to voluntary registration, and suggestions are made for improvement.

Consideration and Suggestions for Alternatives

Comparisons are often made between voluntary and automatic registration systems for the purposes of initial registration and updating the register. As mentioned above, a voluntary system is one in which those who possess the required qualifications have to take the initiative to enter their names on the register; an automatic system, on the other hand, places the responsibility on registration officers to ensure both optimal registration and an accurate register. While various automatic schemes will achieve these goals with different degrees of effectiveness at different costs, automatic registration in general has several advantages.[39] First, assuming that registration personnel are impartial and trustworthy, an automatic registration system should presumably attain the best approximation between the number of eligible and registered voters, hence minimizing the situation where some people have to be turned away from the poll because they have not registered in time. Secondly, because no reliance is placed on the individual elector to report changes in personal particulars, for example, change of address, acquisition of the minimum voting age or change of name upon marriage, a seriously dated register can be avoided if regular updating procedures are instituted. Thirdly, an automatic system is better than a voluntary system in guarding the register against 'padding' or fraud. Voluntary systems make it difficult for particulars in applications to be thoroughly verified. Lastly, automatic registration prevents any attempt to shift the primary political arena from voting to registration, for example, the possibility of potential voters boycotting registration in a voluntary system.

Registration systems elsewhere demonstrate the advantages of automatic over voluntary systems. In Denmark, for example, the compilation of the electoral register is automatic and continuous. The Ministry of the Interior, which is responsible for electoral registration, also administers the national civil registration system to which municipal authorities continuously convey basic citizen information, including change of address, death and the acquisition of voting rights.[40] The register is 'permanently updated' and only Danish citizens living abroad have to take the initiative to register or correct particulars.

In Canada, there is no standing list of electors. New lists of electors are compiled for each election as soon as the returning officer for an electoral district receives a writ of election. The returning officer then proceeds to appoint two enumerators for each polling division within the electoral district. The enumerators' duties are to 'proceed jointly to ascertain the name and address of every person who is entitled to have his name entered on the list of electors at the pending election...' and to 'obtain the information that they may require by a joint house-to-house visitation...'.[41]

In the United Kingdom, registration officers are required to conduct 'sufficient inquiry' to prepare annually a register of all eligible electors. Short of house-to-house canvassing, this has in practice meant sending out a statutory form to each householder requesting a statement of residents who possess electoral qualifications on the qualifying date. The practice is enforced by making failure to comply an offence.[42]

The successful operation of automatic registration necessarily depends on a multitude of factors including, for example, the readiness to commit resources and the existence of large-scale collections of personal information. The Danish system requires the continuous availability of relevant citizens' records to registration authorities while enumeration on the Canadian model is time-consuming and costly and may lead to the inclusion of household residents not eligible to vote. Population characteristics may also impinge upon the effectiveness of the system. For a society with a high illiteracy rate, for example, to send statutory forms, as in the United Kingdom, would not be very practical.

Voluntary registration may appear to be less costly and less burdensome to electoral officials than any variety of automatic registration. There are, however, hidden costs, depending on how inaccurate the register is, how fast it degenerates and what kind of remedial measures are needed to rectify the records. Weaknesses in the system can, in addition, result in inestimable damage to public faith in representative government.

Suggestions that the feasibility of automatic registration should be explored in Hong Kong have been raised in different quarters, although no specific arrangements have been suggested.[43] In fact, while Hong

Kong principally adopts voluntary registration, the process is not totally devoid of 'automatic' elements. Door-to-door enumeration was conducted in some districts in past elections, although only in a limited and unsystematic way; the updating of the electoral register is also partially automatic. Apart from information obtained from driving licences and public housing occupancy, the Registration of Persons (ROP) Division of the Immigration Department, which registers births, deaths and marriages, is another source against which the REO matches its own register.

The government has not been oblivious to calls for the introduction of automatic registration. Both the Secretary for Constitutional Affairs and the Secretary for Home Affairs have made public reference to the issue but have insisted that ROP records are not adequate for determining the eligibility of an individual for registration.[44] Neither, however, elaborated on the cause of the shortcomings. As both Secretaries appeared, in these instances, to have in mind automatic initial registration from records in the government's possession rather than enumeration or something akin to the British model, one possible difficulty may be the legal questions involved if information on criminal records kept by the police were to be transferred to the REO for validation for voter registration.[45]

This brings us to the potential perils of automatic registration using records and the maintenance of a permanent electoral register for a free society. For electoral authorities to be able to perform these functions would probably imply the compilation of a population register which *combines* personal data currently kept in separate government data banks for different purposes: for example, health records, drivers' records, citizen and resident documentation, change-of-address notices from various sources and perhaps even census forms. Some degree of linkage of personal information across data banks is already a measure employed by the REO to update the electoral register. Such practices, however, may be a potential threat to human rights and freedoms. The danger is that, once installed, there would be strong pressure to open the register to all branches of government for unrelated uses and it would not be easy to ensure that the data were used exclusively for electoral purposes and kept absolutely confidential. This is already a concern in Canada, where the Privacy Commissioner has remarked that:

it would be ironic if the electoral process — the heart of the democratic way of life — became the vehicle which tipped the scales
further from the individual to the state.[46]

To the extent that Hong Kong is anxious that its current freedoms
should be fortified against prospective transgression, automatic
registration and updating using other government records is probably
not a desirable option.

Some Suggestions for Improvement

If no radical reform of the existing registration and updating practices
is considered and the essentially voluntary system is to be retained,
some improvements are still possible. One way might be to make it
easier to update information and to publicize the means of doing so.
The suggestion has also been made that electoral registration forms
should be redesigned to make them more 'consumer friendly' and more
available.[47] Before a decision is made to conduct large-scale enumeration,
occasional surveys of small random samples can help to gauge the extent
of the accuracy of the register.

To the extent that the registration process has attracted much public
concern and that its accuracy does affect the level of public participation
in the democratic process, more fundamental reforms are in order.
Given the mobility of the Hong Kong population both within and
out of the territory,[48] as discussed earlier, it should be obvious that
periodic re-registration is desirable. If door-to-door enumeration before
each election and annual exercises are considered too costly and time-
consuming, arrangements for complete re-registration every few years
should be seriously studied. It is possible that regular registration could
come to be regarded as inconvenient and drive away registered electors
rather than retaining them. This makes it even more important that
the government should assume more responsibility and take more
initiative to encourage registration and ensure accurate records.
Registration forms could be sent to household heads requesting their
co-operation in providing information on eligible voters. For example,
to save costs such forms could perhaps be mailed with water bills; and,
for households which do not have to pay for water, with some other

government correspondence. To ensure a high return and proper records, enumerators might be needed to collect the forms and also to make sure that all required information was supplied.

Despite the cost of such schemes and the burden placed on administrators these measures are necessary if the government is to make a success of the political reform programme started in 1984 whose aim was to:

> develop progressively a system of government the authority for which is firmly rooted in Hong Kong, which is able to represent authoritatively the views of the people of Hong Kong, and which is more directly accountable to the people of Hong Kong.[49]

While a high registration rate does not necessarily entail a high turnout, a sufficiently inclusive and accurate register is none the less a prerequisite to any hope of a high turnout in relation to the potential electorate. As far as door-to-door canvassing is concerned, it should also be noted that Hong Kong already possesses an advantage over some other countries in that its population is concentrated in a limited land area.

CONSTITUENCIES AND BOUNDARY DELIMITATION

In the September 1991 elections, Hong Kong was divided into nine double-seat constituencies, the sizes of which varied greatly. The largest constituency, Hong Kong East, with an estimated population of 794,900, was more than twice the size of the smallest constituency, New Territories North, which had a population of only 392,400.[50] Hong Kong's population is estimated at 5.8 million. The average population for each of the nine constituencies should have been about 644,000. Hong Kong East, with 794,900 inhabitants, was 123.4% of the average, while New Territories North was 60.9%.

The differences in constituency populations prompted a member of the Legislative Council to introduce a bill demanding that a legislative framework be set out to determine the future demarcation of constituencies. It was suggested that, in line with practices in the United Kingdom, Canada and Australia, a criterion should be set such that a constituency's population did not differ from the electoral quota by more than 10% and that the difference in population between two neighbouring constituencies should not exceed the same percentage.[51]

In Hong Kong, the power to define the size, the precise boundaries and the number of vacancies for members of each constituency rests with the Governor-in-Council.[52] In his speech announcing the constituency boundaries, the Chief Secretary stated the reasons behind the government's decision on the boundaries:

> First we want to build on the sense of district identity, while providing the opportunity for participation across the whole community without favouring any particular group. Secondly, there is a practical need to avoid the disruption which a change in boundaries would produce.[53]

These considerations are not very different from those applying in other countries. Usually, constituency boundaries represent a compromise between often conflicting concerns: for example, the maintenance of complete administrative units, community integrity and the near equality of population between constituencies. There may also be considerations of geographical features and communications. When a government is inexperienced in holding elections, there may even be functional reasons for drawing constituency boundaries on the basis of existing administrative units to facilitate the work of electoral administrators. In the long run, however, numerical equality in constituency population must be given more prominent consideration if only because principles of democracy demand that the value of votes be equal. In the United Kingdom, boundary commissioners are required to report every 15 years to take into account population movements across constituencies.[54]

In Hong Kong, as a result of agreements between the British and Chinese governments, the number of directly elected members to the Legislative Council may progressively increase up to the year 2003.[55] This may well require revision of constituency boundaries prior to each election. The Hong Kong government held the decennial census in March 1991 while the next Legislative Council elections are scheduled for 1995. Clear criteria for future delimitation should be laid down and the most recent census data should be utilized to ensure that no individual group in the population enjoys greater political influence than their numbers confer.

The government has emphasized its neutrality on questions of constituency boundaries. The Secretary for Home Affairs, for example, has explained that, in reaching decisions on boundaries, the government took into account present and future population distribution and geographical considerations, as well as existing electoral and administrative boundaries, and assured legislators that 'party politics was no part of our thinking'.[56] Such an official disclaimer of political motivations behind boundaries decisions, however, did not stop the administration from being accused of gerrymandering.[57] The Electoral Reform Society of London described the discrepancies as 'excessive' and observed that 'even allowing for exceptional local circumstances it must be possible to achieve a more equitable delimitation'.[58] The delineation of constituencies is an issue of crucial significance for electoral politics as the chance of a political party gaining or losing representation greatly depends on the manner in which the boundaries of constituencies are drawn. Accounts abound of governments attempting to manipulate poll results through gerrymandering; precise criteria for defining constituency boundaries often have to be worked out between interested parties before elections are held.[59]

There does not yet seem to be great public concern about the possible political implications of the Hong Kong government manipulating constituency boundaries. One commentator has argued that there is no reason for the government to want to influence election results through such practices.[60] To the extent that the Hong Kong administration is still perceived to be politically neutral, this observation may be valid. But, in the longer term, as local politics intensifies, too much government involvement and intervention in an area as potentially explosive as the delimitation of constituency boundaries is probably undesirable. In politically sensitive times, it is important for the government not only to be fair and impartial but to be perceived as such. Otherwise, Hong Kong's new-born 'democracy', already precarious, might encounter even more difficulties. In such circumstances, it would be advisable to entrust the important tasks of overseeing constituency delimitation, alignment and realignment to an independent boundary commission.

ELECTORAL EDUCATION OF THE PUBLIC

The government's publicity and public education programme on the elections was greatly criticized.[61] This section examines what the government did, what the major inadequacies of the programme were and what improvements can be made in the future.

The government body responsible for publicity was the election publicity steering committee, chaired by the Deputy Secretary for Constitutional Affairs and including officials from Radio Television Hong Kong and the Government Information Service.[62] According to the Deputy Secretary, the government's central election publicity programme was managed in several stages. The first stage, in late August, was the so-called 'motivation stage' during which publicity efforts concentrated on telling people what voting could do for them. By the end of August, new advertisements were launched specifically to address the feeling that 'one vote does not carry much weight'. Then, two weeks before the 15 September polling day, the programme entered the 'information stage' when publicity focused on providing basic information on the elections: for example, that each voter could cast two votes and that a poll card was not absolutely essential at the polling station. One week before polling day, the emphasis was shifted to reminding voters when polling day was.

All forms of media were used during the campaign, including television, radio and the printing press. Numerous other campaigns conveyed the government's message through other means. The City and New Territories Administration put up 8,000 coloured flags on street lampposts throughout the territory; 600,000 publicity boards were located in prominent locations such as roundabouts and shopping arcades; 20,000 posters were distributed and 500,000 leaflets were handed out at banks, subway and train stations and in shops. Advertisements were shown in cinemas.[63] Other promotion activities sponsored by the government included fun fairs, bus parades, gala shows and even some home visits.

In the month prior to polling day, Radio Television Hong Kong also hosted a series of televised constituency-by-constituency debates in both functional and direct elections, which were simultaneously translated into English on radio. Video and radio tapes of the programmes were kept in the City Hall library for those people who missed the original broadcast.[64]

In terms of quantity and variation of media, the advertisements and publicity on the elections put out by the government were probably sufficient. The inadequacy of the programme lay in the content of the campaigns. There were only two major messages put across in television and newspaper advertisements: one voter had two votes and 'voting is power'. The slogan was very misleading[65] and the first message alone was hardly adequate to inform the public of the specifics of the elections. People were told they had two votes but were never informed they could cast just one and there was no mention of the different implications of going to the polling station and casting a blank vote and not going to vote at all. The public was not informed that constituency boundaries for the Legislative Council elections were different from those used in District Board and Municipal Council elections. Opinion polls showed that a substantial number of registered voters were unaware of this.[66] Nor was there sufficient education on what constituted corrupt electoral activities or on the differences in voting procedures between functional and other constituencies.

All in all, the public education programme was highly inadequate. There was little effort to inform the public on the various stages in the electoral process, ranging from registration to nomination of candidates to casting ballots and the counting of votes. People were just told to vote without any information on the powers and limitations of the Legislative Council.

The government has to enter into more substantive areas of public electoral education if it wishes to have a more active electorate. Exhortations to vote are not sufficient. There should be a continuous education process tied in with other parts of the general civic education programme in an attempt to generate a stronger sense of civic responsibility and an identity with Hong Kong. The purpose of civic education is not only to promote democracy as a political system but to develop democracy as a way of life that permeates the daily activities of every member of society.[67]

CONCLUSIONS

The Hong Kong government's performance in the September 1991 elections left much to be desired. We have concentrated specifically on voter registration, constituency delimitation and electoral education, but other areas of the electoral process could also be improved. Encouragement of younger electors to register, the definition of campaign expenditure, provision for absentee voting and fair and adequate access of candidates to the media are some of the additional aspects that require careful consideration. The critical need for these, as well as the other areas of electoral administration that we have considered, is for an independent electoral commission. This would relieve civil servants of making decisions with important political implications which are not and should not be their responsibility.

NOTES

1. See, for example, Vucina Vasovic, 'Problems of Designing Democratic Election Administration With Reference to the Situation in Yugoslavia' and Stanislaw Gebethner, 'Imperfect Free Elections in Central and Eastern European Countries in 1989 and 1990', papers presented at the symposium on 'Election Administration in Comparative Perspectives' at Tokai University European Centre, Copenhagen, Denmark, 27 and 28 March 1991.

2. Mr. Gilbert Leung Kam-ho allegedly paid money to fellow regional councillors for their votes in September's elections. He is charged with bribery and incurring electoral expenses exceeding the legally sanctioned limit. See *SCMP*, 12 March 1992.

3. For two comments on electoral administration, see Louie Kin-sheun, 'The Electoral System of Hong Kong: Problems and Prospects', paper presented at a seminar on 'Elections and Electoral Politics', Hong Kong Foundation, 8 December 1990, and Michael Meadowcroft and Patrick Bradley, *Report of Delegation,* presented to the Hong Kong Democratic Foundation (London: The Electoral Reform Society, 1991).

4. There are two separate but interrelated electoral registers in Hong Kong, the General Electoral Roll for direct elections and the Legislative Council Electoral Roll for indirect elections through government-designated functional constituencies. This chapter deals solely with the direct elections.

5. Terms of reference as provided by the REO.

6. Information provided by the REO.

7. *EPO,* 1989, ss.6-10 and 1990 Amendment, s.6. Exceptions are convicts, the insane, members of the regular armed forces of the crown and those who have been convicted of corrupt offences.

8. *EPO,* 1990 Amendment, s.9.

9. *SCMP,* 30 June 1990.

10. *SCMP,* 20 March 1990.

11. See *SCMP,* 14 and 20 March 1990 and 20 May 1990.

12. *EPO,* 1989, s.18.

13. *EPO,* 1989, s.21(2) and 1990 Amendment, s.11.

14. *Candidates Manual 1991* (Hong Kong: Registration and Electoral Office, Constitutional Affairs Branch). For the September 1991 elections, the deposit was $10,000, which was refundable only under certain conditions, one being that candidates secured not less than 5% of the valid votes.

15. Information in this section is based mainly on the *Candidates Manual 1991.*

16. The ban was applied when one of the political groups contesting the elections, the United Democrats of Hong Kong, tried to air an advertisement on a fund-raising concert on the local radio and this led to charges of infringement of freedom of expression and association. See *SCMP,* 20 and 21 August 1991.

17. *CIPO,* 1987, s.29.

18. *EPO,* 1989, s.44.

19. *EPP,* 1987, s.47 and 1989 Amendment, s.7. A 'tendered' ballot paper is one cast by an elector who, presenting himself as a particular registered elector and applying for a ballot paper after another person has voted as such elector, satisfies the presiding officer as to his identity and is allowed to mark a ballot paper as any other elector (s.35). It is interesting to note, however, that in this case, if the first ballot is cast by an impostor, it is the impostor's ballot that will be counted and the 'tenderee' who is penalized. While the 'tenderee' will be allowed to vote, the tenderee's ballot will not be counted.

20. *EPP,* 1989 Amendment Regulations, s.9 and 1990 Amendment Regulations, s.20.

21. *EPP,* 1987, ss.54-55.

22. Ibid., s.57.

23. Social Sciences Research Centre, The University of Hong Kong, 'POP Poll 1-6 September 1991' (sponsored by the *South China Morning Post*).

24. *Sing Tao Daily,* 5 September 1991.

25. Robert Chung, 'What Went Wrong With the Turnout Rate?' (unpublished manuscript). See also Chapter 6 above.

26. *Representation of the People Act 1983* (London: Her Majesty's Stationery Office), Chapter 2, s.10(a).

27. Figures provided by the REO.

28. One has to be, *inter alia,* a registered elector to qualify to stand as a candidate in the elections. See *EPO,* 1989, s.18.

29. *SCMP,* 31 July 1991 and 1 August 1991. REO officials said fresh registration forms had been sent to people involved to ensure that changes of addresses were notified but the candidate denied having received any form.

30. *SCMP,* 8 August 1991.

31. *SCMP,* 5 August 1991.

32. *SCMP,* 16 September 1991.

33. Rowena Y.F. Kwok, 'Electoral Administration in Hong Kong', *Journal of Behavioral and Social Sciences,* 37 (1992): 84–105.

34. *SCMP,* 23 September 1991.

35. Robert Chung, *SCMP,* 23 September 1991.

36. Chung, 'What Went Wrong'.

37. *Hong Kong 1991 Population Census: Tabulations for District Board Districts and Constituency Areas: Living Quarters, Households and Population by Type of Living Quarters* (Hong Kong: Census and Statistics Department, 1991), p.13.

38. *SCMP,* 14 September 1991; *Hong Kong Standard,* 15 September 1991.

39. T.E. Smith, *Elections in Developing Countries* (London: Macmillan & Co. Ltd., 1960), Chapter 4.

40. Jorgen Elklit and Anne Birte Pade, *Election Administration in Denmark* (Copenhagen, Denmark: Ministry of the Interior, 1991).

41. *Canada Elections Act,* 1990, Schedule IV, Rule 12.

42. H.F. Rawlings, *Law and the Electoral Process* (London: Sweet & Maxwell, 1988), Chapter 3.

43. *Hansard* (Proceedings of the Legislative Council), 28 November 1990, *passim;* Louie, 'The Electoral System of Hong Kong'; and *SCMP,* 7 August 1991.

44. Michael M.Y. Suen, 'The Hong Kong Electoral System and Its Future Development', paper presented at a conference on 'Democracy and Political Development: Hong Kong Characteristics', Hong Kong Democratic Foundation, 19 May 1991, and the Secretary for Home Affairs, *Hansard,* 28 November 1990, p.595.

45. *Hansard,* 28 November 1990, p.572.

46. Privacy Commissioner, *Annual Report 1990-1991* (Canada: Minister of Supply and Services, 1991), p.20.

47. Meadowcroft and Bradley, *Report of Delegation.*

48. See also the Secretary for Home Affairs, *Hansard,* 28 November 1990, p.595.

49. *White Paper: The Further Development of Representative Government in Hong Kong* (Hong Kong: Government Printer, 1984), p.3.

50. Figures provided by the REO.

51. Martin Lee, *Hansard,* 16 January 1991, pp.874-875.

52. *EPO,* 1990 Amendment, s.4.

53. *Hansard,* 21 March 1990, p.1122.

54. Robert J. Waller, 'The 1983 Boundary Commission: Policies and Effects', *Electoral Studies,* 2, 3(1983): 195-206.

55. *The Basic Law of the Hong Kong Special Administrative Region of the People's Republic of China* (Hong Kong: The Consultative Committee for the Basic Law of the Hong Kong Special Administrative Region of the People's Republic of China, 1990), Annex II.

56. *Hansard,* 28 November 1990, p.595.

57. Martin Lee, *Hansard,* 28 November 1990, p.576.

58. Meadowcroft and Bradley, *Report of Delegation,* para.4.6.5.

59. Smith, *Elections in Developing Countries,* Chapter 3.

60. Louie, 'The Electoral System of Hong Kong'.

61. See *SCMP,* 23 August 1991 and *Sing Tao Daily,* 26 September 1991.

62. *SCMP,* 26 August 1991.

63. *Ming Pao,* 1 September 1991.

64. *SCMP,* 18 August 1991.

65. As the directly elected members, 18 in all, were to constitute less than one-third of the full council of 60 members, to tell the electorate 'voting is power' was nothing short of pathetic.

66. *SCMP,* 17 July 1991.

67. Monica Jiménez de Barros, 'Citizen Education: Its Importance in Latin America and Central Europe', paper presented at a symposium on Central European electoral systems in Budapest, Hungary, 30 July to 2 August 1991.

Appendices

APPENDIX A

ELECTION RESULTS

1. Direct Elections

Constituency	Registered electorate	Turnout (%)	Candidates (group affiliation)	Number of votes	Percentage of the vote in the constituency
1. Hong Kong Island East	261,573	103,028 (39.4)	*Lee Chu-ming, Martin (UDHK)	76,831	40.2
			*Man Sai-cheong (UDHK)	43,615	22.8
			Cheng Kai-nam (HKCF)	29,902	15.6
			Chan Ying-lun (HKDF)	19,806	10.4
			Leung Wai-tung, Diana (I)	15,230	8.0
			Chow Kit-bing, Jennifer (I)	5,805	3.0
2. Hong Kong Island West	171,052	68,979 (40.3)	*Yeung Sum (UDHK)	45,108	34.8
			*Huang Chen-ya (UDHK)	31,052	24.0
			Chan Yuk-cheung, David (I)	29,413	22.7
			Chang Yau-hung, Alex (LDF)	12,145	9.4
			Wong Man-chiu, Ronnie (NHKA)	6,113	4.7
			Cheung Wai-sun, Winnie (NHKA)	5,821	4.5

Constituency	Registered electorate	Turnout (%)	Candidates (group affiliation)	Number of votes	Percentage of the vote in the constituency
3. Kowloon East	217,117	82,405 (38.0)	*Szeto Wah (UDHK)	57,921	37.8
			*Li Wah-ming (MP)	49,643	32.4
			Hau Shui-pui (I)	21,225	13.9
			Poon Chi-fai (I)	16,625	10.9
			Chan Cheong (I)	3,431	2.2
			Li Ting-kit (TUC)	3,393	2.2
			Li Koi-hop, Philip (LDF)	86	0.6
4. Kowloon Central	287,373	110,043 (38.3)	*Lau Chin-shek (UDHK)	68,489	34.2
			*Lam Kui-shing, Conrad (UDHK)	56,084	28.0
			Chan Yuen-han (FTU)	44,894	22.4
			Chan Chi-kwan, Peter (HKCA)	14,145	7.1
			Yeung Lai-yin, Cecilia (HKRC)	8,257	4.1
			Young, Dragon John (I)	6,273	3.1
			Cheung Chung-ming, Justin (I)	2,158	1.1
5. Kowloon West	213,345	69,483 (32.6)	*Fung Kin-kee, Frederick (ADPL)	36,508	28.9
			*To Kun-sun, James (UDHK)	26,352	20.9
			Lee Yu-tai, Desmond (I)	21,471	17.0
			Sit Ho-yin, Kingsley (I)	18,634	14.8
			Law Cheung-kwok (ADPL)	17,145	13.6
			Ng Kin-sun (LDF)	6,098	4.8

Constituency	Registered electorate	Turnout (%)	Candidates (group affiliation)	Number of votes	Percentage of the vote in the constituency
6. New Territories East	197,614	96,637 (49.0)	*Lau Wai-hing, Emily (I)	46,515	26.3
			*Wong Wang-fat, Andrew (I)	39,806	22.5
			Kan Chung-nin, Tony (I)	37,126	21.0
			Lau Kong-wah (UDHK)	26,659	15.1
			Wong Hong-chung, Johnston (UDHK)	26,156	14.8
			Choi Man-hing (I)	348	0.2
			Leung Ka-ching, Eric (I)	306	0.2
7. New Territories South	248,045	91,780 (37.0)	*Lee Wing-tat (UDHK)	52,192	32.0
			*Chan Wai-yip, Albert (UDHK)	42,164	25.9
			Leung Yiu-chung (I)	38,568	23.7
			Yeung Fuk-kwong (I)	30,095	18.5
8. New Territories West	198,817	81,468 (41.0)	*Ng Ming-yum (UDHK)	42,319	29.4
			*Tai Chin-wah (I)	30,871	21.5
			Wong Wai-yin, Zachary (MP)	27,243	19.0
			Tang Siu-tong (I)	23,389	16.3
			Tso Shiu-wai (LDF)	20,018	14.0

Constituency	Registered electorate	Turnout (%)	Candidates (group affiliation)	Number of votes	Percentage of the vote in the constituency
9. New Territories North	121,989	46,644 (38.2)	*Fung Chi-wood (UDHK)	23,267	27.3
			*Tik Chi-yuen (MP)	21,702	25.5
			Cheung Hon-chung (LDF)	16,221	19.1
			Wong Chi-keung, Johnny (LDF)	15,350	18.0
			Chow Mei-tak, Ronald (ADPL)	7,117	8.4
			Tong Wai-man (I)	1,429	1.7
			Total	1,369,313	

*Elected candidate.
Note: Percentages of the vote in each constituency do not add up to 100% as a result of rounding.

2. Functional Constituency Elections

Constituency	Electoral division	Registered electorate	Turnout(%)	Candidates (group affiliation)	Number of votes	Percentage of the vote in the division
Commercial	First Commercial	1,609	911 (56.6)	*McGregor, James David (HKDF)	487	54.0
				Cheng Ming-fun, Paul	416	46.1
	Second Commercial	2,348	Uncontested	Wong Yu-hong, Philip		
Industrial	First Industrial	460	Uncontested	Cheong Kam-chuen, Stephen		
	Second Industrial	1,366	390 (28.6)	*Ngai Shiu-kit	216	56.5
				Seto Fai	166	43.5
Finance and Financial Services	Finance	234	Uncontested	Li Kwok-po, David		
	Financial Services	694	556 (80.1)	*Chim Pui-chung	281	47.6
				Wong Po-hang, Alex	200	33.9
				Cham Yau-tong	59	10.0
				Chan Po-fun, Peter	36	6.1
				Chum Ting-pong	9	1.5
				Wong Wun-wing, David	5	0.8

Constituency	Electoral division	Registered electorate	Turnout(%)	Candidates (group affiliation)	Number of votes	Percentage of the vote in the division
Teaching		38,678	17,034 (44.0)	*Cheung Man-kwong (UDHK)	15,193	89.8
				Ho King-on	886	5.2
				Wou Tchong-hong	836	5.0
Labour (2 seats)		378	Uncontested	Pang Chun-hoi (TUC)		
				Tam Yiu-chung (FTU)		
Social Services		181	Uncontested	Hui Yin-fat		
Medical and Health Care	Medical	4,031	Uncontested	Leong Che-hung (HKDF)		
	Health Care	10,636	Uncontested	Ho Mun-ka, Michael (UDHK)		
Legal		1,240	714 (57.6)	*Ip Sik-on, Simon	542	77.4
				Miller, John William	158	22.6

Constituency	Electoral division	Registered electorate	Turnout(%)	Candidates (group affiliation)	Number of votes	Percentage of the vote in the division
Engineering, Architectural, Surveying and Planning	Engineering	2,805	1,511 (53.9)	*Wong Ping-wai	1,334	89.8
				Tang Ka-fat	151	10.2
	Architectural, Surveying and Planning	1,481	1,039 (70.2)	*Ho Sing-tin	552	53.7
				Lau Shiu-kwan	246	24.0
				Kan Fook-yee	136	13.2
				Brooke, Charles Nicholas	94	9.1
Accountancy		2,276	Uncontested	Wong Hong-yuen (LDF)		
Real Estate and Construction		373	Uncontested	Ronald Arculli		
Tourism		847	728 (86.0)	*Young, Howard	338	40.7
				Wu Tan, Harold	318	38.3
				Yuen Ka-chai	175	21.0
Urban Council		40	Uncontested	Elsie Tu		

Constituency	Electoral division	Registered electorate	Turnout(%)	Candidates (group affiliation)	Number of votes	Percentage of the vote in the division
Regional Council		36	36 (100.0)	*Leung Kam-ho	20	40.0
				Chow Yick-hay	15	30.0
				Lam Wai-keung	10	20.0
				Chau Chun-wing	5	10.0
Rural		112	Uncontested	Lau Wong-fat		

Source: Compiled from *The Hong Kong Government Gazette Extraordinary*, 133(41), 20 September 1991, and statistics provided by the Registration and Electoral Office of the Hong Kong government.

*Elected candidate.

Note: Percentages of the vote in each electoral division do not add up to 100% as a result of rounding.

Abbreviations:

ADPL	Association for Democracy and People's Livelihood	I	Independent
FTU	Federation of Trade Unions	LDF	Liberal Democratic Federation
HKCA	Hong Kong Civic Association	MP	Meeting Point
HKCF	Hong Kong Citizen Forum	NHKA	New Hong Kong Alliance
HKDF	Hong Kong Democratic Foundation	TUC	Trades Union Council
HKRC	Hong Kong Reform Club	UDHK	United Democrats of Hong Kong

APPENDIX B   RESEARCH DESIGN

Fred Yeung

The objectives of this research were twofold. First, we wanted to explore various aspects of voting behaviour in the 1991 Legislative Council direct elections. Secondly, we wished to examine certain methodological questions stemming from the problems of conducting electoral research in Hong Kong.

Prior to the present survey, we conducted a pilot study with two-wave panel interviews of the March 1991 District Board elections in the Hong Kong South district, comprising eight constituencies. From the 190 electors sampled, 53 respondents were successfully interviewed before the elections and 37 after the elections. The pilot study helped to test the research instrument and to anticipate situations and difficulties which might arise in conducting the September survey.

We based our research for the Legislative Council elections on face-to-face interviews with the electorate in the Kowloon Central constituency, providing each interviewer with a structured questionnaire which was to be administered to the respondents. In addition, two samples were selected. The first was a panel sample with whom a pre-election interview was conducted. After the elections, a second-wave interview was administered to those respondents with whom we had conducted the pre-election interview successfully. The second sample was interviewed only after the elections.

QUESTIONNAIRE DESIGN

We devised three sets of questionnaires (see Appendix C). The pre-election questionnaire contained 60 items designed to obtain information on voting intention, intended vote choices, criteria for selecting candidates, political attitudes and stances on various issues and the respondents' personal backgrounds. The two post-election questionnaires asked key questions on voting turnout, actual vote choices and criteria for selecting candidates. The second sample was also asked questions on personal backgrounds and political attitudes. The questionnaire was in Chinese but, where necessary, an English version was also available.

SAMPLING METHOD

The Kowloon Central electorate constituted our sampling pool. We decided to focus on this particular constituency rather than all nine constituencies because the pattern of candidate competition clearly varied among constituencies and we wanted to test for a potentially wide range of political orientations and attitudes.

Kowloon Central was chosen because it provided a balanced mix of candidate types which would facilitate comparisons along a number of dimensions, including candidates' political affiliation, attitudes towards China and ideological orientation.

Information on the sampling pool was provided by the Registration and Electoral Office (REO) in July 1991. We were given the names and addresses of the electorate in both Chinese and English. The record included information on a total of 267,362 registered electors.[1]

We aimed at obtaining 1,000 successful responses for the pre-election interview, 500 for the post-election interview of the panel sample and 200 for the second sample, with whom only a post-election interview was planned. Based on a 45% response rate for the pre-election interview in the pilot study, we estimated that we would need to contact 2,230 and 450 electors for the two samples respectively.

We employed the method of 'two-stage systematic cluster sampling' with a random start.[2] First, a number was assigned to each elector record provided by the REO. The records were arranged by address. Secondly, we generated a random number as the first selection pointer. Based on this, we then took a systematic interval of 1,200 to locate other selection pointers, resulting in a total of 223 pointers. Then, on each pointer, we selected a cluster of electors. We systematically selected each tenth elector on the list and included them in our sample. Our potential respondents were then grouped into 223 clusters, each with ten electors.

The use of clusters enhances administrative efficiency in interviewing, shortening the time needed for moving from one address to the other between interviews. The use of a systematic interval of ten was to prevent successive interviewing within one household and was designed to avoid possible family influences on the respondent when a household had two or more electors.

INTERVIEWING

We sent a letter to our sampled respondents one week before fieldwork began to notify them of the purpose of the research and to solicit favourable responses from them. The pre-election survey was conducted between 7 September, about one week before polling day, and 14 September. The post-election survey was conducted between 16 and 18 September.

We recruited 86 interviewers, who were all students of The University of Hong Kong or other tertiary institutions in the territory. In early September, a training session was held, the content of which included methods of survey research, skills in interviewing, characteristics of the constituency and role-playing sessions which were intended to familiarize interviewers with the questionnaires and to identify any difficulties of interpretation which might arise.

Interviewers were instructed to conduct interviews each day from six to ten o'clock in the evening.[3] They were required to report the reason for an unsuccessful visit. A maximum of three visits was made to guarantee a reasonable response rate for those who were not at home at the time of the initial visit.

SURVEY RESPONSES

The response rates are shown in Table B.1. We obtained successful interviews with about half of the electors we had selected. There were several types of unsuccessful responses. Taking the pre-election survey of the panel sample as an example, one type was that the address information of the elector was defective either because the address was incomplete or wrong or because the elector had moved, emigrated or was deceased. Such responses constituted 31.3% (369 cases) of the total unsuccessful responses, or 16.5% of the total sample size, and have been excluded from the effective sample. The second type consisted

Table B.1 Response rates of surveys

	Pre-election	Post-election(1)	Post-election(2)
Sample size	2,230	1,052	450
Defective sample size	369	0	101
Effective sample size[a]	1,861	1,052	349
Successful responses	1,052	631	171
Response rate[b]	56.5%	60.0%	49.0%

Note: 'Pre-election' and 'post-election(1)' refer to the surveys of the panel sample. 'Post-election (2)' refers to the survey of the second sample, with whom we conducted interviews only after the elections.

[a] The effective sample excludes electors whose information was identified to be defective either because the address information was wrong or incomplete, or because the elector had moved, or emigrated, or was deceased. The effective sample size equals sample size minus defective sample size.

[b] 'Response rate' equals the number of successful responses divided by the effective sample size.

of respondents who refused to be interviewed, and those absent at the time of the visits. The reason for the third type of unsuccessful response was unidentifiable because there was no answer to the three visits made by our interviewers. The second and third types constituted the unsuccessful responses.

Table B.2 contains the classification of invalid responses. We checked the returned questionnaires and controlled for the quality of the responses by telephoning a random sample of the respondents. Returned questionnaires which were considered to have been administered in a manner inconsistent with the requirements of the research were classified as invalid and were excluded. After completing this exercise, we had in hand 1,046 cases for the pre-election survey, 570 cases for the post-election survey of the panel sample and 141 cases for the second sample. These constitute the data on which our analysis is based.

Table B.2 Classification of invalid responses

	Pre-election	Post-election(1)	Post-election(2)
Telephone interview	0	18	2
Not a designated respondent	0	2	0
Interviewer problem[a]	1	39	27
Expatriate respondent[b]	4	0	0
Others	1	2	1
Total	6	61	30

[a] Some interviewers were found to have used unreliable practices in conducting interviews. These responses were invalidated.

[b] There were expatriate respondents in our samples. We conducted interviews with them using an English version of the questionnaire. However, since the number of cases was very small, these responses were excluded from the final analysis.

NOTES

1. The actual number of electors in the Kowloon Central constituency at the time was 276,032. The record obtained comprised only 267,362 electors. The discrepancy was the result of a technical problem encountered in transferring data files from the Registration and Electoral Office.

2. See E. Babbie, *Survey Research Methods* (Belmont, California: Wadsworth, 1990), pp.84-91.

3. The fieldwork on Saturdays was conducted from two o'clock in the afternoon to ten o'clock in the evening.

APPENDIX C QUESTIONNAIRES*

1. PRE-ELECTION SURVEY

I. Personal Particulars and Voting Behaviour

1. How old are you?

    | Fill in the exact age if possible. |

    1 [ ] 21-29 years
    2 [ ] 30-39 years
    3 [ ] 40-49 years
    4 [ ] 50-59 years
    5 [ ] 60 years or above   _____

2. Sex

    1 [ ] Male
    2 [ ] Female

3. What is your marital status?

    1 [ ] Single
    2 [ ] Married
    3 [ ] Widowed
    4 [ ] Divorced/separated

4a. What is your current occupation?

    | Record the answer. |

    1 [ ] Sector ————————
             Position/rank ————— ⊢ Go to Q. 5
    2 [ ] I am not employed at the moment

---

* Translated from the original Chinese version.

4b. How would you describe your status?

    1   [ ]   Housewife
    2   [ ]   Student
    3   [ ]   Unemployed/looking for employment
    4   [ ]   Retired
    5   [ ]   Others (please specify)_____

5. What is your level of education?

    1   [ ]   No formal education/below primary level
    2   [ ]   Primary level
    3   [ ]   Secondary level
    4   [ ]   Matriculation level
    5   [ ]   Tertiary: non-degree programmes
    6   [ ]   Tertiary: degree programmes/post-graduate level
                  (e.g. Masters/Doctorate programmes, etc.)

6. How long have you been living in this constituency?

> If the respondent is unable to specify the exact number of years, record the closest approximation.

    1   [ ]   Under 1 year
    2   [ ]   1 year to less than 3 years
    3   [ ]   3 years to less than 5 years
    4   [ ]   5 years to less than 10 years
    5   [ ]   10 years or over

7a. Have you voted before?

    1   [ ]   Yes
    2   [ ]   No ──────────────┐
    3   [ ]   Can't remember ────┴── Go to Q. 8a

7b. Have you voted 3 times or more in the past?

    1   [ ]   Yes
    2   [ ]   No
    3   [ ]   Can't remember

8a. Do you intend to vote in the coming Legislative Council elections?

    1   [ ]   Yes ── Answer Q.8b, then go to Q.9
    2   [ ]   No ── Answer Q.8c-12, then go to Q.32
    3   [ ]   Not yet decided ── Answer Q.9-14, then go to Q. 15c

8b. Please specify and rank in order of importance three
major reasons why you intend to vote.

> If the respondent can only think of one or two reasons,
> the interviewer should press on by asking: 'Any more?' If
> no further reason can be identified, the interviewer should
> record the answer as it is given. Ask the respondent to
> rank the most important reason as '1' and proceed down-
> wards to '2' and '3'.

Order

01 [ ] _____ To support the political group that I favour
02 [ ] _____ To fulfil my civic responsibility
03 [ ] _____ To influence government policies
04 [ ] _____ To protect my personal interests
05 [ ] _____ Voting is a channel for me to express
my views on government policies
06 [ ] _____ Influenced by family members/friends
07 [ ] _____ Influenced by the leader(s) of a
particular political group
08 [ ] _____ There is a candidate in my constituency
whom I admire/support
09 [ ] _____ My neighbours are all going to vote
10 [ ] _____ Others (please specify) _____
11 [ ] _____ I am not sure/don't know

8c. What is the main reason that you are not going to vote?

> Tick one answer only.

1 [ ] No time
2 [ ] No interest
3 [ ] There is no suitable candidate in my
constituency
4 [ ] The powers of the Legislative Council are
too limited to influence government policies
5 [ ] It is useless to go and vote because Hong Kong
will eventually come under China's control
6 [ ] Others (please specify) _____

9. Can you tell me the exact date of this year's Legislative Council elections?
(The correct date is: 15 September)
    1   [ ]   Correct
    2   [ ]   Incorrect
    3   [ ]   Don't know

10. Do you know how many Legislative Council directly elected seats there are in the whole of Hong Kong?
(The correct number is: 18)

    1   [ ]   Correct
    2   [ ]   Incorrect
    3   [ ]   Don't know

11. Do you know which constituency you belong to?
(The correct answer is: Kowloon Central)

    1   [ ]   Correct
    2   [ ]   Incorrect _____

    | Record the respondent's answers |

    3   [ ]   Don't know

12. Do you know how many candidates are contesting the directly elected seats in your constituency?
(The correct number is: 7)

    1   [ ]   Correct
    2   [ ]   Incorrect
    3   [ ]   Don't know

II. Personal Attributes of Candidates

13. In an ideal situation, what factors would you take into account when choosing your Legislative Council candidate?

> Ask the respondent to mention 3 factors and rank them in order of importance, with '1' as the most important. If the respondent identifies only 1 or 2 factors, the interviewer should press on by asking: 'Any more?'

Order

01	[ ] _____	Educational attainment
02	[ ] _____	Age
03	[ ] _____	Occupation
04	[ ] _____	Sex
05	[ ] _____	Residence in the district
06	[ ] _____	Membership of a particular political group
07	[ ] _____	Membership of a particular social/community organization
08	[ ] _____	Charisma/appearance
09	[ ] _____	Social status/prestige
10	[ ] _____	Style of work
11	[ ] _____	Willingness to serve society/us
12	[ ] _____	Policy stance/platform
13	[ ] _____	Past performance/experience
14	[ ] _____	Acquaintance with candidate
15	[ ] _____	Candidate is supported by a particular political group
16	[ ] _____	Candidate is supported by a particular social/community organization
17	[ ] _____	Candidate is supported by renowned individuals
18	[ ] _____	My family members/friends/neighbours are all going to vote for this candidate
19	[ ] _____	Others (please specify) _____
20	[ ] _____	No particular criterion in my mind

14. If there are two candidates, one male and one female, who are equal in all other respects, would you vote for the male or female candidate?

    1   [ ]   Male
    2   [ ]   Female
    3   [ ]   No strong preference one way or the other

15a. Have you decided who to vote for in this month's Legislative Council elections?

    1   [ ]   Yes
    2   [ ]   No —— Go to Q.15c

15b. So who do you intend to vote for? Who else?

> As far as possible, try to solicit and record two names from the respondent.
>
> (i)   If the respondent gives two names, go to Q.16.
> (ii) If the respondent gives only one name, go to Q.16, then proceed to Q.18.
> (iii) If the respondent gives two names, neither of which is of candidates running in the Kowloon Central constituency, go to Q.32.

Names of candidates: (1) _____
(2) _____

15c. If you were to cast your votes now, which two candidates would you vote for?

> As far as possible, try to solicit and record two names from the respondent.
>
> (i) If the respondent cannot decide, go to Q.22.
> (ii) If the respondent gives two names, neither of which is of candidates running in the Kowloon Central constituency, go to Q.32.

Names of candidates: (1) _____
(2) _____

16. Why would you choose candidates (1) _____/
and (2)_____? Any further reasons?

> The respondent should identify and rank three reasons, with '1' as the most important. If the respondent gives only one or two reasons, the interviewer should ask: 'Any more?' If the respondent has chosen only one candidate, only fill in the relevant sections.

Candidate (1)	*Candidate (2)*
Order	*Order*

#			#		
01	[ ] _____	Educational attainment	[ ] _____	Educational attainment
02	[ ] _____	Age	[ ] _____	Age
03	[ ] _____	Occupation	[ ] _____	Occupation
04	[ ] _____	Sex	[ ] _____	Sex
05	[ ] _____	Residence in the district	[ ] _____	Residence in the district
06	[ ] _____	Membership of a particular political group	[ ] _____	Membership of a particular political group
07	[ ] _____	Membership of a particular social/ community organization	[ ] _____	Membership of a particular social/ community organization
08	[ ] _____	Charisma/ appearance	[ ] _____	Charisma/ appearance
09	[ ] _____	Social status/ prestige	[ ] _____	Social status/ prestige
10	[ ] _____	Style of work	[ ] _____	Style of work
11	[ ] _____	Willingness to serve society/us	[ ] _____	Willingness to serve society/us
12	[ ] _____	Policy stance/ platform	[ ] _____	Policy stance/ platform
13	[ ] _____	Past performance/ Experience	[ ] _____	Past performance/ Experience
14	[ ] _____	Acquaintance with candidate	[ ] _____	Acquaintance with candidate
15	[ ] _____	Candidate is supported by a particular political group	[ ] _____	Candidate is supported by a particular political group
16	[ ] _____	Candidate is supported by a particular social/ community organization	[ ] _____	Candidate is supported by a particular social/ community organization
17	[ ] _____	Candidate is supported by renowned individuals	[ ] _____	Candidate is supported by renowned individuals

18 [ ] _____ My family   [ ] _____ My family
           members/friends/   members/friends/
           neighbours are all   neighbours are all
           going to vote for   going to vote for
           this candidate   this candidate

19 [ ] _____ Others (please   [ ] _____ Others (please
           specify)   specify)

           _____   _____

20 [ ] _____ No particular   [ ] _____ No particular
           criterion in my mind   criterion in my mind

17. If you could only vote for one candidate, would you rather choose
candidate (1) _____ or
candidate (2) _____ ?

    1   [ ]   Name of candidate: _____

> The respondent should answer questions Q.18-21 on
> the basis of this chosen candidate.

    2   [ ]   Don't know how to choose ——— Go to Q. 22

18. How good is your understanding of _____'s
overall election platform?

    1   [ ]   Very good
    2   [ ]   Good
    3   [ ]   Partial
    4   [ ]   Not very good ——┐
    5   [ ]   Not good at all ——┴ Go to Q. 20

19. Now we would like your views on _____.
First, we will talk about his/her election platform.
Please choose one answer from this card.

> SHOW RED CARD

1	2	3	4	5	6
Strongly agree	Agree	Neutral	Disagree	Strongly disagree	Not sure/ no opinion

You think his/her election platform is

	1	2	3	4	5	6
a. Clear	☐	☐	☐	☐	☐	☐
b. Practicable	☐	☐	☐	☐	☐	☐
c. Compatible with your own view	☐	☐	☐	☐	☐	☐

20. _____'s past service records are very impressive.

1	2	3	4	5	6
☐	☐	☐	☐	☐	☐

21. _____'s sincerity in serving the society and the public cannot be questioned.

1	2	3	4	5	6
☐	☐	☐	☐	☐	☐

III. Political Groups

22. Can you identify from this list those candidates who are running in your constituency?

> SHOW YELLOW CARD. If the respondent cannot recognize any name from the answer card, go to Q.32.

Can correctly identify _____ names

23. Can you specify the political stance/inclination of those candidates whom you have just identified?

> Ask the respondent to answer this question in relation to every individual candidate he/she has identified. If the respondent is unclear about the meaning of 'political stance/inclination', or if the respondent confuses political stance with political groups such as the United Democrats of Hong Kong and the Liberal Democratic Federation etc., the interviewer should explain that political stance refers to whether the candidate is, for example, liberal or pro-China, etc.

Names of candidates	Political stance/ inclination
LAU Chin-shek	_____
Conrad LAM Kui-shing	_____
Peter CHAN Chi-kwan	_____
Cecilia YEUNG Lai-yin	_____
CHAN Yuen-han	_____
John YOUNG	_____
Justin CHEUNG Chung-ming	_____

24. Can you specify if they belong to any political group, or are they running as independents?

Names of candidates	Name of political group(s)	Independent ($\sqrt{}$)
LAU Chin-shek	_____	_____
Conrad LAM Kui-shing	_____	_____
Peter CHAN Chi-kwan	_____	_____
Cecilia YEUNG Lai-yin	_____	_____
CHAN Yuen-han	_____	_____
John YOUNG	_____	_____
Justin CHEUNG Chung-ming	_____	_____

> Q.25-Q.26c should be answered with reference to the chosen candidates as indicated in Q.15b or Q.15c. If the respondent has not chosen any candidate in those two questions, go to Q.28. If the respondent has chosen only one candidate, fill in the relevant sections only in Q.25-Q.26c.

25. You mentioned just now that you intended to vote for candidate (1) _____ and/(2) _____. Is your choice based on his/her/their political stance?

Candidate (1)	Candidate (2)	
[ ]	[ ]	1. Yes
[ ]	[ ]	2. No

26a. Is your choice based on the political group(s) to which he/she/
they belong?

Candidate (1)   Candidate (2)

   [ ]   [ ]   1. Yes
   [ ]   [ ]   2. No ——— Go to Q.27

26b. If yes, are you thinking of the characteristics of the group(s)(e.g.
their organization, their stance, etc.) or those of the leader(s) of
the group(s)?

Candidate (1)   Candidate (2)

   [ ]   [ ]   1. Characteristics of the
                                 group(s) ⌐
   [ ]   [ ]   2. Personal qualities   ⊢ Go to
                                 of leader(s) ⌐   Q. 27
   [ ]   [ ]   3. Both
   [ ]   [ ]   4. Don't know——— Go to Q.27

26c. Which is more important?

Candidate (1)   Candidate (2)

   [ ]   [ ]   1. Characteristics of the group
   [ ]   [ ]   2. Personal qualities of leader(s)
   [ ]   [ ]   3. Both/don't know

27. When you choose your candidates, how much influence do you
think the following groups of people will have on your choice?

┌────────────────────────┐
│   SHOW GREEN CARD   │
└────────────────────────┘

1	2	3	4	5
Not influential	Fairly influential	Very influential	Extremely influential	No opinion/ not sure

	1	2	3	4	5
a. Family members	□	□	□	□	□
b. Friends/colleagues	□	□	□	□	□
c. Neighbours	□	□	□	□	□

	1	2	3	4	5
d. Political groups/community leaders	☐	☐	☐	☐	☐
e. Mass media	☐	☐	☐	☐	☐
f. Others (please specify) _____	☐	☐	☐	☐	☐

IV.   *Stance on Public Policies*

28. In your opinion, what are the two most important problems confronting Hong Kong at the moment?

> If the respondent identifies less than two problems, the interviewer should press on by asking: 'Any more?' Ask the respondent to prioritize the relative importance of the two problems, with '1' as the more important. If the respondent fails to mention any problem, go to Q.32.

The most important problems   Order of
confronting Hong Kong   importance

(a) _____   _____
(b) _____   _____

> If the respondent mentions only one problem, proceed to Q.29; if he/she mentions two problems, go to Q.30. If the problems mentioned fall outside the list identified in Q.32-Q.41, go to Q.32.

29. As regards problem (a) _____, do you think that the candidates in this constituency hold very different positions or have very different approaches to the problem?

    1   [ ]   Yes ———————————— Go to Q.31
    2   [ ]   No
    3   [ ]   Not sure
    4   [ ]   The candidates' positions/   Go to Q.32
                approaches to the problem
                are not very clear

30. As regards these two problems, do the candidates in your constituency hold very different positions or have very different approaches to the problems?

Problem *Problem*
  (a)   *(b)*

[ ]	[ ]	Yes ——————————— Go to Q.31
[ ]	[ ]	No
[ ]	[ ]	Not sure
[ ]	[ ]	The candidates' positions/ ⎱ Go to Q.32
		approaches to the problem
		are not very clear

> If the respondent has made no choice of candidates in the answer to Q.15b or Q.15c, go to Q.32. If the respondent has chosen only one candidate in those two questions, fill in the relevant sections only.

31. You mentioned just now that you would vote for candidate(s) (1)_____ /and (2) _____.Regarding the (two) important problem(s) you have identified, do you think he/she/they would agree with the following statement(s)?

> Read out from among Q.32-Q.41 the statement(s) which is/are relevant to the problem area(s) identified by the respondent. Let him/her choose the answer.
> SHOW BLUE CARD

Problems	Candi-date(s)	Strongly agree	Agree	Neutral	Disagree	Strongly disagree	Not sure about candidate's position	Candidate's position not clear
		1	2	3	4	5	6	7
(a)	(1)	☐	☐	☐	☐	☐	☐	☐
	(2)	☐	☐	☐	☐	☐	☐	☐
(b)	(1)	☐	☐	☐	☐	☐	☐	☐
	(2)	☐	☐	☐	☐	☐	☐	☐

The following is a list of questions relating to various areas of public policy in Hong Kong. We would like to know your views on these issues. Please choose one answer from this card.

> SHOW WHITE CARD

1	2	3	4	5
Strongly agree	Agree	Disagree	Strongly disagree	Don't know/ no opinion

32. *Inflation*

If economic growth results in inflation, I would rather have the government control inflation, even if it means having to slow down the growth of the economy.

1	2	3	4	5
☐	☐	☐	☐	☐

33. *Law and order*

The death penalty should not be reintroduced in Hong Kong.

1	2	3	4	5
☐	☐	☐	☐	☐

34. *Vietnamese boat people*

Hong Kong should immediately abolish the first asylum policy for Vietnamese boat people.

1	2	3	4	5
☐	☐	☐	☐	☐

35. *Sino-Hong Kong relations*

China should not play a decision-making role in the internal affairs of Hong Kong; the most it can do is to express its views.

1	2	3	4	5
☐	☐	☐	☐	☐

36. *Foreign labour*

Hong Kong should continue to import foreign labour.

1	2	3	4	5
☐	☐	☐	☐	☐

37. *Housing*   1   2   3   4   5

The government should immediately   ☐   ☐   ☐   ☐   ☐
introduce a capital gains tax on property
transactions to curb speculation in the
property market.

38. *Social security/welfare*   1   2   3   4   5

Hong Kong cannot at the moment   ☐   ☐   ☐   ☐   ☐
afford to spend more on social
security.

39. *Taxation*   1   2   3   4   5

If taxes have to be increased, the   ☐   ☐   ☐   ☐   ☐
increase should first be applied to
profits tax.

40. *Medical services*   1   2   3   4   5

The charges for medical services   ☐   ☐   ☐   ☐   ☐
should not be linked to cost
considerations.

41. *Environmental protection*   1   2   3   4   5

Protection of the environment is a   ☐   ☐   ☐   ☐   ☐
worthy cause, even if it means a rise
in the cost of industrial production.

V. Political Attitudes

We would like to find out your opinions on the following statements. Please choose one answer from this card.

SHOW ORANGE CARD

1	2	3	4	5	6
Strongly agree	Agree	Neutral	Disagree	Strongly disagree	Don't know/ no opinion

42. Generally speaking, Hong Kong citizens can influence government policies.

|1|2|3|4|5|6|
|☐|☐|☐|☐|☐|☐|

43. It is useful to make a complaint if you are dissatisfied with a government policy.

|1|2|3|4|5|6|
|☐|☐|☐|☐|☐|☐|

44. You trust that the Hong Kong government will protect the interests of the Hong Kong people.

|1|2|3|4|5|6|
|☐|☐|☐|☐|☐|☐|

45. You are generally satisfied with the social policies pursued by the government.

|1|2|3|4|5|6|
|☐|☐|☐|☐|☐|☐|

46. You are prepared to pay more taxes so as to enable the government to provide more social welfare services.

|1|2|3|4|5|6|
|☐|☐|☐|☐|☐|☐|

47. You believe that the Hong Kong government is able to maintain the territory's stability and prosperity during the transitional period.

|1|2|3|4|5|6|
|☐|☐|☐|☐|☐|☐|

48. In handling conflicts between China and Hong Kong, the acceptance of China's opinion is of predominant importance.

|1|2|3|4|5|6|
|☐|☐|☐|☐|☐|☐|

49. You believe that Hong Kong will continue to be stable and prosperous after 1997.

|1|2|3|4|5|6|
|☐|☐|☐|☐|☐|☐|

50. It is better to leave government to a capable leader than to require citizens to scrutinize it constantly.

1	2	3	4	5	6
☐	☐	☐	☐	☐	☐

51. You will definitely leave Hong Kong if the opportunity arises.

1	2	3	4	5	6
☐	☐	☐	☐	☐	☐

VI. Personal Particulars (continued)

Finally, we would like to know more about your personal particulars.

> For Q.52 and Q.53, show respondent the range of options if he/she appears hesitant.

52. What is your personal monthly income?

       1   [ ] No income
       2   [ ] Under $3,000
       3   [ ] $3,000 – $5,999
       4   [ ] $6,000 – $9,999
       5   [ ] $10,000 – $14,999
       6   [ ] $15,000 – $19,999
       7   [ ] $20,000 – $49,999
       8   [ ] $50,000 and above
       9   [ ] Refuse to answer

53. What is your total monthly household income?

       1   [ ] Under $3,000
       2   [ ] $3,000 – $5,999
       3   [ ] $6,000 – $9,999
       4   [ ] $10,000 – $14,999
       5   [ ] $15,000 – $19,999
       6   [ ] $20,000 – $49,999
       7   [ ] $50,000 – $79,999
       8   [ ] $80,000 and above
       9   [ ] Refuse to answer

54. Do you have any religious beliefs?

    1   [ ] Protestant
    2   [ ] Catholic
    3   [ ] Buddhist
    4   [ ] Muslim
    5   [ ] Others (please specify) _____
    6   [ ] No religious belief

55. How long have you been living in Hong Kong?

    1   [ ] Under 10 years
    2   [ ] 10 - 20 years
    3   [ ] Over 20 years

56. When you think of your identity, do you see yourself more as a Hongkonger, or more as a Chinese?

    1   [ ] Chinese
    2   [ ] Hongkonger
    3   [ ] Both
    4   [ ] Neither
    5   [ ] No opinion/refuse to answer

57. What type of housing are you living in?

> The interviewer should observe by himself/herself. This question should be raised only if the interviewer is uncertain of the answer.

    1   [ ] Public housing — Go to Q.59
    2   [ ] Private sector housing
    3   [ ] Home ownership scheme housing
    4   [ ] Villa/bungalow
    5   [ ] Temporary housing/squatter
    6   [ ] Others (please specify) _____

58. Do you own or rent this place?

    1   [ ] Self-ownership (no need to pay instalments)
    2   [ ] Ownership through instalments
    3   [ ] Rented
    4   [ ] Housing benefits/staff quarters
    5   [ ] Others (please specify) _____

59. Do you belong to any groups/organizations?

> The respondent should first be allowed to answer on his/her own. The interviewer should then follow up by going through the following list.

01   [ ]   Religious organizations
02   [ ]   Professional organizations
03   [ ]   Labour organizations/unions
04   [ ]   Political groups (United Democrats, Liberal Democratic Federation, etc.)
05   [ ]   Pressure groups (livelihood concern groups, etc.)
06   [ ]   Kaifong associations
07   [ ]   Neighbourhood organizations (mutual aid committees, owners' associations, etc.)
08   [ ]   Community organizations (youth clubs, Caritas, etc.)
09   [ ]   Recreational organizations (Football Association, Country Club, etc.)
10   [ ]   Others (please specify) _____

60. Which social class do you see yourself as belonging to?

1   [ ]   Lower class
2   [ ]   Lower-middle class
3   [ ]   Middle class
4   [ ]   Upper-middle class
5   [ ]   Upper class
6   [ ]   Don't know

> Thank you very much for your co-operation.

2. POST-ELECTION SURVEY (1)

1. Did you vote on Sunday, 15 September?

    1   [ ]   Yes
    2   [ ]   No ——————— Go to Q.11

2. Please specify and rank in order of importance three major reasons why you voted.

    > If the respondent can only think of one or two reasons, the interviewer should press on by asking: 'Any more?' If no further reason can be identified, the interviewer should record the answer as it is given. Ask the respondent to rank the most important reason as '1' and proceed downwards to '2' and '3'.

    Order

    01   [ ] _____   To support the political group that I favour
    02   [ ] _____   To fulfil my civic responsibility
    03   [ ] _____   To influence government policies
    04   [ ] _____   To protect my personal interests
    05   [ ] _____   Voting is a channel for me to express my views on government policies
    06   [ ] _____   Influenced by family members/friends
    07   [ ] _____   Influenced by the leader(s) of a particular political group
    08   [ ] _____   There is a candidate in my constituency whom I admire/support
    09   [ ] _____   My neighbours are all going to vote
    10   [ ] _____   Others (please specify) _____
    11   [ ] _____   I am not sure/don't know

3. Who did you vote for? Who else?

    > If the respondent has voted for only one candidate, skip Q.5 and Q.6.

1 _____ (1)
2 _____ (2)
3 Blank vote. (Specify reason for casting such a vote, then end the interview.)

_____

_____

4. Please list and rank in order of importance the three most important reasons why you voted for Candidate (1) _____ ?

> '1' is the most important reason. If the respondent can only think of one or two reasons, the interviewer should press on by asking: 'Any more?'

Order

01	[ ] _____	Educational attainment
02	[ ] _____	Age
03	[ ] _____	Occupation
04	[ ] _____	Sex
05	[ ] _____	Residence in the district
06	[ ] _____	Membership of a particular political group
07	[ ] _____	Membership of a particular social/community organization
08	[ ] _____	Charisma/appearance
09	[ ] _____	Social status/prestige
10	[ ] _____	Style of work
11	[ ] _____	Willingness to serve society/us
12	[ ] _____	Policy stance/platform
13	[ ] _____	Past performance/experience
14	[ ] _____	Acquaintance with candidate
15	[ ] _____	Candidate is supported by a particular political group
16	[ ] _____	Candidate is supported by a particular social/community organization
17	[ ] _____	Candidate is supported by renowned individuals
18	[ ] _____	My family members/friends/neighbours are all going to vote for this candidate
19	[ ] _____	Others (please specify) _____
20	[ ] _____	No particular criterion in my mind

5. Please also list and rank in order of importance the three most important reasons why you voted for candidate (2) _____?

> '1' is the most important reason. If the respondent can only think of one or two reasons, the interviewer should press on by asking: 'Any more?'

Order

01	[ ]	_____	Educational attainment
02	[ ]	_____	Age
03	[ ]	_____	Occupation
04	[ ]	_____	Sex
05	[ ]	_____	Residence in the district
06	[ ]	_____	Membership of a particular political group
07	[ ]	_____	Membership of a particular social/ community organization
08	[ ]	_____	Charisma/appearance
09	[ ]	_____	Social status/prestige
10	[ ]	_____	Style of work
11	[ ]	_____	Willingness to serve society/us
12	[ ]	_____	Policy stance/platform
13	[ ]	_____	Past performance/experience
14	[ ]	_____	Acquaintance with candidate
15	[ ]	_____	Candidate is supported by a particular political group
16	[ ]	_____	Candidate is supported by a particular social/community organization
17	[ ]	_____	Candidate is supported by renowned individuals
18	[ ]	_____	My family members/friends/neighbours are all going to vote for this candidate
19	[ ]	_____	Others (please specify) _____
20	[ ]	_____	No particular criterion in my mind

6. Of the two candidates you voted for, whom did you like better?

1	[ ]	Please specify name of candidate: _____
2	[ ]	Don't know how to choose between the two

> If the respondent did not vote for the candidate whom he/
> she expressed an intention to vote for at the last inter-
> view, go to Q.7; if the candidates chosen were the same
> as the ones named at the previous interview, go to Q.8.

7. You mentioned at the last interview that you intended to vote for
   (1)_____ and (2)_____. Why didn't you vote
   for them eventually?

   Specify reasons: Candidate (1) _____
                     Candidate (2) _____

8. When did you decide to vote for him/her/them? Was it right after
   the government announced the list of candidates? Was it one
   week before the elections? Or was it on your way to the polling
   station?

   1   [ ]   Right after the government announced the list of
              candidates
   2   [ ]   One week before the elections
   3   [ ]   On my way to the polling station
   4   [ ]   Can't remember
   5   [ ]   Others (please specify) _____

   > Fill in the corresponding number of the chosen option for
   > each candidate.

                Candidate (1)_____
                Candidate (2)_____

9. How influential were the following factors upon your vote
   decision(s)?

   > SHOW GREEN CARD

1	2	3	4	5
Not influential	Fairly influential	Very influential	Extremely influential	No opinion/ not sure

		1	2	3	4	5
1	The personal qualities of the candidate(s)	☐	☐	☐	☐	☐
2	His/her/their stance on public policies	☐	☐	☐	☐	☐
3	The political group to which he/ she/they belong(s)	☐	☐	☐	☐	☐
4	The leader(s) of the political group to which he/she/they belong(s)	☐	☐	☐	☐	☐

10. Of the four factors listed, how would you rank their importance?

> Interviewer should read out the four factors once more. '1' is the most important factor.

Order of importance

1 The personal qualities of the candidate(s) _____
2 His/her/their stance on public policies _____
3 The political group to which he/she/ they belong(s) _____
4 The leader(s) of the political group to which he/she/ they belong(s) _____

> For those who have voted, skip Q.11 and go to Q.12.

11. What is the main reason that you did not go to vote?

> Give one answer only.

1 [ ] No time
2 [ ] No interest
3 [ ] There is no suitable candidate in my constituency
4 [ ] The powers of the Legislative Council are too limited to influence government policies
5 [ ] It is useless to go and vote because Hong Kong will eventually come under China's control
6 [ ] Others (please specify) _____

12. Can you name the two candidates who have won the Legislative Council seats in your constituency? _____
    (The correct answers are: LAU Chin-shek and Conrad LAM kui-shing.)

    | 1 | [ ] | Both names correctly identified |
    | 2 | [ ] | One name correctly identified |
    | 3 | [ ] | No name correctly identified/don't know |

    > For those who have voted, proceed to Q.13; otherwise end interview here.

13. Are you aware of the fact that the directly elected legislators only comprise a minority in the Legislative Council, so that they can play only a limited role in the political system?

    | 1 | [ ] | Yes, I am aware of that |
    | 2 | [ ] | No, I am not aware of that ── End of Interview |

14. So why did you still decide to vote?
    Please specify reason(s) _____
    _____

> Thank you very much for your co-operation.

3. POST-ELECTION SURVEY (2)

1. How old are you?

   | Fill in the exact age if possible. |

   1   [ ]   21-29 years
   2   [ ]   30-39 years
   3   [ ]   40-49 years
   4   [ ]   50-59 years
   5   [ ]   60 years or above   _____

2. Sex

   1   [ ]   Male
   2   [ ]   Female

3. What is your marital status?

   1   [ ]   Single
   2   [ ]   Married
   3   [ ]   Widowed
   4   [ ]   Divorced/separated

4a. What is your current occupation?

   | Record the answer. |

   1   [ ]   Sector ———————————
                 Position/rank —————————— Go to Q. 5
   2   [ ]   I am not employed at the moment

4b. How would you describe your status?

   1   [ ]   Housewife
   2   [ ]   Student
   3   [ ]   Unemployed/looking for employment
   4   [ ]   Retired
   5   [ ]   Others (please specify) _____

5. What is your level of education?

1   [ ]   No formal education/below primary level
2   [ ]   Primary level
3   [ ]   Secondary level
4   [ ]   Matriculation level
5   [ ]   Tertiary: non-degree programmes
6   [ ]   Tertiary: degree programmes/post-graduate level
                  (e.g. Masters/Doctorate programmes, etc.)

6. How long have you been living in this constituency?

> If the respondent is unable to specify the exact number of years, record the closest approximation.

1   [ ]   Under 1 year
2   [ ]   1 year to less than 3 years
3   [ ]   3 years to less than 5 years
4   [ ]   5 years to less than 10 years
5   [ ]   10 years or over

7. Did you vote on Sunday, 15 September?

1   [ ]   Yes ———— Go to Q.9
2   [ ]   No ———— Continue Q.8, then go to Q.19

8. What is the main reason that you did not go to vote?

> Give one answer only.

1   [ ]   No time
2   [ ]   No interest
3   [ ]   There is no suitable candidate in my constituency
4   [ ]   The powers of the Legislative Council are too limited to influence government policies
5   [ ]   It is useless to go and vote because Hong Kong will eventually come under China's control
6   [ ]   Others (please specify) _____

9. Can you specify and rank in order of importance three reasons why you have voted?

> If the respondent can only think of one or two reasons, the interviewer should press on by asking: 'Any more?' If no further reason can be identified, the interviewer should record the answer as it is given. Please ask the respondent to rank the most important reason as '1' and proceed downwards to '2' and '3'.

Order

01 [ ] _____ To support the political group that I favour
02 [ ] _____ To fulfil my civic responsibility
03 [ ] _____ To influence government policies
04 [ ] _____ To protect my personal interests
05 [ ] _____ Voting is a channel for me to express my views on government policies
06 [ ] _____ Influenced by family members/friends
07 [ ] _____ Influenced by the leader(s) of a particular political group
08 [ ] _____ There is a candidate in my constituency whom I admire/support
09 [ ] _____ My neighbours are all going to vote
10 [ ] _____ Others (please specify) _____
11 [ ] _____ I am not sure/don't know

10. Who did you vote for? Who else?

> If the respondent has voted for only one candidate, skip Q.12 and Q.13.

1 _____(1)
2 _____(2)
3 Blank vote. (Specify reason for casting such a vote, then go to Q.19.) _____
   _____

11. Please list and rank in order of importance the three most impor-
    tant reasons why you voted for candidate (1) _____ ?

> '1' is the most important reason. If the respondent can
> only think of one or two reasons, the interviewer should
> press on by asking: 'Any more?'

Order

01	[ ] _____	Educational attainment
02	[ ] _____	Age
03	[ ] _____	Occupation
04	[ ] _____	Sex
05	[ ] _____	Residence in the district
06	[ ] _____	Membership of a particular political group
07	[ ] _____	Membership of a particular social/ community organization
08	[ ] _____	Charisma/appearance
09	[ ] _____	Social status/prestige
10	[ ] _____	Style of work
11	[ ] _____	Willingness to serve society/us
12	[ ] _____	Policy stance/platform
13	[ ] _____	Past performance/experience
14	[ ] _____	Acquaintance with candidate
15	[ ] _____	Candidate is supported by a particular political group
16	[ ] _____	Candidate is supported by a particular social/community organization
17	[ ] _____	Candidate is supported by renowned individuals
18	[ ] _____	My family members/friends/neighbours are all going to vote for this candidate
19	[ ] _____	Others (please specify) _____
20	[ ] _____	No particular criterion in my mind

12. Can you list the three most important reasons why you voted for
    candidate (2) _____ ?

> '1' is the most important reason. If the respondent can
> only think of one or two reasons, the interviewer should
> press on by asking: 'Any more?'

Order

01 [ ] _____ Educational attainment
02 [ ] _____ Age
03 [ ] _____ Occupation
04 [ ] _____ Sex
05 [ ] _____ Residence in the district
06 [ ] _____ Membership of a particular political group
07 [ ] _____ Membership of a particular social/
           community organization
08 [ ] _____ Charisma/appearance
09 [ ] _____ Social status/prestige
10 [ ] _____ Style of work
11 [ ] _____ Willingness to serve society/us
12 [ ] _____ Policy stance/platform
13 [ ] _____ Past performance/experience
14 [ ] _____ Acquaintance with candidate
15 [ ] _____ Candidate is supported by a particular
           political group
16 [ ] _____ Candidate is supported by a particular
           social/community organization
17 [ ] _____ Candidate is supported by renowned
           individuals
18 [ ] _____ My family members/friends/neighbours are
           all going to vote for this candidate
19 [ ] _____ Others (please specify) _____
20 [ ] _____ No particular criterion in my mind

13. Of the two candidates you voted for, whom did you like better?

1 [ ] Please specify name of candidate: _____
2 [ ] Don't know how to choose between the two

14. When did you decide to vote for him/her/them? Was it right after the government announced the list of candidates? Was it one week before the elections? Or was it on your way to the polling station?

1 [ ] Right after the government announced the list
        of candidates
2 [ ] One week before the elections
3 [ ] On my way to the polling station
4 [ ] Can't remember
5 [ ] Others (please specify) _____

Fill in the corresponding number of the chosen option(s) for each candidate.

Candidate (1)_____
Candidate (2)_____

15. How influential were the following factors upon your vote decision(s)?

SHOW GREEN CARD

1	2	3	4	5
Not influential	Fairly influential	Very influential	Extremely influential	No opinion/ not sure

	1	2	3	4	5
1 The personal qualities of the candidate(s)	☐	☐	☐	☐	☐
2 His/her/their stance on public policies	☐	☐	☐	☐	☐
3 The political group to which he/she/they belong(s)	☐	☐	☐	☐	☐
4 The leader(s) of the political group to which he/she/they belong(s)	☐	☐	☐	☐	☐

16. Of the four factors listed, how would you rank their importance?

Interviewer should read out the four factors once more. '1' is the most important factor.

Order of importance

1 The personal qualities of the candidate(s)   _____
2 His/her/their stance on public policies   _____
3 The political group to which he/she/they belong(s) _____
4 The leader(s) of the political group to which he/she/ they belong(s) _____

17. Are you aware of the fact that the directly elected legislators only comprise a minority in the Legislative Council, so that they can only play a limited role in the political system?

    1   [ ]   Yes, I am aware of that
    2   [ ]   No, I am not aware of that ⸺ Go to Q.19

18. So why did you still decide to vote? Please specify reason(s)

_____

_____

19. Can you name the two candidates who have won the Legislative Council seats in your constituency?
(The correct answers are: LAU Chin-shek and Conrad LAM Kui-shing.)

    1   [ ]   Both names correctly identified
    2   [ ]   One name correctly identified
    3   [ ]   No name correctly identified/don't know

Finally, we would like to know more about your personal particulars.

> For Q.20 and Q.21, show respondent the range of options if he/she appears hesitant.

20. What is your personal monthly income?

    1   [ ] No income
    2   [ ] Under $3,000
    3   [ ] $3,000 – $5,999
    4   [ ] $6,000 – $9,999
    5   [ ] $10,000 – $14,999
    6   [ ] $15,000 – $19,999
    7   [ ] $20,000 – $49,999
    8   [ ] $50,000 and above
    9   [ ] Refuse to answer

21. What is your total monthly household income?

    1   [ ] Under $3,000
    2   [ ] $3,000 – $5,999
    3   [ ] $6,000 – $9,999
    4   [ ] $10,000 – $14,999
    5   [ ] $15,000 – $19,999

6   [ ] $20,000 – $49,999
7   [ ] $50,000 – $79,999
8   [ ] $80,000 and above
9   [ ] Refuse to answer

22. Do you have any religious beliefs?

1   [ ]   Protestant
2   [ ]   Catholic
3   [ ]   Buddhist
4   [ ]   Muslim
5   [ ]   Others (please specify) _____
6   [ ]   No religious belief

23. How long have you been living in Hong Kong?

1   [ ]   Under 10 years
2   [ ]   10 - 20 years
3   [ ]   Over 20 years

24. When you think of your identity, do you see yourself more as a Hongkonger, or more as a Chinese?

1   [ ]   Chinese
2   [ ]   Hongkonger
3   [ ]   Both
4   [ ]   Neither
5   [ ]   No opinion/refuse to answer

25. What type of housing are you living in?

> The interviewer should observe by himself/herself. This question should be raised only if the interviewer is uncertain of the answer.

1   [ ]   Public housing — Go to Q.27
2   [ ]   Private sector housing
3   [ ]   Home ownership scheme housing
4   [ ]   Villa/bungalow
5   [ ]   Temporary housing/squatter
6   [ ]   Others (please specify) _____

26. Do you own or rent this place?

1	[ ]	Self-ownership (no need to pay instalments)
2	[ ]	Ownership through instalments
3	[ ]	Rented
4	[ ]	Housing benefits/staff quarters
5	[ ]	Others (please specify) _____

27. Do you belong to any groups/organizations?

> The respondent should first be allowed to answer on his/her own. The interviewer should then follow up by going through the following list.

01	[ ]	Religious organizations
02	[ ]	Professional organizations
03	[ ]	Labour organizations/unions
04	[ ]	Political groups (United Democrats, Liberal Democratic Federation, etc.)
05	[ ]	Pressure groups (livelihood concern groups, etc.)
06	[ ]	Kaifong associations
07	[ ]	Neighbourhood organizations (mutual aid committees, owners' associations, etc.)
08	[ ]	Community organizations (youth clubs, Caritas, etc.)
09	[ ]	Recreational organizations (Football Association, Country Club, etc.) _____
10	[ ]	Others (please specify)

28. Which social class do you see yourself as belonging to?

1	[ ]	Lower class
2	[ ]	Lower-middle class
3	[ ]	Middle class
4	[ ]	Upper-middle class
5	[ ]	Upper class
6	[ ]	Don't know

> Thank you very much for your co-operation.

APPENDIX D PROFILE OF SURVEY RESPONDENTS

	Pre-election (%)	Post-election(1) (%)	Post-election(2) (%)
Age			
21-29 years	14.7	13.2	10.6
30-39 years	26.7	25.3	28.4
40-49 years	16.3	16.5	18.4
50-59 years	18.7	18.8	20.6
60 years and above	23.5	26.3	22.0
(N)	(1,046)	(570)	(141)
Sex			
Male	50.7	47.4	48.9
Female	49.3	52.5	51.1
(N)	(1,046)	(570)	(141)
Education			
Below primary	21.4	23.9	26.2
Primary	26.2	27.7	31.9
Secondary	35.9	32.3	28.4
Matriculation	4.1	4.0	2.8
Tertiary: non-degree	6.1	6.0	5.0
Tertiary: degree	6.3	6.1	5.7
(N)	(1,046)	(570)	(141)
Occupation			
Businessman	5.8	6.9	10.4
Professional	21.8	24.3	14.3
Administrator	7.4	7.2	10.4
Clerical	16.3	13.0	9.1
Sales	5.3	5.1	5.2
Service	11.0	9.4	19.5
Agricultural	0	0	0
Production	30.3	31.9	29.9
Unclassifiable	2.1	2.2	1.3
(N)	(565)	(276)	(77)

	Pre-election (%)	Post-election(1) (%)	Post-election(2) (%)
Not employed			
Housewife	61.5	64.9	69.0
Student	1.5	1.5	1.7
Unemployed	3.9	2.3	5.2
Retired	32.2	31.3	22.4
Others	1.0	0	1.7
(N)	(413)	(262)	(58)
Personal monthly income			
No income	36.8	43.7	38.1
Under $3,000	6.4	6.9	9.4
$3,000 – $5,999	16.5	15.3	15.1
$6,000 – $9,999	19.1	15.1	15.8
$10,000 – $14,999	11.8	10.2	10.1
$15,000 – $19,999	3.4	3.3	5.0
$20,000 – $49,999	4.1	4.0	3.6
$50,000 and over	0.6	0.2	0.7
Refuse to answer	1.3	1.2	2.2
(N)	(1,043)	(568)	(139)
Monthly household income			
Under $3,000	5.1	4.9	3.0
$3,000 – $5,999	9.6	9.9	10.4
$6,000 – $9,999	20.8	22.4	16.4
$10,000 – $14,999	25.1	24.2	21.6
$15,000 – $19,999	10.7	10.1	9.7
$20,000 – $49,999	15.7	15.0	22.4
$50,000 – $79,999	1.3	1.2	0
$80,000 and over	0.5	0.4	0.7
Refuse to answer	11.2	11.8	15.7
(N)	(1,036)	(566)	(134)
Housing type			
Public housing	63.1	63.3	58.9
Private housing	25.1	24.2	31.9
Home ownership scheme	9.8	10.8	9.2
Villa/bungalow	0.3	0.4	0

	Pre-election (%)	Post-election(1) (%)	Post-election(2) (%)
Temporary housing/ squatter	0.3	0.4	0
Others	1.4	1.1	0
(N)	(1,040)	(567)	(141)

Group membership

	Pre-election (%)	Post-election(1) (%)	Post-election(2) (%)
Religious groups	10.1	10.4	9.9
Professional groups	3.4	3.9	2.3
Trade unions	9.6	9.4	8.4
Political groups	0.5	0.2	0.8
Pressure groups	1.0	0.2	0
Kaifong associations	1.4	1.4	0
Neighbourhood associations	5.4	5.3	3.8
Community associations	4.7	5.5	1.5
Recreational associations	2.5	1.6	3.1
Others	1.6	1.6	0
No group membership	68.2	67.7	77.1
(N)[a]	(1,035)	(566)	(131)

Note: 'Pre-election' and 'post-election(1)' refer to the surveys of the panel sample. 'Post-election(2)' refers to the survey of the second sample, with whom we conducted interviews only after the elections. [a]The percentage total exceeds 100% because respondents could claim membership of a maximum of three groups.

Bibliography of Hong Kong Electoral Materials ▬

OFFICIAL DOCUMENTS

An Agreement Between the Government of the United Kingdom of Great Britain and Northern Ireland and the Government of the People's Republic of China on the Future of Hong Kong (Hong Kong: Government Printer, 1984).

Arrangements for Testing the Acceptability in Hong Kong of the Draft Agreement on the Future of the Territory, report of the Assessment Office and the Independent Monitoring Team (Hong Kong: Government Printer, November 1984).

The Basic Law of the Hong Kong Special Administrative Region of the People's Republic of China (Hong Kong: The Consultative Committee for the Basic Law of the Special Administrative Region of the People's Republic of China, April 1990).

Candidates Manual 1991 (Hong Kong: Registration and Electoral Office, Constitutional Affairs Branch).

Corrupt and Illegal Practices Ordinance (Cap 288).

Electoral Provisions Ordinance (Cap 367).

Electoral Provisions (Procedure) Regulations (Cap 367).

Electoral Provisions (Registration of Electors) Regulations (Cap 367).

Green Paper: A Pattern of District Administration in Hong Kong (Hong Kong: Government Printer, June 1980).

Green Paper: The Future Development of Representative Government in Hong Kong (Hong Kong: Government Printer, July 1984).

Green Paper: The 1987 Review of Development in Representative Government (Hong Kong: Government Printer, May 1987).

Legislative Council (Electoral Provisions) Ordinance (Cap 381).

Legislative Council (Electoral Provisions) (Procedure) Regulations (Cap 381).

Legislative Council (Electoral Provisions) (Registration of Electors and Appointment of Authorized Representatives) Regulation (Cap 381).

Public Response to the Green Paper: The 1987 Review of Development in Representative Government, Parts I, II and III, report of the Survey Office (Hong Kong: Government Printer, October 1987).

White Paper: District Administration in Hong Kong (Hong Kong: Government Printer, January 1981).

White Paper: The Development of Representative Government: The Way Forward (Hong Kong: Government Printer, February 1988).

White Paper: The Future Development of Representative Government in Hong Kong (Hong Kong: Government Printer, November 1984).

SECONDARY SOURCES

Catholic Institute for Religion and Society, 'Views of Catholics on Political Participation', report of a survey in two sub-parishes, November 1990. (Original in Chinese. 教友對政治參與的看法).

Chai Wan Caritas, 'Research on the Voting Behaviour of the Electorate in the 1988 North Chai Wan District Board Elections', 1988. (Original in Chinese. 一九八八年柴灣北區區議會選民投票行為研究).

Chan, David K.K., 'Local Administration in Hong Kong', in Alex Y.H. Kwan and David K.K. Chan, eds., *Hong Kong Society: A Reader* (Hong Kong: Writers' and Publishers' Cooperative, March 1986), Chapter 5.

Chan, Rosanna, *Is the Hong Kong District Board a Channel for Popular Citizen Participation* (Hong Kong: Research and Resource Press, 1982).

Chang, Chak-yan, 'The Mechanics of Democracy in Hong Kong', paper presented at a conference on 'Democracy and Political Development: Hong Kong Characteristics', Hong Kong Democratic Foundation, 19 May 1991.

Cheng, Joseph Y.S., 'The 1985 District Board Elections in Hong Kong', in Joseph Y.S. Cheng, ed., *Hong Kong in Transition* (Hong Kong: Oxford University Press, 1986), pp.67-87.

————, 'The Democracy Movement in Hong Kong', *International Affairs*, 65, 3(Summer 1989): 443-462.

————, 'The 1988 District Board Elections: A Study of Political Participation in the Transitional Period', in Kathleen Cheek-Milby and Miron Mushkat, eds., *Hong Kong: The Challenge of Transformation* (The University of Hong Kong, Centre of Asian Studies, 1989), pp.116-149.

Cheung, Adrian, 'Role of Appointed Legislators Confused', *The Foundation* (a monthly publication of the Hong Kong Foundation Limited), 16, August 1991, p.1.

————, 'When Success Is Not a Success', *The Foundation*, 17, September 1991, p.1.

Cheung, Bing-leung, 'Problems in the Executive—Legislative Relationship Under Constitutional Changes', paper presented at a conference on 'Democracy and Political Development: Hong Kong Characteristics', Hong Kong Democratic Foundation, 19 May 1991.

————, 'Democracy and the Democratic Movement in Hong Kong: Origin and Prospects', Norwich, University of East Anglia, Centre for Public Choice Studies, Discussion Paper 10, July 1991.

Chinese University Students' Union, United College Students' Union, New Asia College Students' Union and Chung Chi College Students' Union, 'A Study of Voting Behaviour and Voter Attitudes', 1985.

Chow, King W., 'Hong Kong in Turbulence After the Legislative Council Direct Elections?' *The Foundation,* 19, December 1991, p.11.

Christian Family Service Centre, 'An Opinion Survey of Hong Kong's System of Representative Government: Report', with The University of Hong Kong, Students' Union, Social Service Society, 1984. (Original in Chinese. 香港代議制民意調查報告書).

Chui, Ernest W.T., 'An Exploratory Study on the Voting Behaviour of Hong Kong Citizens in the District Board Election 1988', City Polytechnic of Hong Kong, Department of Social Administration, 1988 (mimeo).

————, 'A Study of Voting Behaviour of Hong Kong Citizens in the 1989 Urban Council and Regional Council Elections', City Polytechnic of Hong Kong, Department of Applied Social Studies,1989 (mimeo).

Chung, Robert, 'What Went Wrong With the Turnout Rate?' (unpublished manuscript).

'Democracy Squeezed Out in Hong Kong', *Hong Kong Monitor* (the Journal of the Friends of Hong Kong Committee, London), March 1990, p.1.

Electoral Reform Society (London), 'Report of Delegation', presented to the Hong Kong Democratic Foundation, 1991 (mimeo).

Hong Kong Christian Service, Li Cheng Uk Friendship Association, Hong Kong Federation of Youth Groups, So Uk Youth Centre and Office of Urban Councillor Li Chik-yuet, 'A Study of Voters' Views of Ideal District Board Members', 1985.

Hong Kong Council of Social Service, 'Social Workers' Participation in Politics', April 1988.

————, Working Group on International Youth Year, 'Opinion Survey of Young People's Political Participation: Report', 1986.

Hong Kong Democratic Foundation, 'Electoral Reform Proposals', November 1991 (mimeo).

Hong Kong Federation of Students, Social Affairs Committee, 'A Survey Report on the Legislative Council Elections', 1985. (Original in Chinese. 立法局選舉調查結果).

Hong Kong Federation of Youth Groups, 'A Survey of Youth Opinions on the "1987 Review of Development in Representative Government": Report', 1987. (Original in Chinese. 「一九八七代議政制發展檢討」青年意見調查報告書).

————, Cho Yiu Youth Centre, 'A Survey Report on the Attitudes of Voters in South Kwai Chung', 1985. (Original in Chinese. 葵涌南區投票選民態度調查報告書).

————, Cho Yiu Youth Centre, 'A Report on the Attitudes of the Electorate in Regional Council Elections', 1986. (Original in Chinese. 區域議局選民態度研究報告書).

Hong Kong Forum, 'A Survey of Candidates' Platforms and Political Orientations in the 1985 District Board Elections: Report', 1985. (Original in Chinese. 八五年區議會選舉候選人政綱及政治心態調查報告).

Hong Kong Methodist Oi Wah Estate Service Centre, 'An Opinion Poll of the Chai Wan District on the Legislative Council Elections', 1985. (Original in Chinese. 立法局選舉柴灣區民意調查報告).

Hong Kong Policy Review, 'A Survey of Hong Kong Citizens: Opinions on the System of Representative Government', 1984. (Original in Chinese. 香港市民對代議制意見調查報告書).

'Hong Kong Politicians Won't Lie Down', *The Guardian Weekly*, 15 December 1991, p.12.

Hong Kong University Students' Union and Social Sciences Society, 'A Study of Voter Attitudes', 1985.

Hong Kong University Students' Union, Social Service Group, Promotion of Youth Participation in District Board Administration Society, 'A Study of Voter Attitudes in the Second District Board Elections', 1985.

Hong Kong University Students' Union, Social Service Group and Social Sciences Society, 'A Study of Voting Behaviour in the 1985 District Board Elections', 1985.

Hung, Citi, 'Research in Aid of Election Campaigns', paper presented at a conference on 'Politics and the 1991 Elections in Hong Kong', City Polytechnic of Hong Kong, 27 October 1991.

Junk Bay Medical Relief Council, Rennie's Mill Community Development Section, 'An Opinion Survey of the Rennie's Mill Electorate in the Regional Council Elections 1986', 1986. (Original in Chinese. 區域議局調景嶺選民意見調查報告書).

Kam, Ping-Kwong *et al.*, 'Research Report on Candidates' Views on Political Accountability in the 1991 District Board Elections', City Polytechnic of Hong Kong, Department of Applied Social Studies, Research Group, July 1991. (Original in Chinese. 九一年區議會選舉候選人看政治交代研究報告書).

Kirby, Stephen, 'The Future of Hong Kong: Democracy Versus Autonomy', *Hong Kong Monitor*, March 1988, pp. 9-14.

Kwok, Hong-kin and K.K. Chan, 'A Public Opinion Survey of the "Green Paper: The 1987 Review of Developments in Representative Government": A Case Study of Local Residents' Views in the Central and Western District', Hong Kong, Central and Western District Board, Committee on Public Opinion and Political Development, September 1987. (Original in Chinese. 中西區居民對 1987 年代議政制發展檢討綠皮書的意見調查).

Kwok, Rowena Y.F., 'The 1991 Legislative Council Elections in Hong Kong', *Representation*, 30, 112(Winter 1991–92):68–71.

———, 'Electoral Administration in Hong Kong', *Journal of Behavioral and Social Sciences,* 37 (1992): 84–105 .

Lam, Jermain T.M. and Jane C.Y. Lee, 'Research Report on the Political Culture of the Voters in Hong Kong: Part I: A Study of the Professional Constituencies of the Legislative Council', City Polytechnic of Hong Kong, Department of Public and Social Administration, November 1991.

Lau, Emily, 'No Vote on Voting', *Hong Kong Monitor,* March 1988, p. 2.

Lau, Siu-kai, 'Public Attitude Towards Political Parties in Hong Kong', paper presented at a conference on 'Politics and the 1991 Elections in Hong Kong', City Polytechnic of Hong Kong, 27 October 1991.

———— and Kuan Hsin-chi, 'The District Board Elections in Hong Kong', The Chinese University of Hong Kong, Institute of Social Studies, December 1983.

———— and Kuan Hsin-chi, 'The 1985 District Board Elections in Hong Kong: The Limits of Political Mobilization in a Dependent Polity', *Journal of Commonwealth and Comparative Politics,* 25, 1(March 1987): 82-102.

Law, Chi-kwong, 'A Research Report on the Factors Which Influenced Electoral Results in the 1985 District Board Elections', The University of Hong Kong, Department of Social Work, 1985.

Lee, Jane C.Y., 'The Politics of Transition in Hong Kong: Elections and the Mobilization Process 1982-1985', unpublished Ph.D. thesis, Australian National University, 1989.

Lee, Ming-kwan, 'Politicians', in Richard Y.C. Wong and Joseph Y.S. Cheng, eds., *The Other Hong Kong Report 1990* (Hong Kong: The Chinese University Press, 1990), pp.113-130.

————, 'Issue Positions Assumed by Candidates Standing for Elections to the Legislative Council, 1991', paper presented at a conference on 'Politics and the 1991 Elections in Hong Kong', City Polytechnic of Hong Kong, 27 October 1991.

Leung, Clarence, 'Hedging Against a Bellicose Chamber', *The Foundation,* 16, August 1991, p. 1.

————, 'Voter Turn-out', paper presented at a conference on 'Politics and the 1991 Elections in Hong Kong', City Polytechnic of Hong Kong, 27 October 1991.

Leung, Joan Y.H. and Rowena Y.F. Kwok, 'Electorate Perception of Political Groupings in Hong Kong', paper presented at a conference on 'Politics and the 1991 Elections in Hong Kong', City Polytechnic of Hong Kong, 27 October 1991.

Lingnan College, Political Science Department, Public Opinion Polls, 13-19 August 1991 (commissioned by *Sing Dao Yih Pao, Sing Dao Wan Pao, Tin Tin Daily News* and the *Hong Kong Standard*); 6-10 September 1991, 15 September 1991 (sponsored by Television Broadcasts Limited).

Lo, Chi-kin, 'Do Parties Matter?' paper presented at a conference on 'Politics and the 1991 Elections in Hong Kong', City Polytechnic of Hong Kong, 27 October 1991.

————,'Constitution and Administration', in Sung Yun-wing and Lee Ming-kwan, eds., *The Other Hong Kong Report 1991* (Hong Kong: The Chinese University Press, 1991), pp.1-15.

Lo, Shiu-hing, 'Colonial Policy-Makers, Capitalist Class and China: Determinants of Electoral Reform in Hong Kong's and Macau's Legislatures', *Pacific Affairs,* 62, 2(1989): 204-218.

Louie, Kin-sheun, *An Exploration of Hong Kong's Politics and Political System* (Hong Kong: Commercial Press, 1987).

————, 'The Electoral System of Hong Kong: Problems and Prospects', paper presented at the seminar on 'Elections and Electoral Politics', Hong Kong Foundation, 8 December 1990.

————, 'Political Parties', in Sung Yun-wing and Lee Ming-kwan, eds., *The Other Hong Kong Report 1991* (Hong Kong: The Chinese University Press, 1991), pp. 55–75.

'Lu Ping on the Elections', *Wen Wei Po,* 20 September 1991.

Man, Sze-wai, 'Anti-democratic Aspects of the Election Results', paper presented at a conference on 'Politics and the 1991 Elections in Hong Kong', City Polytechnic of Hong Kong, 27 October 1991.

Meeting Point, Committee on Politics and Law, 'A Survey Report on the Voting Behaviour of the Electorate in the 1985 District Board Elections', 1985. (Original in Chinese. 1985 年區議會選舉選民投票行為問卷調查報告書).

Mosher, Stacy, 'Selective Suffrage', *Far Eastern Economic Review*, 29 August 1991, pp.16-20.

————, 'Liberal Landslide', *Far Eastern Economic Review*, 26 September 1991, pp.19-20.

New Hongkong Society, 'The New Hongkong Society's Opinion Survey of Whether the Legislative Council Should Have More Elected Seats', 1984. (Original in Chinese. 新香港學會「立法局應否增設民選議席」民意調查結果報告).

'An Owl Swoops', *The Economist*, 7 September 1991, pp.27-28.

'A Rebuke for Mother', *The Economist*, 21 September 1991, p.26.

'Representing the Right Interests: A Legislative Dilemma?' *Hong Kong Monitor*, December 1990, p.8.

Scott, Ian, 'Functional Constituencies and Representation', paper presented at a conference on 'Democracy and Political Development : Hong Kong Characteristics', Hong Kong Democratic Foundation, 19 May 1991.

Scott, Janet Lee, 'Local-level Election Behaviour in an Urban Area', The Chinese University of Hong Kong, Institute of Social Studies, January 1985.

Shepherd, James, 'Democracy Postponed', *Hong Kong Monitor*, March 1989, p.1.

Suen, Michael M.Y. (Secretary for Constitutional Affairs, Hong Kong), 'Hong Kong's Electoral System and Laws in This Voting Year', *Hong Kong Monitor*, March 1991, pp.13-16.

————, 'The Hong Kong Electoral System and Its Future Development', paper presented at a conference on 'Democracy and Political Development: Hong Kong Characteristics', Hong Kong Democratic Foundation, 19 May 1991.

Tam, Fau-chuen, Thomas, 'A Study of Political Participation of Youth Leaders in Shatin', Hong Kong, Shatin District Board, 1990.

Tsang, Steve, 'A Triumph for Democracy?' *Hong Kong Monitor*,

December 1991, p.1 and 12.

Tsang, Tak-shing, 'Election Results', paper presented at a conference on 'Politics and the 1991 Elections in Hong Kong', City Polytechnic of Hong Kong, 27 October 1991.

The University of Hong Kong, Social Sciences Research Centre, 'Public Opinion Programme', 7-12 July 1991 (commissioned by *Ming Pao* and the *South China Morning Post);* 12-13 August 1991, 15-19 August 1991, 1-6 September 1991, 11-13 September 1991 (sponsored by Asia Television Limited (mimeo).

'Why Hong Kong Needs to Develop a Culture of Free Institutions', *The Spectator,* 20 January 1990.

Yeung, Agnes and Chui Wing-tak, 'The 1991 Elections Year: Perspectives of the Hong Kong Citizens', paper presented at a conference on 'Politics and the 1991 Elections in Hong Kong', City Polytechnic of Hong Kong, 27 October 1991.

Young Women's Christian Association, Hong Kong Headquarters, Youth Work and Community Service Department, 'A Survey of the Electorate's Political Consciousness', 1988. (Original in Chinese. 選民意識問卷調查報告書).

————, Choi Wan Social Service Centre, 'A Survey Report on the Voting Behaviour of the 1985 District Board Electorate', 1985. (Original in Chinese. 1985 區議會選民投票行為調查報告書).

———— with S.K.H. Holy Cross Social Service Centre and Baptist Oi Kwan Social Service Centre, 'A Study of the 1985 District Board Elections', 1985.

CHINESE PRESS REPORTS OF OPINION POLLS

Hong Kong Economic Journal
17 July 1991
    (poll conducted by *Hong Kong Economic Journal,* January to May 1991)

14   August 1991
(poll commissioned by *Hong Kong Economic Journal* and
conducted by Hong Kong Polling Services Limited, mid-July to
12 August 1991)
14   September 1991
(poll conducted by Hong Kong Polling and Business Research
Company, 28 August 1991 to 6 September 1991)
15   September 1991
(poll conducted by *Hong Kong Economic Journal,* 15 September
1991)

Hong Kong Economic Times
14 - 16 August 1991
(poll conducted by *Hong Kong Economic Times,* 12 August
1991)

Ming Pao
6   July 1991
(poll conducted by City and New Territories Administration,
13-17 May 1991)
11   July 1991
(poll conducted by two lecturers from the City Polytechnic
of Hong Kong and The University of Hong Kong, 29 April 1991
to 4 May 1991)
18   July 1991
(poll commissioned by *Ming Pao* and conducted by Hong Kong
Polling Services Limited, 18 July 1991)
30   July 1991
(poll conducted by Survey Research of Hong Kong, July 1991)
8   August 1991
(poll conducted by the United Democrats of Hong Kong,
August 1991)
7   September 1991
(poll conducted by a group of District Board members and one
former Urban Councillor, 18 August 1991 to 1 September
1991)

15 September 1991
(poll conducted by Hong Kong Polling and Business Research
Company, 9-13 September 1991)

Oriental Daily News
8   August 1991
(poll conducted by *Oriental Daily News,* August 1991)

Sing Dao Yih Pao
4   May 1991
(poll conducted by five women's organizations, May 1991)
(poll conducted by the Liberal Democratic Federation of
Hong Kong, May 1991)
12 September 1991
(poll conducted by Asia Commercial Research Company,
January, June and August 1991)
(poll conducted by Asia Commercial Research Company,
mid-August 1991)
30 September 1991
(poll conducted by Kam Ping-kwong, City Polytechnic of Hong
Kong and residents' organizations in two public housing
estates in Kwai Chung, July 1991)

Index

Association for Democracy and People's Livelihood 4, 5, 12, 22

Ballots
  secret 193
  void 193
Basic Law 3, 9, 10, 16, 17, 94
Beijing massacre *see* China, pro-democracy movement 1989
Boundary commissions 204
  commissioners (UK) 203
British government 2, 3, 13, 16, 23, 203
By-elections 5, 15

Campaign
  activities 13, 41-3, 60, 136-7, 138, 192
  expenses 192
  issues 12-14, 44
Campbell, J.E. 80
Candidate evaluation
  affective 102, 112, 114-15, 119, 147
  performance 112, 113, 114-15, 119
Candidate image 113-14, 138
Candidate nomination 192
Candidates, background of 41-4
Canvassing *see* Voter registration, enumeration

Carmines, E.G. 95
Catholic Alliance in Support of the Democratic Movement in China 153, 165-6, 172
Catholic Church, in Hong Kong 151-3, 173, 175-6
  and orientations towards elections and political development 163, 170-2
  and political participation 153-5
  and political values 154, 162
  and the 1991 elections 154-5, 161-3
Catholic Institute for Religion and Society 153, 158, 165-6, 172
Catholic Justice and Peace Commission 166, 172
Catholic voters
  choice of candidates 162, 163, 164, 167-70, 173
  differences with non-voters 164, 167, 171
  knowledge of Church's social teaching 163, 164-5
  socio-economic status 162, 167-70, 171
  turnout 158-163, 165, 173
Catholic Youth Council 166
Census 7, 8, 197, 203
Chan Chi-kwan, Peter 43-5

Chan Yuen-han 6, 42-5, 51, 67, 70-4, 86-8, 94-5
Cheng Kai-nam 6
Cheng Tak-kin 41
Cheung Chung-ming, Justin 43-5
China, pro-democracy movement 1989 5, 6, 15, 17-18, 41, 93, 113
Chinese Communist Party 23
Chinese government 2, 3, 6, 7, 8, 9-13, 15, 16, 17, 18-19, 23, 203
  attitudes towards civil liberties 17
  attitudes towards constitutional reform 3, 9, 11, 24
  attitudes towards the election 9-10, 18-19
  National People's Congress 10
Christian Industrial Committee 44
Civic Association 5, 43, 44, 45
Conservatives 37, 39-41, 96
  business 4, 5, 10, 24, 67, 87
  professionals 4, 5, 10
  rural 4, 5, 14
Constituencies
  delimitation 188, 202-4
  double-seat 3, 103, 111, 136, 146, 202
  population 38, 202
  single-seat 103, 146
Constituency boundaries
  see Constituencies, delimitation
Corrupt and Illegal Practices Ordinance *see* Electoral practices, irregular
Critical elections 1-2, 20-1, 24
Cultural Revolution 15, 16

Dahl, R. 60
Denver, D. 82, 95
Disenfranchisement 8-9, 196-7
District Board elections 14, 15, 39, 41, 52, 54-5, 61, 83, 103-4, 116-17, 138, 146, 147, 160
Downs, A. 60, 113
Durkheim, E. 156

Election deposits 192
Election results 5, 11, 45, 212-19
Electoral boundaries *see* Constituencies, delimitation

Electoral commission 207
Electoral education 188, 205, 206
Electoral environment, variables of 49
  electorate's socio-economic status 57-8, 71-2
  level of economic development 57
  political environment 57, 59-61, 74, 103-4
  see also Legislative Council; Political group affiliation; Political orientations; Political parties
Electoral laws 189-90, 192
Electoral practices, irregular 188, 190, 192
Electoral predictions, on voter turnout 127-9, 134, 139
Electoral procedures, 190, 192–3
  effect on choosing candidates 111–12, 119
Electoral Reform Society (London) 204
Electoral registers 2, 7, 8; *see also* Electoral rolls, General Electoral Rolls
Electoral Registration *see* Voter registration
Electoral rolls
  Functional Constituency Roll 189
  General Electoral Roll 189, 195-7
  see also Electoral registers; Voter registration
Electorate, consistency *see* Voter consistency
Electorate, inconsistency *see* Voter inconsistency
Emigration 8, 15, 60, 85, 91-2
Executive Council 9, 13, 196
Exit polls *see* Surveys, exit polls

Federation of Trade Unions 5, 19, 37, 40, 42, 43, 44, 51, 52, 70, 94
Ford, Sir David 7
Franchise 190
Franklin, M. 81
Functional constituencies 3, 10-11, 23, 40, 60, 187, 188; *see also* Legislative Council
Fung Kin-kee, Frederick 12, 22

Gerrymandering 204
Governor 3, 8, 9, 13

Hong Kong Alliance 18, 41, 44, 93, 166
Hong Kong and Kowloon Department Store Workers Association 44
Hong Kong and Macau Affairs Office 9
Hong Kong Citizen Forum 5
Hong Kong Confederation of Trade Unions 44
Hong Kong Democratic Foundation 10
Hong Kong Federation of Catholic Students 166
Hong Kong government 2, 3, 7, 8, 10, 16, 17, 23, 152
Housing
private 34, 36, 39
public 34, 36, 39

Independent candidates 4-5, 13, 43, 44, 45, 67
Inflation 84, 85-6
Interview effect 134
Issue saliency (1997 issue) 46, 138, 144-5
and autonomy of the Hong Kong government 13, 17, 20, 24, 85, 89-90, 93
and confidence in Hong Kong's political future 17, 85, 89-92, 93
and democratic political development 16-17, 20, 24, 85, 89, 92, 93
see also Political orientations
Issue voting 144-5, 146
definition 79
different levels 82
methodological problems 81-2
necessary conditions 80-2
sufficient conditions 81
see also Issue saliency (1997 issue); Political stance

Joint Meeting of the Catholic Bodies Concerned for the Development of the Hong Kong Government System 170

Kaifongs 40, 41
Key, V.O. 1, 2, 20, 23, 24
Kowloon City 31, 33, 34, 36, 38-40, 43, 53

Kwun Tong Man Chung Friendship Promotion Association 5
Lai King-tim 196
Lam Kui-shing, Conrad 6, 41, 44-5, 51, 67, 69, 70-4, 86-8
Lau Chin-shek 6, 22, 41, 44-5, 51, 67, 69, 70-4, 86-8
Lau Siu-kai 23
Lau Wai-hing, Emily 13, 22
Law Cheung-kwok 12
Lee Chu-ming, Martin 6, 9, 37
Legislative Council
membership 3, 4, 7, 10-11, 24, 60
powers 9, 13, 22, 60, 61, 83, 143
see also Functional constituencies
Liberal Democratic Federation 4, 23, 52,
Liberals 4, 5, 7, 12-15, 18, 20, 22-3, 24, 37, 41, 45, 51, 57, 67, 69-74, 80, 87, 89-95, 96, 144-5, 147; see also Issue saliency (1997 issue); Political stance
Lo Chi-kin 23
Lu Ping 9

Media 21
and electoral education 21, 205-6
influence on catholic voters 163, 168, 169, 173
influence on voters 138
Meeting Point 4, 5, 15
Meier, K.J. 80
Merelman, R. 155
Mutual aid committees 40

New China News Agency 9, 18-19, 40
New Hong Kong Alliance 5
Ng Ming-yum 14
Non-voters
reasons for non-voting 7-8, 60-1
and voters, comparison 62-6, 74

Opinion polls 9, 13, 16, 84-5, 135, 194, 206

People's Liberation Army 17
Political apathy 21, 147
Political efficacy 50, 53-5, 56, 57, 59, 62, 64, 65, 72-3, 74, 143, 146, 147

Political knowledge 50-3, 54, 57, 59, 63, 64, 74-5, 143, 147
Political group affiliation 51, 52, 67-8, 145; *see also* Political parties
Political orientations 49-50, 155
  towards democracy 50, 65-6
  towards the Chinese government 50, 54-7, 59, 63-4, 72-5, 89-92, 94, 143-7
  towards the Hong Kong government 50, 54, 55, 62-5, 72-3, 143, 146
  towards welfare 50, 56-7, 63-5, 73-4
  see also Political efficacy; Political knowledge; Voters, attitude towards China
Political participation 99
Political parties 3, 14, 22-4, 52, 59, 66, 74, 96, 104, 138, 139, 145, 146
  and platform 12-13, 67-8
  see also Political group affiliation
Political socialization 151, 155, 172
Political stance 46, 51, 52, 53, 67-74, 87-9, 144-5, 155
  see also Conservatives; Independent candidates; Issue saliency (1997 issue); Liberals; Pro-China candidates
Polling day 21, 193
Polling hours 193
Polling stations 21, 197
  presiding officers of 197
Postal voting 197
Privacy Commissioner (Canada) 200
Pro-China candidates 12, 18, 19, 37, 39-43, 45, 51, 67, 69-74, 80, 86-7, 89-95, 96, 144-5, 146, 147; *see also* Issue saliency (1997 issue); Political stance
Progressive Hong Kong Society 41
Proxy voting 197

Quasi-political organizations 104
Questionnaires 177-84, 225-58

Reform Club 5, 43, 44, 45
Regional Council elections 14, 52, 83, 103-4, 116-17, 138
Registration and Electoral Office 189, 190, 191, 195, 196, 200

Registration of Persons Division, Immigration Department 200
Registration officers 187, 193
Representation of the People Act (UK) 194
Research design 37, 156-7, 220-4
Respondents, profile of 38, 260-2
Response bias 134, 135, 139
Returning officers 187, 192

St Bonaventure's Church 156-7, 158, 159, 161, 162-3, 170, 171
St Jude's Church 156-7, 159, 161, 170, 171
Shun Lee Estate Catholic sub-parish 156-7, 158, 159, 160, 161, 162, 170, 171
Sino-British agreement 2, 14, 15, 16, 17, 83, 162
Sino-British negotiations *see* Sino-British agreement
South China Morning Post 8
Stimson, J.A. 95
Surveys
  Catholic Institute for Religion and Society survey (1990) 158, 160
  Catholic voters survey (1991) 151, 158
  control group (Kowloon Central survey) 37-8, 134
  exit polls 12, 43
  pre-and post-election surveys (Kowloon Central survey) 37-8, 116, 118, 126, 127, 130-3
  previous research 101-2, 103, 115-17, 146
Szeto Wah 6, 9

Ta Kung Pao 18
Tai Chin-wah 5, 15
Taikoo Shing Catholic sub-parish 156-7, 158–62, 170, 171
Tam Wai-chu, Maria 23
Tam Yiu-chung 40
Trades Union Council 5
Turnout *see* Voter turnout
Turnout enhancement effect 134-5, 139

United Democrats of Hong Kong 4, 5,

10, 12, 14, 20, 22-3, 37, 39, 41, 44, 51, 52, 86, 93, 138
'United front' organizations 3, 5, 6, 16, 18-19
Urban Council elections 14, 39, 43, 52, 61, 83, 103-4, 116-17, 138, 159-60, 162

Vietnamese boat people 13, 84, 85, 86
Vote counting 187, 193
Voter consistency 147
  definition 125
  dimensions 106–7, 111–12, 125, 127-33
  explanations and implications 106-7, 133-9
Voter inconsistency, explanation of 137-9
Voter registration 187, 188
  automatic 190, 198-201
  in Canada 199
  closing date 195
  in Denmark 198-9
  enumeration 199, 201-2
  permanent 195-6, 200
  registration rate 7, 38, 195, 202
  in the United Kingdom 194-5, 199
  voluntary 190, 194-6, 198-200
  see also Electoral rolls
Voter turnout 2, 7-9, 21, 38-9, 49, 54–5, 57, 59-61, 74, 127-9, 148, 194, 196-7
Voters
  attitudes towards China 11-13, 15-20
  attitudes towards policy issues 13, 63-6
  choice of candidates 49, 53, 65, 67-74, 111-12, 135-6, 139, 144-5, 147
  rational 95, 100-1, 113
  reasons for voting 61-2
  structured preferences 14-5, 20, 23, 125, 127, 137, 139, 147
  undecided 127, 135, 139
  see also Catholic voters; Non-voters; Political orientations; Voter consistency; Voter registration;

Voter turnout; Voting criteria
Votes
  paired 12, 70-1, 146
  single 12, 70-1
Voting
  as a civic responsibility 61-2
  as an expressive act 62, 66
Voting age 190
Voting criteria 46, 100-2
  candidates' particulars 14, 102, 114-15, 145-7
  educational attainment 102, 108-9, 115-17, 146
  ideal preferences and actual criteria 102, 105-11, 112, 116-19, 145-6
  latent criteria 118, 119
  performance or experience 69, 102, 107-11, 112, 114, 146-7
  policy stance or platform 69, 70, 107-11, 113, 117, 146-7
  style of work 69, 107-11, 113-14, 116-17, 146, 147
  support of individuals and organizations 102, 114-15
  willingness to serve the public 65, 69, 107-11, 112-13, 114, 146, 147
  see also Candidate evaluation; Candidate image; Voter consistency
Voting inclinations 93-5
Voting intention 126, 128, 135, 147; *see also* Voter consistency, dimensions
Voting system 4, 193

Wong Tai Sin 31, 34, 35, 36, 38-9, 43, 53
Wong Wang-fat, Andrew 13
Wu, John Baptist, Cardinal 153, 154, 165

Yeung Lai-yin, Cecilia 43-5
Young, John Dragon 43-5

Zhang Junsheng 9